VITAL REMNANTS

VITAL REMNANTS

America's Founding and the Western Tradition

Edited by

GARY L. GREGG II

ISI BOOKS

WILMINGTON, DELAWARE

1999

Cataloging-in-Publication Data

Vital remnants : America's founding and the Western tradition / edited by Gary L. Gregg II. -- Wilmington, DE : ISI Books, 1999.

    p. cm.

    ISBN 1-882926-31-5
      1. United States -- History -- Constitutional period, 1789-1809. 2. United States -- Civilization. I. Gregg, Gary L., 1967-

E310 .V58 1999   99-71451
973/.4--dc21   CIP

Published in the United States by:

    ISI Books
    Post Office Box 4431
    Wilmington, DE 19807-0431

Manufactured in the United States of America

For my Mother and Father

CONTENTS

FOREWORD

In June 1998 the Intercollegiate Studies Institute brought together more than sixty of the best undergraduate students, advanced graduate students, and college faculty in the nation to reflect upon the state of higher education and to explore the Western roots of the American Constitutional Order. The present volume had its origin in the lectures delivered at that week-long conference on "America and the Western Tradition" held in Colonial Williamsburg, Virginia.

Both the conference and *Vital Remnants* were inspired by the work of the late Russell Amos Kirk. Kirk did much to awaken our imaginations, rekindle our memory, and remind us of the deep roots of American order. The Williamsburg conference began with a tribute to Kirk and was dedicated to his memory. When considering the substantial works of Kirk's pen, we are reminded with Eliot that "The communication of the dead is tongued with fire beyond the language of the living." He is owed much credit, though indirectly and imperfectly transmitted, for the pages that follow.

A number of individuals deserve considerable thanks for their various roles in making this volume a reality. Ken Cribb, Jeff Nelson, Brooke Daley, and Sam Torode showed early and constant support for the project and Mark Henrie was ready with good advice and encouragement from its earliest stages to its final form. Though a number of program officers at ISI contributed to the conference that made this book possible, Paul Rhein deserves particular credit for masterfully taking an idea and making it a successful event. The authors of each of the essays here collected contributed more to the volume than their chapters alone. For their insight, advice, and gracious acceptance of this editor's meager suggestions, I am appreciative.

Gary L. Gregg II

Parkesburg, Pennsylvania

INTRODUCTION

Gary L. Gregg II

"Long before our time, the customs of our ancestors molded admirable men, and in turn those eminent men upheld the ways and institutions of their forebears. Our age, however, inherited the Republic as if it were some beautiful painting of bygone ages, its colors already fading through great antiquity; and not only has our time neglected to freshen the colors of the picture, but we have failed to preserve its form and outlines."

—Marcus Tullius Cicero

According to Marcus Tullius Cicero, his Rome "inherited the Republic as if it were some beautiful painting of bygone ages, its colors already fading through great antiquity." Like Cicero's Rome, modern America has inherited a most worthy republic whose colors we have allowed to fade "and not only has our time neglected to freshen the colors of the picture, but we have failed to preserve its form and outlines." As our schools have neglected to freshen the colors of the republic for the rising generation, so too the form and outlines of the constitutional order have been undermined by constitutionally pernicious theories and practice. At the dawn of a new century, no task is more important than refreshing the hues and restoring the form of the republic. Only in recovering and restating the timeless and the true can one hope to redeem the times in which one lives. From Edmund Burke in eighteenth-century England to Russell Kirk in twentieth-century America, this has been the heart of the conservative mission and it is this same spirit that informs this collection.

America was a nation blessed from its outset with great natural, moral, intellectual, and spiritual resources. None was purchased cheaply, and none by any one generation on either side of the Atlantic. From the nomadic Hebrew tribes to fifth-century Athens to Christian England and Colonial Virginia, the republic is the descendant not of one age or place, but of many. America is a multicultural nation because it is a Western nation and it is in that Western heritage that our values and our institutions find their roots and continuing vitality.

We are a nation of the West because our Founders were men of the West. They received the language of the English

countryside, the literature of the Latin poets, the rule of prescriptive common law, and the religion of the Cross. In their
schools, in their fields, in their meeting houses, and by the
hearth, they were part of the great Western tradition. In the
fervor of revolution and founding, they could have abandoned
that Western past; they could have severed the great links connecting their world to their heritage. They could have become
radicals of the form that would later strike at the very heart of
France. But, America's Founders were conservative revolutionaries, not radical social tinkerers, and it was in the spirit of
preservation that they worked their revolution.

America's Founders crafted a written constitution upon an
inherited unwritten constitution. A conservative document,
the Constitution presupposed the mores and traditions of the
people for which it was established and could have come from
no other. They accepted the blessings of Providence and of prescription. They built upon the trials and tribulations of the
past. They looked to the ages and to what Patrick Henry called
"the lamp of experience" to light their way. The American
Founders were a generation who understood their place in the
great chain of being and so secured the blessings of liberty to
themselves and their posterity. They were, in short, part of the
rich history of the Anglo-Saxon people and of the great tradition of Western civilization and culture.

All around us now lie the remains of broken civilizations,

the remnants of that upon which our forebears built. Our literature, our politics, the architecture of our public spaces, our religion and family life; scattered about our feet are the remnants upon which we depend but which we too often fail to notice and more often still fail to appreciate. Yet it is these remnants of ages past that help make life tolerable in the modern age.

Some of the remnants that sustain us are European and ancient, but some of them are specifically American. Though the American Founders prudently built upon the achievements of the West and particularly upon English precedent, the Founding generation in turn contributed to the Western tradition. Late-eighteenth-century America was an important time in human history. It marked the birth of a renewed federation of states that would become a large and vital nation spanning a continent. It opened a new realm of self-understanding for a people that would spur untold changes on every other continent around the globe. It demonstrated anew the possibility of ordered liberty at the same time as it chastened man by knowledge of his own eternal weaknesses. But, we must always remember that this was "a revolution not made but prevented," and a foundation not newly laid, but newly restored. We are the children of the Founding generation, but they were the prudential children of the West.

Our inheritance, then, is both Western and American. Our

Constitution was built upon ancient truths and English traditions. Our political rights were forged in the fires of revolution, but tempered in the cooling waters of the traditional Christian moral order of colonial North America. We are the heirs of a well-balanced constitutional order—both written and unwritten alike. But we stand at the dawn of a new century, in grave danger of losing sight of the truths our Founders knew and lived. We are in danger of selling our inheritance for the pottage of the hour.

From the Parthenon of Athens to the ruined stone walls of Roman-occupied Scotland, from the Romance languages of the continent to the great churches and universities of England, the continuity between the antique and the modern is daily more apparent on the far side of the Atlantic. We Americans, however, have few physical reminders of our distant past to enliven our imaginations. Being a "new nation," we are unable to pause among the debris of collapsed societies: there is no medieval Cleveland waiting to be exhumed beneath our Ohio streets. And yet, usually unaware, we continue to walk daily among the remnants of broken civilizations—for ancient worlds continue to work mysteriously through our lives, our books, and our institutions.

From the earliest days of English settlements in North America, those who pilgrimaged across the Atlantic thought of themselves as somehow different and apart from the Old World. After all, had they not proven themselves more pious, industrious, ambitious, and daring in their acts of migration? Such a feeling of special consecration, of being a new nation set apart from and better than Europe, has continued through the generations in North America. This American exceptionalism has in recent years been succeeded by a highly modern understanding that is more pernicious—the hubristic rush to embrace everything new and discard the old. Progress, however, is not inevitable. The timeline of history is not the ruler by which morality or degree of civilization can be measured. What modern man has gained from his pride, he has correspondingly lost in tradition, prudence, and the wisdom of the ages.

The denizens of modern America live in what might be called the "Age of Amnesia." Silently, almost imperceptibly over the decades, we have been losing our ability to remember as a culture and a civilization. Having long ago left the soil of our fathers, the memory of the family fades with each uprooted generation. What it is to be civilized is ill-recalled, as the leveling scythe of relativism infects the textbooks and teachers of the young. The cultural celebration of youth over age, the material over the spiritual, science over history, the immediate over the patiently-achieved, journalistic sensationalism over the life of the mind, all mitigate against public memory. At nearly every turn the contemporary culture constructs barriers to memory. Recent innovations in education are particularly troubling in this regard as teachers have traditionally functioned as one of the chief agents of cultural remembrance. No guns need blare nor books burn for the cultural celebration of neoterism to work its noxious way, severing what Lincoln called "the mystic cords of memory."

With a society's failure to remember its past, all things become possible. Both conservatives and progressives know this essential truth about the fragility of culture. The Left actively attempts to undermine people's knowledge of and *pietas* for the past, for in it they find great obstacles to "progress." Once the foundation is leveled, once the remnants of the cultural and political past have been swept away, progressives will set to the task of building anew a better society founded on "modern" principles and values. In the emptiness they set to raise their own weak timbers of therapeutic history and progressive "feel good" mythology. This is the underlying vision of the contemporary educational establishment. This is the ultimate promise of political correctness, multiculturalism, academic feminism, and cultural and ethical relativism. The war against the past, the assault on absolute values and norms, the attempt to obliterate "dead white European males" from the curriculum are all attacks on our culture's memory. Once we forget, all things will be possible—all things pernicious as well as benign.

Conservatives do not suffer from this particularly prideful

disease of modernity—the unreflective approval of everything new and "modern." They do not suffer under the cult of presentism that finds the new always of more worth than the old and the present superior to the past. They recognize change is not always progress and understand the grave dangers attendant upon any radical societal surgery. They understand that a culture is a complex bundle of traditions that no human mind can fully untangle or any single age replace. They would not trade the solid ground of prudence, tradition, and transcendent truth for the fading shape of the *Zeitgeist* or the shifting sands of human hopes and good intentions.

It has been said that every new generation is a new people. While perhaps not completely and literally true, that notion captures the awesome central duty of each generation to serve the future by remembering the past and preserving the good of the present. It also reminds us of the great hope for our age. If every generation is in some way a new people, hope is justified. For even in our culture, where the educational establishment has maligned the American Founders and the Western tradition, as long as there are some who have kept the tablets, hope remains.

Vital remnants are waiting to be recovered in books unread, ideas unexplored, experiences unremembered. Mostly outside our everyday consciousness, one may discern even to-

day the remnants of the West, connecting man to the permanent things, maintaining civil society, and sustaining the constitutional order. The remorseless scythe of modernity has leveled much of our Western inheritance, but the roots remain.
The essays here collected are all efforts in recollection and recovery. They will help Americans remember those remnants of
the West that informed the Founding generation and to one
degree or another support our polity still. They do not aim at a
comprehensive restatement of Western influences, nor do they
attempt an exhaustive exposition of the main lines of political
and social thought at the Founding. The latter task would be as
difficult as the former would be impossible. The authors here
collected may not even agree on every point, but they are all
united in the effort to revitalize the remnants of our shared
past.

What we refer to as "The Founding" is a complex process
that unfolded over the course of decades, much as its roots
were sowed, pruned, lost, and recovered over millennia. Both
the parent and its offspring defy attempts at simplification. Its
enemies have attempted to reduce the Founding to a few key
buzzwords such as "slave-owning," "male dominated," "aristocratic," and "premodern" in an effort to discard it whole and
thereby pave the way for a new founding based on abstract and
controversial theories of "justice." Some friends of the American tradition have likewise attempted such a simplification by

reducing the Founding to one document or concept, or prun-
ing it to the inspiration of but one political thinker or school
of thought. But, like the Constitution of 1789, which is its
greatest product, the Founding is complex and defies reduction.

Cultures are organic. Fed by the humus of many ages and
many nations, they grow and develop in ways the human mind
can never truly grasp. Attempts to do so have often led the
philosopher down dangerous paths of abstraction and tyranny.
Rather than attempting grand theory, the authors of *Vital Remnants* are engaged in the much more important task of collect-
ing remnants to patch the frayed cloak of the constitutional
order. As Cicero urged his own generation, these authors are
engaged in refreshing the colors of the republic.

Russell Kirk helped us remember that our present is deeply
rooted in the history of five cities—Athens, Jerusalem, Rome,
London, and Philadelphia. Like Kirk's *Roots of American Order*,
the work that inspired the present volume, the following essays
are brief tours through the legacies of these cities. They are not
exhaustive dissertations, but learned expositions of the underlying roots of the American constitutional order.

Wilfred McClay opens *Vital Remnants* with the question,
"Is America an experiment?" The language of experimentation
has been used in American social thought since the Founding.
George Washington and Alexander Hamilton, among others of

the period, may have understood the American project as one of experimentation, but they did not understand by that the radicalism the term has become associated with more recently. Unlike those who view America as a continuing process of re-creating who we are and what we value, for Washington, America was a practical experiment in the preservation of liberty and the success of republican government. In a learned tour through America's self-understanding, McClay finds our own frontier, our own experiment, in the important effort of reappropriating our past—a past that has been obfuscated by the forces of our present.

The history and literature of the Greeks are two particularly important parts of our distant past that are in need of proper reappropriation. However, the role played by classical Greece in the drama of the American Founding is particularly problematic. Like the rest of the Western pantheon, the Greeks have come under fire by the intellectual Left and have been dismissed for the typical "sins" the Left recognizes everywhere they wish to find them. On the other hand, some schools of thought would have us study the works of Athens with the reverence usually reserved for holy writ and would have us seek a return to the *polis* in modern America. The truth of the Greeks' influence on the history of the West and hence on America seems to lie in the middle. Though they gave us no political institutions, they did bequeath to America a rich literature that

was known and studied by the men of the Founding generation. They also provided a panoply of negative lessons of
internecine violence, demogoguery, radical democracy, and class
conflict that informed America's prudential Founders.

Until the current century, one vitally important constant
through the history of Western civilization was the centrality of
farming to the vast majority in every culture, in every age. On
this score, classical Greece was not much different from Revolutionary-era America—where nine out of every ten adult males
were farmers. To ignore or dismiss the importance of life working the land in any endeavor to adequately understand the political theory of the American Founders does violence to the
endeavor. Bruce Thornton connects the American Founding
period to the georgic tradition that begins with the Greek poet
Hesiod in the seventh century B.C., and in so doing amply
demonstrates the importance of the views and virtues of those
who labor in the land to understanding and appreciating the
history of the West, and particularly to understanding the
American Founding. If, as Jefferson wrote in his *Notes on Virginia* and as many others of the Founding generation were profoundly convinced, virtue and free government are best cultivated among those who labor in the earth, modern Americans
might well pause a moment in front of the latest strip mall to
consider the obliteration of the family farm that has occurred
over the last few decades.

More than classical Greece, the example and literature of Rome had a profound impact on the imaginations and the political understandings of the educated men of the Founding. Plutarch, Tacitus, Polybius, Virgil, and Livy were among the most important educators of the men who made the revolution and founded the Constitutional order. It was the literature of the classics to which they turned for precedent and insights. Those who debated the passage of the Constitution of 1787 took for *noms de plume* such Roman names as Publius, Brutus, and Cato. Were the Founding era's ubiquitous citations of classical authors, precedent, and political lessons merely illustrative or did the classical education of colonial America have a more formative impact on their political ideas and their actions? In his contribution, E. Christian Kopff argues that the influence of the classics should not be underestimated when considering the American Founding and further urges modern America to return to the classics which, with John Adams, he finds "indispensable" to republican government.

When considering the influence of classical Greece and Rome, however, one must be steadily aware of the dangers of abstraction and the necessity of context. Americans of the Founding generation did not attempt to reinstitute the polity of Athens, nor did they attempt to refound the Republic of Rome in North America. Rather, the influences of the classical world were mediated by two forces that impacted their thinking more than any others—Christianity and the experience of English and colonial political life.

Christian theology and the daily life of local Protestant congregations were particularly essential in the formation of the minds and hearts of the American Founding generation. To the degree that we fail to comprehend the basic tenets of Christianity, we are distanced from the Founders. Though the disconnection on this score is large in modern American society, it is particularly acute in the academy. As Graham Walker points out, the basic failure to understand and appreciate Christian theology has contributed greatly to our confusion over the nature of the American Founding and the principles that undergird the constitutional order. Rather than finding the regime grounded in classical republicanism or modern liberalism, as are the common and rival academic understandings, Walker articulates a constitutional order grounded in an Augustinian political theology of original sin that the Founders inherited from their Protestant ministers, teachers, and neighbors. It is in the framework created by the theology of creation and fall that we can come to understand such essential elements of the constitutional order as limited government and federalism. It is also such an understanding that provides prudent answers to such contemporary concerns as the public encouragement of virtue and the role of religion in public life.

The concept of natural law has been central to much of the

Western political tradition. Though often in disagreement on its content, many of the figures that most informed Western conceptions of politics believed that standards exist above and beyond humanly created "positive law" that can be used as a basis from which to judge such man-made law. In the American context, debates have raged regarding the degree to which the Founders were committed to such a natural law understanding when creating the American Constitution. In his contribution, Robert George sees the Founders to have been dedicated to a natural law understanding of politics but one fundamentally unlike that which informs much of America's contemporary jurisprudence.

As it did so egregiously in *Griswold v. Connecticut* (1965), the Supreme Court has taken for itself the role of enforcer of its own understanding of natural law and natural rights. It has thereby usurped the legislative authority reserved to Congress and the states. George argues that a belief in natural law does not necessitate any such form of judicial enforcement of principles not found in the Constitution. Indeed, as he makes clear, fidelity to the rule of law, acceptance of the constitutional limits of one's authority, is a necessary ingredient in any proper understanding of justice. Judicial activism in the name of natural justice thereby violates rather than supports what it purports to defend. By accepting natural law but denying to the Court the special role as its guardian, Professor George reconnects us to a superior understanding of the relationship between natural law and constitutional government that should inform our contemporary jurisprudence.

English political experience and Christianity both had profound influence on the minds of the American Founders. One extremely important avenue of their joint influence was found in English common law, which provided the context for the American Constitution and which still influences our understanding of law. Anchored in tradition and developed through experience and reason, common law has been a conserving force during times both of tranquillity and rage. Christianity has always been an important part of the common law, though that fact has often been denied and its importance ignored. In his contribution to this volume, James Stoner explores the relationship of Christianity to the common law in the United States and finds the proper balance struck not in the secularism of the judge-made law of recent decades, but in a series of nineteenth century cases dealing with blasphemy, Sunday closings, and church property disputes. Though it could fully flower again only with time, remembering our common law heritage would do much to add a degree of sanity and balance to our current First Amendment jurisprudence.

Of the most profound losses that attend the failure of a society to remember its own origins, one must surely be that words often lose their meaning and become malleable in the hands of authors, judges, political figures, and teachers. As words lose their meaning, so the documents and institutions of the past slowly disintegrate. Perhaps no single word is more important to the American political tradition than "liberty." Barry Alan Shain asks us to consider how far we have emptied this word of the rich and multifaceted meaning it held for the men of the Founding generation. The radical individualist understanding that contemporary America has of the term, which has led to such pernicious innovations as no-fault divorce, nearly unbridled freedom of license, and loss of corporate rights, were not shared by eighteenth century Americans who penned the various state constitutions, the Declaration of Independence, the Constitution of 1787, and the Bill of Rights. Rather, as Shain clearly demonstrates, their notion of liberty was in keeping with a Western, communally based understanding where rights are married to corresponding responsibilities. Once we have lost the meaning of the words that inspired the republic and formed its foundational document, how long can its fruits be securely enjoyed?

Were the American Revolution and the creation of the Constitution inspired by and grounded in Enlightenment notions of society and politics? Such is often the assertion, but if the preceding chapters do not amply demonstrated the considerable pre-Enlightenment roots of the American order, Donald Livingston's treatment of Enlightenment politics should dispel

such notions of the nature of the American Founding. Com-
paring Enlightenment politics to those espoused by Johannes
Althusius and David Hume, Livingston finds that America was
founded upon a non-Enlightenment idiom that understood
the possibility and necessity of divided sovereignty and recognized the legitimacy of independent social authorities. But the
language of the Founders did occasionally exhibit a youthful
relation to the ideology of the Enlightenment, and Livingston
finds it to have been those germs that would, decades later, be
twisted into a thoroughgoing nationalist understanding of the
American project. It was not the American Founders who were
the children of the Enlightenment, but those who have given
us the modern era of large, centralized government and the
emasculation of local communities.

In a related vein, Bruce Frohnen points out that the American Revolution was not much of a "revolution" at all. Rather
than a cultural and political revolution like that which would
rock the foundations of civilization in France, the American
patriots fought for traditional liberties and relationships that
had been undermined by an overreaching parliament. In this
way, Frohnen makes clear the American Revolution was a conserving war for independence, which sought to reestablish the
balanced constitutional system of post-1688 England—not a
revolution built upon abstractions and attempting to remake
society.

Traditionally, the radical intellectual Left has used tactics that are overtly anti-Western and in many cases unreservedly anti-American. In order to refashion society, they first had to become its most fervent critics. In this mode, at least they were easily spotted and their project was routinely unmasked. But the academic left now seems poised to take a potentially more dangerous tact in its effort to obliterate our past. Richard Rorty, the dean of American philosophers, now urges the Left to embrace American national pride and engage in practical political innovations. They should appropriate the language of national pride and love America, but not the America that actually exists or has ever existed, but the America of the Left's greatest hopes. In this way, by casting aside all tradition, experience, and truth itself, but simultaneously seeming to embrace "America," the Left, it is asserted, can achieve a limitless improvement in society and in the human condition itself. Peter Augustine Lawler penetrates this post-modern attempt at creating a therapeutic society, and he unmasks it as a direct and pernicious threat to human liberty. Lawler concludes *Vital Remnants* with a defense of the constitutional order and the Western view of the human condition upon which it was established. At the heart of that understanding is the synthesis of Socratic reason and biblical revelation that Lawler finds to be the secret of the West's vitality.

The American constitutional order grew from roots sunk

deep in the history of Western civilization. The Free Society is a precious and fragile inheritance from ages past and cultures broken. Vital remnants still work through us, but for how long? Current cultural trends mitigate against memory and many of our professional educators have surrendered to the politically correct forces of amnesia. Nevertheless, as these essays all attest, hope remains as some scholars and teachers keep the tablets and seek to enliven moral imaginations with revitalized remnants of our shared inheritance. May they help, in some small way, to freshen the colors of our republic.

Is America an Experiment?

Wilfred M. McClay

Some of the most valuable work in the field of American history these days is being done by the men and women who restore and preserve historical sites. Though such work is often disdained as antiquarian or subscholarly by academic historians, in fact it serves an immensely important public purpose. It helps us remember our origins, and thereby remember who we are. Whenever one visits a reconstructed colonial American setting—and here I am thinking not only of a relatively elegant town like Williamsburg, but also of somewhat more spare or rugged places such as Jamestown or Old Sturbridge Village or Plimoth Plantation or St. Mary's City—one is forcibly reminded of the tentativeness and fragility of the entire American undertaking.

That impression follows one even into the more famous venues. Go to Independence Hall in Philadelphia, Faneuil Hall or the Old North Church in Boston, the Old Senate Chamber at the State House in Annapolis. All are lovely, well-kept sites. Yet one is struck not by their grandeur, but their tininess, their almost self-effacing modesty. Even the most jaded among us may feel compelled to pause for a moment, and ponder the astounding fact that a nation so colossal could have grown from seeds so small. When one thinks about the chaotic and tumultuous social history of Jamestown and early Virginia, or contemplates the half-mad audacity of the New England Puritans, who were convinced that their lonely adventure huddled together in a remote and frigid wilderness was a divinely appointed mission of world-historical importance, one does not sense historical inevitability or destiny. Far from it. The longer and more deeply one studies the American past, the easier it is to imagine that matters could have turned out very differently.

Yet it would be a mistake to see this American enterprise—and it would be a long time before it had sufficient coherence to be called anything like an enterprise—as a quirky, *sui generis* thing, independent of the great movements of Western history. Lewis Mumford once rightly observed that "the settlement of America had its origins in the unsettlement of Europe," an insight that neatly compresses a great deal of history into a single phrase.[1] Nevertheless, there has always been a strong tendency, perhaps never stronger than in the present day, to detach our discussions of the American past from discussions of what we call Western civilization, and thereby to neglect the specifically American slant upon, and contribution to, that larger subject. It is almost as if we presume that the relationship between the great traditions of European thought and the realities of modern American life is so clear-cut—or so hopelessly severed—as to need no comment.

This is nothing new. It is, in fact, one of the central themes of American history. For no question has bemused and bedeviled American writers from the nation's beginnings more persistently than the question of how America was related, intellectually and culturally, to Europe. The question has always tended to be posed in stark, either/or terms. In declaring political independence, had America declared something approaching cultural independence? Or was it still mired down in a kind of colonial mentality, even as its political and social institutions, and its galloping commercial and industrial economy, were vaulting ahead into previously unimagined territory? One sees this dichotomy all the time, an opposition between what Philip Rahv called palefaces and redskins—"palefaces" being writers who attempted to produce a high-toned American literature, worthy of comparison in both form and content with the great literatures of Europe; and "redskins" being those who believed that it was the destiny of American culture to produce something dramatically different, something indigenous, something as bold and distinctive as the facts of American social and political democracy.[2]

The heart of the redskin author was well expressed by Ralph Waldo Emerson, in his famous address "The American Scholar" in 1837, when he complained that "we have listened too long to the courtly muses of Europe."[3] By speaking of "courtly" muses, Emerson wished to remind his listeners of the fiercely antimonarchical and antiaristocratic premises undergirding American political life. But the thrust of his remarks went deeper. It urged would-be American writers to find their own way, and treat their European heritage not as a sacred legacy but as an exploitable (and dispensable) resource. In a different but complementary way, the influential American historian Frederick Jackson Turner propounded a theory of American origins that discounted the "germs" of European culture, and instead found the genius of American democracy arising directly out of the life of the American frontier.[4] Either of these views was likely to lend considerable support to the idea of America as a land of experiment: an ever-unfolding enterprise that was not tied down to any enduring principles or precepts or institutions drawn from the past, but was instead committed to an understanding of human life as open-ended improvisation and unfettered exploration, a perpetual trial-and-error undertaking.

For whatever reason, this idea—the idea of America as an experiment—has taken hold with a vengeance in our contemporary discourse. It is, in fact, so ubiquitous that one stumbles on it virtually every day, without even looking for it. Let me cite two representative examples.

Marjorie Heins, director of the Arts Censorship Project of the American Civil Liberties Union, casually invoked the idea during the course of a March 1998 C-SPAN appearance, in connection with the suit brought against the National Endowment for the Arts (NEA) by controversial performance artist Karen Finley and several others who had been denied NEA grants on the grounds that they offended general standards of decency. Of course, Ms. Heins thought the NEA's denial of funding to Ms. Finley was deplorable, and marshaled all the most familiar arguments as to why this was the case. But the clinching argument, in her mind, was contained in her declaration that "we are as a nation collectively involved in a great experiment," and that our national commitment to free experimentation demands that we be "mature" enough to "contribute" some portion of our tax dollars to the subsidizing of forms of expression that we do not like.[5] (That it might be more logical to demand such "maturity" first from those who receive and distribute such federal monies, rather than from the taxpayers who pony them up, was an unexplored alternative, though one that the Supreme Court now appears to have endorsed.[6])

Another, rather more chilling example of the language of

experiment appeared in a December 1997 op-ed piece in the
New York Times by the eminent Harvard law professor Laurence
Tribe, dealing with the possibility of human cloning. Tribe argued that it was premature and perhaps unwise for us as a nation to move to prohibit such cloning, and he adduced a variety of grounds for this assertion. At the head of the list was the
need to preserve the central importance of experimentation in
American culture. A society that privileges certain behaviors as
"natural" and stigmatizes others as "unnatural" runs the risk of
"cutting itself off from vital experimentation," including experimentation with alternative lifestyles. The prohibition of
cloning in particular might serve to open a Pandora's box of
reactionary sentiment, ultimately serving to cast a pall of doubt
over all those who are experimenting with "unconventional ways
of linking erotic attachment, romantic commitment, genetic
replication, gestational mothering, and the joys and responsibilities of child rearing."[7] The great experiment that is America
must be permitted to go on, no matter what.

In both cases, then, we see the idea of America-as-experiment offered as a last refuge of the otherwise unthinkable or
indefensible. One often sees the partisans of the most extreme
forms of multiculturalism, or advocates of a transformation in
the standards of American citizenship, or other opponents of
the very idea of a common American culture, making a similar
flourish: America is not, in their view, a set of fixed beliefs or

standards or customs or laws or codes or institutions. *America is an experiment.* And what, one can almost hear the average contemporary American say, could possibly be wrong with that? Is not experimentation a healthy and wonderful thing? Is not America at its best a nation devoted to individual liberty, and to the pursuit of all the things that inquiring minds want to know?

Even Neil Postman, one of the most sensible and perceptive critics of American education and popular culture, suggests in his most recent book that we ought to install the idea of America as an experiment as *the central narrative of American history.* This means for him that we will now define America as "a perpetual and fascinating question mark," "a series of stunning and dangerous questions" that "will always remain unanswered." Or, as he says in another place, we have always been a nation "formed, maintained, and preserved on the principle of continuous argumentation."[8]

I would submit that, far from being desirable, this is truly a ghastly idea, unrealistic and unappealing. It envisions our national life as something resembling an academic seminar, or an endless television talk show. One might be forgiven for thinking this sounds more like something out of Dante than Tocqueville. It mistakes the means for the end, supposing that continuous argumentation itself can be a *substitute* for truth, rather than a means of discerning truth.

What may make Postman's view attractive to many of us is the favorable view we all have of the idea of "experiment." One may in fact be taking on one of the few remaining shibboleths of American life in questioning the idea of America as an experiment. Experimentation, we tend to feel, is a salutary thing, a trademark of individual liberty, the sign of a curious and questioning mind—a quality more inclusive than motherhood, and certainly much healthier than apple pie. A life lived without experiment, we imagine, is doomed to be hidebound, unimaginative, nasty, prudish, and short.

Perhaps. But such statements beg the question of what an experiment is, and of what it might mean to live in a country that embodies an experimental spirit. Is the spirit of experiment the same thing as an endless process of asking "why not?" Is it a sort of endless project of deconstructing the stable, reconfiguring the given, overturning the traditional, and driving our carriages over the bones of the dead, in William Blake's grisly phrase? Is America the land of antitraditional tradition, of what Irving Howe called "the American newness"? Is that what we mean by liberty, the liberty to declare independence of everything that has come before us, to discard the tried and embrace the untried—exercising our creativity even if it means reinventing the wheel?

Clearly this imprecise and sentimental idea of America as an experiment needs to be examined. To do so, we first have to take a closer look at the idea of experiment itself. Dictionaries define experiment in three ways: first, as a test made to demonstrate a known truth; second, as a test to examine the validity of a hypothesis; and third, as a test to determine the efficacy of something previously untried. The Latin roots of the word strongly suggest the guiding idea of *trying* or *testing*. But what should be obvious, in all three definitions, is the fact that "experiment" is always related to some specific end, some well-defined goal, some truth, hypothesis, pattern, or principle to be confirmed or disconfirmed. Even trying the efficacy of something untried, which might seem to include the "why not?" school of experimentation, actually does not include it on closer examination. It does not because the concept of "efficacy" is necessarily related to some very particular and carefully circumscribed end. (When Roman Catholics speak of the "efficacy" of the sacraments, they do not mean that the wine makes you drunk.) Experiment is the indispensable core of modern science, which is in turn a Western product par excellence. But the key to an effective scientific experiment lies in the careful definition of the problem, a definition that does not swerve in midstream, and that always seeks to identify, understand, and harness the real and objective laws of nature, rather than seek to transform or obliterate those laws.

In that sense, the American nation most definitely *was* an experiment at the outset. In particular, it is crystal clear that the Framers of the Constitution, and the early generations of American national political leaders, thought of their handiwork in precisely this way. Alexander Hamilton began the first number of *The Federalist* with the famous speculation that it "seemed to have been reserved to the people of this country, by their conduct and example, to decide the important question, whether societies of men are really capable or not of establishing good government from reflection and choice, or whether they are forever destined to depend for their political constitutions on accident and force."[9] The word "experiment" is not used here, but the concept most certainly is; and the word itself occurs in twenty-four of the papers in *The Federalist*—always in a very practical and unmystical way, with the clear implication that experiments succeed, experiments fail, and that is the process by which knowledge progresses.

In contrast, it is revealing to ask ourselves whether someone in the position of Marjorie Heins would ever be willing to concede that the "experiment" of subsidizing broadly offensive art had failed. Is there any conceivable evidence that she and others like her would find persuasive? In Mr. Tribe's case, can one identify a purpose or end for all this social experimentation—or for that matter, any conceivable set of common values that could take precedence over the sovereign right of self-determining individuals to live experimentally? In that case, what do these two individuals *really* mean by "experiment"? And what, in general, do contemporary Americans understand it to mean?

In any event, the word "experiment" was used quite conspicuously by George Washington, in his first inaugural address, where he echoed Hamilton's view almost exactly, remarking that "The preservation of the sacred fire of liberty and the destiny of the republican model of government are justly considered, perhaps, as deeply, as finally, staked on the *experiment* intrusted to the hands of the American people."[10]

So Washington himself thought of America as an experiment; but this was best understood as a careful and focused practical experiment, not an open-ended utopian foray in human engineering or consciousness-transformation. The ends of the experiment are made clear in Washington's statement. They are the preservation of liberty and the republican model of government—that is, freedom and self-governance—or as we sometimes put it, ordered liberty. They were not talking about an open-ended commitment to achieving absolute equality of condition, let alone the satisfaction of every desire and the drying of every tear. They had very specific goals in view. The Framers by and large saw this new constitutional order as an informed, realistic, and focused effort to use the knowledge of history and human nature in order to *defy* the known effects of history and human nature.

This was, in itself, a bold and imaginative effort, whose outcome was far from certain. History seemed to teach the doleful lesson that the fate of even the best free republics was the fate of Rome, America's exemplar *and* its warning.[11] Human nature was perverse and incorrigible, a fact that ensured that the republican form of government would be exceptionally unstable and corruptible. The example of Rome hung over the early nation, as if it were one of Neil Postman's gigantic question marks. Everywhere one looked, the adulation of Roman models was evident—in the neoclassical architecture, in the public statuary, and even in the classical *noms de plume* (Publius, Brutus, Cato) chosen by both proponents and opponents of the Constitution. But since even Rome had succumbed, in the end, to the corruptions and ambitions of human nature, that adulation was inevitably double-edged and laced with profound doubt.

There was plenty to be nervous about in the American experiment. Yet by 1838, when Abraham Lincoln gave a speech entitled "The Perpetuation of our Political Institutions" before the Young Men's Lyceum of Springfield, Illinois, the results of the experiment were in. "America had been felt to be an undecided experiment," said Lincoln; "now, it is understood to be a successful one," having conclusively proved "the capability of a people to govern themselves." But success, he continued, brought its own perils. As the "patriots of Seventy-Six" who had created the new nation passed away, and a postrevolutionary generation came of age, there was the danger that the commitment to the republic would flag, now that the success of the experiment was no longer at issue, and the younger generation was left without a proper field of activity for its own heroic aspirations. Lincoln worried that "the temple must fall" unless "other pillars" be provided to take the place of the Founding generation, pillars "hewn from the solid quarry of sober reason" rather than the powerful but unsustainable passions that had motivated the first patriots.[12] In a sense, then, Lincoln saw a perpetuation of the spirit of experimentalism, and of experimental urgency, as a part of any effort to perpetuate our political institutions. Perhaps this was why, twenty-five years later at Gettysburg, he recurred to the idea that the Civil War itself was a "testing" of whether the product of such a republican experiment "can long endure."[13] It was one thing to make a democratic republic work; it was quite another to sustain its working.

Lincoln was right to raise these issues. Part of the value of the idea of "experiment" is the sense of alertness and responsibility for our own lives that it awakens in us. If we do not hold up the walls, who will? Whatever one thinks of his formulation, it seems hard to escape the fact that the scope and character of the experiment were also being slightly redefined by Lincoln, and arguably expanded beyond what Washington had in mind—most notably in the Gettysburg Address's invocation of the war's call for a "new birth of freedom." Yet such language seems mild compared to the distended language of Franklin D. Roosevelt, often praised as an example of the pragmatist spirit in American politics. The economic conditions of the day, he declared, demanded "bold, persistent experimentation." One should not get too fancy about it; instead, "take a method and try it: if it fails, admit it frankly and try another. But above all, try something."[14] With such language we have come a long way from the notion that the aim of the experiment is the cultivation of a regime built around ordered liberty. And yet, to give him his due, Roosevelt still clearly linked the process of experimentation with results. Like a good pragmatist, he recognized that an experiment can produce negative results, or even fail altogether.

The important point to bear in mind is that these examples illustrate how pliable are the uses of the idea of "experiment." Roosevelt's language was pointing toward the sense of experiment that we increasingly hear expressed today, one that is more than willing to entertain the transformation of the American people and nation and institutions into something radically different from what they are and have been. In this view, the American project, to the extent we can even talk about such a thing, is unfinished and nothing to take any great pride in—yet. Fortunately, however, nothing is static or fixed. We are continually remaking, reinventing, and recreating ourselves as a people. Democratic ideals are being recast; civic identity is in flux. This is America—anything is possible. Ours is, as the title of a popular textbook has it, an "unfinished nation."[15]

Of course, these things are true to some extent. We are indeed always changing and adapting. America is still a land of extraordinary possibility. To call America an "unfinished nation" can be viewed as a form of honest affirmation, a way of endorsing an enterprise that has repeatedly fallen far short of its professed ideals, perhaps most notably and shamefully in its treatment over several centuries of African slaves and their descendants. The question, however, is whether everything is therefore to be open to transformation. A proper experiment requires stability in the object and means by which the experiment is conducted, and in the ends the experiment is designed to achieve. It is one thing to argue that the experiment needs to be conducted more faithfully, and quite another to say that it needs to be redefined or junked altogether. In the historian John Fonte's telling words, we need to be on our guard about the concept of America as an "unfinished nation," since this can be employed as "a blank check to argue for the reinvention of the American nation-state from its origins as an experiment in self-government tempered by constitutional liberty, to a permanent cultural revolution."[16] Thus would the concept of America-as-experiment be transformed into Experimental America.

A salient expression of this theme appears in philosopher

Richard Rorty's new book, *Achieving Our Nation*, an attempt to revive the fortunes of leftist thought in American political life by urging American academic intellectuals to stop theorizing so much, and simply to get back to the business of social transformation. Had the words not already been used by Nike and Jerry Rubin, the book's title ought to have been *Just Do It*. That we all "know" what needs to be done, and that the past three decades of debates over economic and social policy are not even worth noticing, are only two of the book's staggering assumptions. But let that pass. For our present purposes, it is more useful to focus on a passage from near the end of the book that illuminates the landscape with the suddenness of a lightning bolt. This book has been warmly received by those who want to see in it an affirmation of America, and an effort, in accents recalling the glory days of the Popular Front, to recover the mantle of patriotism for the Left. Yet this hope simply does not bear up under scrutiny. Rorty has the considerable virtue of being a clear writer, a virtue that makes it hard to hide the real thrust of what he is saying:

> Nobody has yet suggested a viable leftist alternative to the civic religion of which Whitman and Dewey were prophets. That civic religion centered around taking advantage of traditional pride in American citizenship by substituting social justice for individual freedom as

our country's principal goal. We were supposed to love our country because it showed promise of being kinder and more generous than other countries.... This was a counsel of perfection rather than description of fact. But you cannot urge national political renewal on the basis of descriptions of fact.... You have to be loyal to a dream country rather than to the one to which you wake up every morning. Unless such loyalty exists, the ideal has no chance of becoming actual.[17]

There is a lot to ponder here. Consider, for example, the implications of the words "taking advantage." But the last two sentences are especially startling. What makes them particularly fascinating is the fact that they come from a leading advocate of pragmatism, a philosophy that, whatever else it means, is committed to an emphasis upon the actual, the immediate, the concrete, the particular, as opposed to the ideal or fantastical. One would have thought that a pragmatist would be less of an idealist, would have more respect for the way things are.

Rorty's statement serves to make the point that there are some respects in which America is *not* an experiment, and it is pernicious to talk as if it is. There is a big difference between saying, as Lincoln did, that the great achievements of our fathers are fragile, and ever in need of support and bolstering, and saying that our country does not exist yet, because it does

not yet correspond with the dreams of enlightened intellectuals. This is the language of "unfinished nation" taken to its
extreme. "Achieving" our country is the sort of ungrammatical
phrase that always should be a tip-off that an intellectual heist
is taking place. We do not use the word "achieve" in the way
Rorty has tried to use it. One accomplishes a task, one does
not "accomplish" a country. One lives in it. Unless, that is,
one is a pragmatist who urges us to live in a dream country,
rather than in the one that actually sustains us.

A more serious way of making this point is to say that we
cannot live in the world provisionally. Otherwise, we will reach
the ends of our lives without ever having begun them. A far
better pragmatist, William James, understood this fully.[18] We
must make choices, ultimate choices, merely to live. We are not
born into a vacuum, or on probation from reality. We have
specific fathers and mothers, contexts in which our duties and
obligations are shaped. Our duties are to them, not to the fathers, mothers, and others that we would have preferred to
have, had we been able to create the universe in a manner more
after our own hearts. We cannot say, with Herman Melville's
haunted character Bartleby the Scrivener, "I would prefer not
to."[19] We cannot withhold ourselves from our country until it
meets USDA standards of purity. We do not have it in our
power to reinvent the world first, and then and only then begin
to live in it. The past has a reality, has inescapable sway, has

authority over us; and we cannot be nurtured by that past until we acknowledge its reality.

Some of these realizations were memorably captured by Robert Frost in "The Gift Outright," a very great American poem that reflects upon the historical evolution of American national identity.

THE GIFT OUTRIGHT

The land was ours before we were the land's.

She was our land more than a hundred years

Before we were her people. She was ours

In Massachusetts, in Virginia,

But we were England's, still colonials,

Possessing what we still were unpossessed by,

Possessed by what we now no more possessed.

Something we were withholding made us weak

Until we found out that it was ourselves

We were withholding from our land of living,

And forthwith found salvation in surrender.

Such as we were we gave ourselves outright

(The deed of gift was many deeds of war)

To the land vaguely realizing westward,

But still unstoried, artless, unenhanced,

Such as she was, such as she would become.[20]

The idea of American civilization as "colonial," and the image of the "land vaguely realizing westward" are powerfully evocative of Emerson and Turner, of the idea that American civilization needs to find its own distinctive voice, rather than live off the inheritance of its European patrimony. This is the redskin element in American intellectual history. However, the phrase "something we were withholding made us weak" seems to me a phrase that Rorty might want to take to heart. Maybe the thing that makes Rorty's Left weak, aside from its ideas, is what it is withholding. It is the very withholding that Frost warns against, and Rorty, notwithstanding his praise of isolated figures like John Dewey and Walt Whitman, urges us to persist in. In fact, many of us who have spent our lives moving away from the Left were first nudged in that direction by a sense that the ideas and the withholding were part of one and the same problem. A reading of *Achieving Our Country* will not change anyone's mind about that.

A primal love of one's country, like the primal and inexplicable love of Being itself, constitutes an enormous emotional and spiritual resource, to be drawn upon in all the endeavours of one's life by those fortunate enough to have it. Such love is neither synonymous with complacency, nor synonymous with any particular ideological commitment or political identification. But it is incompatible with the idea of America as an open-ended experiment, an entity yet to be achieved, in which all options are open, all traditions are subject to dissolution, and all claims are revocable. It is incompatible with the idea of treating the Constitution as a *living* document that means what our robed masters and law professors tell us it means today, when they are not creating new things out of whole cloth. If everything is open to change, then nothing finally matters but the narcissistic self, the one still point left in a turning world. Or perhaps even that narcissism will give way to Robert Jay Lifton's "protean man," which unapologetically celebrates the postmodern conception of the self as an ensemble of endlessly changing roles.[21] But this is a recipe for disaster, a recipe for lives stunted by the false excitement of a provisionality that is, at best, nothing more than an extended adolescence. Experimentation cannot be an end in itself; the very concept disintegrates at the first analytical touch. The experiment of America, like all experiments, means nothing unless it is undertaken for the sake of what is not experimental, for the sake of those convictions, beliefs, and fundamental commitments embodied in the term "ordered liberty."

There is one more insight to be gleaned from Frost, and that is in his notion of the Gift Outright. "Such as we were, we gave ourselves outright," he says. An "outright" gift is one given wholly, without reserve or qualification. Well, what are we to make of this? Do we *ever* really have that power of self-endowment, the power to make ourselves? Certainly not, and perhaps

Frost is guilty of an overstatement here, guilty of succumbing to his own redskin and Turnerian prejudices. But at the same time, what Frost has captured here for our contemplation is a struggle that is intrinsic to American history, and to the relationship between what we are as Americans and what we are as part of Western civilization. The same ambivalence is at the heart of the idea of experiment in American history. On the one hand, experiment is a controlled, rational, truth-seeking process that takes seriously the conditions in which one has been placed and our natural or God-given power to act, and thereby to influence our world. The recognition of the power of the past should not be a counsel of passivity; on the contrary, it should be a goad to action. It is *that* sense of experiment that Washington, Hamilton, Lincoln, and even Rorty's hero John Dewey, invoked.

But there is also the sense of experiment that Rorty's other hero, Walt Whitman, invoked, experiment as the search for a condition of boundlessness and unconstraint, of Promethean rebellion against the dead-hand authority of God and nature— the song of the open road, and of the land "vaguely realizing westward." There is quite a lot of that in the American intellectual tradition, going back at least to Jefferson, with his conceit that America was to be "nature's nation," free from the confining artifices and corrupting hierarchies that disfigured all other nations, a nation in which the individual is set free from all ascriptions of birth and heritage, free to make himself. Going forward, we find it in our modern and postmodern fantasies of self-construction, in which individual persons are to be regarded as self-originating sources of valid claims. Let me admit, too, that I deeply cherish the sense of fluidity, the sense of sheer possibility, in American life. It would be both blind and ungrateful to fail to do so. But it is also blind and ungrateful to pretend that one has no antecedents, and that one's present existence is a gift outright from one's self.

To put this same point in a rather different way, the redskin strain in our intellectual history suffers from a prickly defensiveness, even immature defiance, a tendency that one sees in, for example, Mark Twain—a tendency to try just a little too hard, to counterpunch too much against "courtly muses," whether real or imaginary, and thereby to show too little confidence in the possibility of an Americanness that is comfortable with its European heritage. Sometimes a redskin can even sound like a redneck. To be sure, there are worse things than being a redneck. But these are not our only choices, and we should never imagine that they are. We have a more goodly and various heritage than that. The American vs. European conflict is an important historical element in that heritage, but we ought to be mature enough to understand that the grounds for that conflict are now largely past. America will continue to have, as it has had since at least 1945, an essential role to play in the protection and perpetuation of that European heritage. At the same time, if it is to play the role effectively, America will also need to attend, more closely and carefully than it has in the past, to parts of that heritage it has increasingly neglected. We may need to reflect on why so much of the rest of the world now finds the American experiment to be something worrisome, and even morally unsettling.

Professor James Kurth of Swarthmore wrote an interesting article four years ago, in which he argued, against the Harvard political scientist Samuel Huntington, that the real "clash of civilizations" in the future would not be between the West and one or more of the Rest, but instead "between the West and the Post-West, within the West itself."[22] This clash, he argued, "has already taken place within the brain of Western civilization, the American intellectual class." The term "Post-West" is a felicitous one for our purposes, since it implies a combination of dependency and departure. What we mean by "Post-West" is a massive intensification of certain very Western ideas, to the exclusion of others. The hypertrophy of the idea of "rights," detached from notions of individual limitations or accountability, is perhaps the most vivid example of the sort of thing I mean.

But at the very center of the Post-Western idea is a redefinition of the meaning of the nation. We have come from fancying ourselves Nature's Nation to seeking to achieve the Denatured

Nation. America is no longer to be thought of as an entity whose cohesion is based on a shared set of values, shared social and institutional arrangements, a shared legal structure, a shared history, a shared culture, and a shared standard of citizenship. Or, to the extent that it is so conceived, and a modernist rather than postmodernist ideal prevails, all such desiderata are considered subordinate to certain international and universalistic values: humanitarianism, egalitarianism, democracy, international equity. Either way, the nation-state is understood to be inadequate, and ideas of national sovereignty obsolete. There is a strong overriding sense of experiment in the Post-West, though a sense one cannot find in Frost, and rarely in the great American tradition: a sense of "experiment" as the promise of total and open-ended human transformation, a sense that (as Rorty makes explicit) amounts to an unrelenting war against any constraints upon the human will, and particularly against the limiting conceptions of God and nature.[23]

That project is, of course, also Western, based as it is on Western notions of the systematic relief of man's estate through the exercise of instrumental reason. Arguably, Karl Marx was the modern Western philosopher, *par excellence*. He certainly was not anything else *but* Western. That fact should give us pause when we think about Western civilization as a benign or inert body of knowledge in any simple sense, rather than as a peculiarly charged, dynamic, and self-questioning activity, one that can go badly astray even within its own terms. The West is no one thing; the roots of American order are astonishingly various, and in tension with one another. Merely to think about the fundamental incompatibility of Athens and Jerusalem, and about the equally indispensable role that each plays in the sustenance of this civilization, is to realize how complicated a task it is to describe the West.

At the risk of oversimplification, I think we can say one thing. Today, when we think of the West, we tend to think of such ideals as individual liberty, private property, democratic polity, economic growth, and the transforming power of applied science. All these things are indeed characteristics of the modern West. They have, however, been successful only because they arose in a larger and longer context, the moral context of what some call the Old West—the premodern cultural inheritance built up over many centuries by the successive influences of Judaism, classical Greece and Rome, Christianity, and the ever-underestimated institutions of the medieval period.[24] We have forgotten this fact. Instead, we act as if the West is modernity pure and simple—and the rest of the world is only too inclined to agree.

There are consequences to this mistaken belief. Consider some of the pathologies afflicting the world we now live in: its hard and inhuman techno-rationality; its growing disregard for the intrinsic value of human life; and its fanatical desire to conquer and manipulate nature for no proportionate purpose. Consider its shameless compulsion to make private what should be public, and make public what should be private; its willingness to put a price tag on anything for which there is a potential buyer; and its inability to conceive a higher calling in life than the pursuit of individual pleasure.

One could go on. The point is that each of these pathologies represents a grotesque intensification of tendencies and values that were benign, even admirable, so long as they were embedded in and restrained by a deeper set of metaphysical convictions, particularly convictions that stressed that the human being is created in the image of God and is ultimately answerable, in some way, to that Creator. Virtues become vices when they are disconnected from their proper points of reference. This is precisely why experimentation cannot be a sufficient end in itself.

I do not, however, want to conclude in a way that appears to disparage the idea of experiment, properly understood. That would be an error just as great as the uncritical exaltation of experiment. There is still one great experiment ahead of us now, and its outlines are becoming clearer and clearer as time goes by. There has been a growing division in the Western soul between the Old West and New West—between those who embrace either the *imago Dei* or a normative conception of nature, with the inherent limits upon the human will and human condition that such conceptions impose, and those who disdain such limits in the name of boundless revolutionary or technological transformation. It seems increasingly likely that this division, as it grows and deepens, will correspond less and less to the usual divisions of left and right, liberal and conservative. This is another way of saying that both ends of the ideological spectrum, as it exists in our own time, will need to take stock of themselves, and of how they stand with respect to these matters.

The stakes are high, as high as they were in 1787, if not far more so. If the West is to survive and thrive, and if it is not to devolve into a doomed pseudo-civilization of soulless hedonists and consumers, a dystopia less like George Orwell's than Aldous Huxley's, a way of life that will earn, and deserve, the world's contempt, it must recover its lost Old Western dimension, the framework of meaning within which the New Western achievements can find their proper measure. The moral revulsion that most—though not all—of us feel at the now-looming prospect of human cloning, taken along with the inability of many of us, from President Clinton on down, to provide a persuasive justification for this revulsion, should be a warning sign to us that Western man cannot live for long by New Western bread and circuses alone.

So we, too, are embarked upon an experiment—a great experiment in cultural recovery. No one knows whether it is possible. There is no real precedent for it, at least not on the scale required now. One sees precisely this concern weaving in and out of the highly interesting, if abstract and tentative, reflections of a European figure like Vàclav Havel.[25] But America will have to be a central focus of this experiment of cultural recovery, and the task will be especially difficult here. When Nathaniel Hawthorne complained that America had no ruins and castles, he was pointing not only to the nation's youthfulness, but to the fact that the American relationship to premodern institutions was extraordinarily weak.[26] Consequently, we will not be able to stumble into this transformation. We will not find it by rummaging around in our basements and attics. We will not be able to find it, as Turner said the frontiersmen found democratic freedom, by exchanging our leather shoes for moccasins, and our automobiles for birch canoes. We are going to have to engage in an arduous process of consciously reappropriating the past, a past that has very nearly slipped out of our reach, and to do so not out of antiquarianism but in a fresh and unprecedented way, knowing that our lives depend on it.

It is a formidable experiment. It will be the great task of the rising generations. As in any experiment, the possibility of failure is very real, very palpable. But we can take some inspiration from those words of Hamilton, and from the fact that the experiment he and Washington described *has* succeeded, by any reasonable standard that one can apply to things here below.

Moreover, there are other aspects of our American past on which we can profitably build. One of the enduringly suggestive features of Turner's view of American history, notwithstanding all its faults, is its energizing idea of a *frontier*. That was why John Kennedy called his program the New Frontier, as an effort to borrow some of that word's resonance, and mark the coming of a new generation. Well then, here is a new frontier, for us, now. Our very own experiment, every bit as exciting, and challenging, as the one our forebears embraced. Yet a very different kind of experiment. May we fare as well as they did.

NOTES

This article appeared in somewhat altered form in *The Public Interest*, no. 133 (Fall 1998): 3-22, and appears by permission.

1. Lewis Mumford, *The Golden Day: A Study in American Experience and Culture* (New York: Boni and Liveright, 1926), 11.

2. Philip Rahv, "Paleface and Redskin," in *Essays on Literature and Politics, 1932-72*, ed. Arabel J. Porter and Andrew J. Dvosin (Boston: Houghton Mifflin, 1978), 3-19.

3. Ralph Waldo Emerson, "The American Scholar," in *Ralph Waldo Emerson*, ed. Richard Poirier (New York: Oxford University Press, 1990), 37-52.

4. Frederick Jackson Turner, *The Frontier in American History* (New York: Holt, 1920), 1-38.

5. "NEA Decency Standards," C-SPAN Washington Journal, March 31, 1998, ID# 102740, Tape 98-03-31-06-1, Purdue University Public Affairs Video Archives.

6. See *National Endowment for the Arts v. Finley*, 118 S. Ct. 2168 (No. 97-371) (June 1998).

7. Laurence H. Tribe, "Second Thoughts on Cloning," *New York Times*, December 5, 1997, A23.

8. Neil Postman, *The End of Education: Redefining the Value of School* (New York: Alfred A. Knopf, 1995).

9. Alexander Hamilton, *Federalist* no. 1, in *The Federalist*, ed. Jacob E. Cooke (Middletown, Conn.: Wesleyan University Press, 1961), 3.

10. *The Papers of George Washington*, Presidential Series, ed. W. W. Abbot (Charlottesville, Va.: University Press of Virginia, 1987), 2:175.

11. There is a profusion of studies of these matters, written over many years; some recent and valuable ones include Carl J. Richard, *The Founders and the Classics: Greece, Rome, and the American Enlightenment* (Cambridge, Mass.: Harvard University Press, 1994); M.N.S. Sellers, *American Republicanism: Roman Ideology in the United States Constitution* (New York: New York University Press, 1994); William L. Vance, *America's Rome* (New Haven, Conn.: Yale University Press, 1990).

12. Abraham Lincoln, "Address to the Young Men's Lyceum of Springfield, Illinois, January 27, 1838," in *Abraham Lincoln: Speeches and Writings, 1832-1858*, ed. Don E. Fehrenbacher (New York: Library of America, 1989), 28-36.

13. Abraham Lincoln, "Address at Gettysburg, Pennsylvania," in *Abraham Lincoln: Speeches and Writings, 1859-1865*, ed. Don E. Fehrenbacher (New York: Library of America, 1989).

14. Quoted in Arthur M. Schlesinger, "America: Experiment or Destiny?" in *Historical Viewpoints*, ed. John A. Garraty (New York: Harper and Row, 1985), 2:390-400.

15. Alan Brinkley, *The Unfinished Nation: A Concise History of the American People*, 2nd ed. (New York: Alfred A. Knopf, 1997).

16. John Fonte, "The Progressive Project," unpublished manuscript in author's possession.

17. Richard Rorty, *Achieving Our Country: Leftist Thought in Twentieth-Century America* (Cambridge, Mass.: Harvard University Press, 1998), 101.

18. William James, *The Varieties of Religious Experience: A Study in Human Nature: Being the Gifford Lectures on Natural Religion Delivered at Edinburgh in 1901-1902* (New York: Modern Library, 1994).

19. Herman Melville, "Bartleby the Scrivener," in *Herman Melville*, ed. Harrison Hayford (New York: Library of America, 1985), 635-72.

20. Robert Frost, "The Gift Outright," in *The Poetry of Robert Frost*, ed. Edward Connery Lathem (New York: Holt, 1970), 348. Copyright 1942 by Robert Frost. © 1969 by Henry Holt and Co., © 1970 by Lesley Frost Ballantine. Reprinted by permission of Henry Holt and Company, Inc.

21. Robert Jay Lifton, *The Protean Self: Human Resilience in an Age of Fragmentation* (New York: Basic Books, 1995). See also Paul Leinberger and Bruce Tucker, *The New Individualists: The Generation After the Organization Man* (New York: Harper and Row, 1991); Kenneth Gergen, *The Saturated Self: Dilemmas of Identity in Contemporary Life* (New York: Basic, 1992); and Walter Truett Anderson, *The Future of the Self: Inventing the Postmodern Person* (New York: Putnam, 1998).

22. James Kurth, "The Real Clash," *The National Interest*, no. 37 (Fall 1994): 3-22.

23. See Rorty, *Achieving Our Country*, 14-23.

24. For example, see David Gress, *From Plato to NATO: The Idea of the West and Its Opponents* (New York: Free Press, 1998).

25. Vàclav Havel, *The Art of the Impossible: Politics as Morality in Practice: Speeches and Writings, 1990-1996*, trans. Paul Wilson et al. (New York: Alfred A. Knopf, 1997); and *Open Letters: Selected Writings 1964-1990* (New York: Alfred A. Knopf, 1991).

26. See the comments both of Hawthorne and James reflected in James's little gem of a book, *Hawthorne*, which can be found in *The Shock of Recognition*, ed. Edmund Wilson (New York: Farrar, Straus and Cudahy, 1955), 427-565.

FOUNDERS AS FARMERS: THE GREEK GEORGIC TRADITION AND THE FOUNDERS

Bruce S. Thornton

That the ancient Greeks and Romans influenced immeasurably the political philosophy of the American Founders should be a historical truism. Yet the advent of multiculturalism, with its version of history as a therapeutic melodrama designed to boost the self-esteem of selected "victims," has called into question a historical fact once the common knowledge of every schoolboy. Today the roots of American political freedom and order are often traced to the Iroquois League, whose council sachems are the alleged architects of American democracy and federalism. This historical falsehood crops up in countless textbooks, was asserted in a Concurrent Resolution of the U.S. Congress in 1988, and was given the presidential imprimatur when Bill Clinton said to several hundred Indian tribal leaders, "Because of your ancestors, democracy existed here long before the Constitution was drafted and ratified."[1]

This official endorsement of patently false knowledge on the part of political officials whose Latinate titles and offices testify to their classical roots, would alone justify a return to the question of classical influences on the Founders. The fact is, eighteenth-century Americans were steeped in the language, ideas, texts, speeches, people, and history of the Greeks, particularly as these were refracted through the Roman lens. As Carl J. Richard reminds us, "The classics supplied mixed government theory, the principal basis for the U.S. Constitution. The classics contributed a great deal to the founders' conception of human nature, their understanding of the nature and purpose of virtue, and their appreciation of society's essential role in its production.... In short, the classics supplied a large portion of the founders' intellectual tools."[2] Perhaps as important, the history of the Greeks' political failures provided the Founders with monitory lessons, "a cautionary tale," as Russell Kirk puts it, "of class conflict, disunity, internecine violence, private and public arrogance and selfishness, imperial vainglory, and civic collapse: what to shun."[3]

Whether the Greeks provided models to emulate or mistakes to avoid, their culture and the Romans' permeated the minds of eighteenth-century educated (and even half-educated) Americans, if only because the classics provided the bulk of the typical curriculum.[4] Even those who opposed classical learning because it was impractical and irrelevant to the new conditions of America, or because it was tainted with elitism, heathenism and slavery, nonetheless were saturated with the poets and politicians, the history and literature of the ancients. Benjamin Franklin may have groused that it was "better to bring back from Italian travel a receipt [recipe] for Parmesan cheese than copies of ancient historical inscriptions," yet he still endorsed the study of classics because it would "fix in the minds of youth deep impressions of the beauty and usefulness of virtue of all kinds."[5] And for all his attacks on the classical curriculum, Benjamin Rush was familiar enough with Greek history to have the sixth-century Athenian statesman Solon appearing in his dreams.[6] Given the ubiquity of classics in education and public life, most educated Americans at some level could have sympathized with Jefferson's encomium to classical learning: "To read the Latin & Greek authors in their original, is a sublime luxury.... I thank on my knees, him who directed my early education, for having put into my possession this rich source of delight; and I would not exchange it for anything which I could then have acquired, & have not since acquired."[7]

Given the importance, then, of Greek and Roman ideas and history for the Founders, a discussion of the georgic tradition can remind us of a neglected example of that influence. Yet the georgic tradition is worthy of examination for another important reason. Since it is concerned with farming and its values and conditions, the georgic ideal spoke more directly and concretely to the experience of the Founders than it can to us moderns who have little or nothing to do with the production of food. In contrast, the life and values of farming were more intimately known to most people before the twentieth century simply because most people were directly engaged in agriculture. At the time of the revolution, nine out of every ten people were farmers,[8] as were many of the Founding generation. "During the whole of the American Enlightenment," Henry Steele Commager notes, "every President was a countryman."[9] In the lives and writings of the Founders we repeatedly happen upon fond encomia to the farming life, testifying not just to its ubiquity but to its moral value. John Adams would find respite from the rigors of law school in laboring on the family farm in order "to put the mind into a stirring, thoughtful mood." And George Washington, who was frequently characterized as Cincinnatus, the late-sixth-century Roman leader who temporarily left his plow to turn back the invading Gauls, enthused, "To see plants rise from the earth and flourish by the superior skill and bounty of the laborer fills the contemplative mind with ideas which are more easy to be conceived than expressed."[10] These sentiments, which link farming to contemplation, labor, and virtue, go right to the heart of the georgic vision. Hence an examination of the georgic tradition recovers for us a portion of the intellectual and material contexts of the American political revolution.

GEORGIC VS. PASTORAL

One problem that arises in discussions of American agrarianism is that it is confused with pastoral at the expense of georgic ideas.[11] Pastoral and georgic thought are very different, both in their conception of the natural world and in the ethic and values that each conception engenders.[12] Pastoral thought views the natural world from a sophisticated urban perspective, as an artifical *locus amoenus*, a pleasant landscape of peace, natural beauty, and harmony with humans, a fitting locale for love and art and particularly the *otium* or leisure in which to practice both. Georgic thought, on the other hand, sees nature as harsh and destructive, a congeries of forces attacking humanity and hence necessitating *labor*, the hard work needed to create order and virtue in order to keep the forces of disorder at bay. The representative figure of pastoral poetry is the idealistic shepherd, lounging in the shade of the tree while he pipes songs about his lovers. The typical character of georgic poetry is the practical farmer, plowing beneath the harsh sun as he eyes the gathering clouds.

The georgic tradition begins with the Greek poet Hesiod (ca. 700 B.C.). In his *Works and Days*, with its vivid descriptions of harsh winter and scorching summer, he gives us a vision of a cruel and indifferent natural world in which the "gods keep livelihood hidden from men," an Iron-Age world filled with predators and pests, famine and storms, and human passions and appetites like sex or greed or violence that militate against human order as much as nature's forces do. Hence the need for hard work to create order and virtue: "The immortals decreed that man must sweat/to attain virtue," Hesiod says, since "for mortals order is best, disorder is worst." "Work, work," the poet advises his wastrel brother Perses, "and then Hunger will not be your companion.... Hunger and the idling man are bosom friends.... If you work, you will be dearer to immortals / and mortals; they both loathe the indolent." This imperative to labor in turn creates virtues such as duty, piety, and self-control: "Do not postpone for tomorrow or the day after tomorrow; / barns are not filled by those who postpone / and waste time in aimlessness. Work prospers with care; / he who postpones wrestles with ruin." Moreover, self-sufficiency and independence can be achieved only by work: "Work, foolish Perses, / for this is what the gods have decreed for men; / otherwise sad-hearted, you will drag your wife and children along / to beg support from neighbors deaf to your pleas." Labor and virtue together create order, both the order of the controlled soul and the orders of culture projected onto a chaotic natural world.[13]

The Roman poet Virgil, whose works were well-known to the Founders,[14] continued the georgic tradition in his *Georgics* (37-30 B.C.), drawing out further the implications of the georgic ethic for political order and virtue. Like Hesiod, Virgil describes

a natural world of plagues, storms, passions, and predators constantly encroaching on the hard-won space of human civilization: "So it is," Virgil sums up the inherent chaos of nature,
"for everything by nature's law / Tends to the worse, slips ever
backward, backward."[15] Also like Hesiod, Virgil recognizes that
only labor can prevent these destructive natural forces from
sweeping away human civilization: "Toil [labor] mastered everything, relentless toil / And the pressure of pinching poverty"
(I.145-46). This labor is an improving one, for the mind must
create skills, crafts, and technologies that compensate for human physical weakness and bend nature's destructive forces to
its will, forces Jove intentionally inflicts on people so "that
step by step practice and taking thought / Should hammer out
the crafts" (I.133-34). Labor and technology together create a
civilization that allows human beings collectively to overcome
their natural weakness and conquer a cruel, indifferent environment. The representative figure of this civilizing process is the
farmer, who daily struggles with a recalcitrant nature to provide
the means for survival, and whose values of hard work, self-
control, and duty undergird civilization's social and political
order.

The political dimension of georgic thought reflects its historical context. It is no accident that Hesiod's work appeared,
as Victor Hanson argues, at the same time as a rising class of
middling hoplite-farmers. These independent yeomen owned

and worked their own land, and their regimen of hard work, self-sufficiency, and distrust of merchant and aristocrat alike created the foundation of the Greek city-state and its unique blend of consensual government of land-owners, militia warfare, and an ethic of middling values, all of which reflected and sustained the experience of small farming.[16] This political dimension of agrarian values is implicit throughout Hesiod, as in his condemnation of the "gift-devouring kings," the aristocrats who know nothing of "how asphodel and mallow mature."[17] Virgil, however, explicitly develops the connection between the small farmer and political order. After all, the Roman republic was a nation of citizen-farmers, and Roman national ideology glorified the rural past and its values even as the collapse of the republic called them into question. The Romans themselves made this connection between small farmers and national greatness a truism, from Cato the Censor (234-149), who said that the old Romans praised a man by calling him a "good farmer" and that farming is the "most highly respected calling," to Cicero, who remarked that the Romans' ancestors "busily worked their own land and did not push for that of others. In this way they augmented with territory and cities and nations this republic, this empire, and the fame of the Roman people."[18]

That the republic's political disintegration followed the abandonment of the simple lifestyle and values of the citizen-soldier was by Virgil's time another commonplace. At the end of the first *Georgic*, Virgil links the political and social disorder of the decaying republic to the abandonment of small farming: "So many wars, so many shapes of crime / Confront us; no due honour attends the plough, / The fields, bereft of tillers, are all unkempt, / And in the forge the curving pruning-hook / Is made a straight hard sword" (I.506-10). At the end of the second *Georgic*, he contrasts his portrait of the peaceful, self-sufficient life of the small farmer with the political disorder of a Rome corrupted by luxury and greed and torn by civil strife, a place where "men revel steeped in brothers' blood" (II. 510). Virgil ends the second *Georgic* by linking the small farmer's life to Roman greatness: "Thus it was / That Rome became the fairest thing in the world" (II.534-35). In Virgil the farmer who works his own land and supports his family is made the building-block of political stability, justice and order, for the values and ethics that farming daily demands—frugality, duty, self-control—are the same ones that create and sustain a participatory political order in which citizens rule rather than aristocratic or plutocratic elites.

Georgic thought's emphasis on nature's harshness, however, does not preclude an appreciation of its beauty. Hesiod and Virgil both have scenes describing the loveliness of nature, and it is perhaps such scenes, particularly Virgil's famous and oft-imitated encomia to Italy and its farms in the second *Georgic*, that mislead many into characterizing them as pastoral. When

Nathaniel Ames III, arguing for the agricultural life in 1767, quotes Virgil's second *Georgic*—"Oh! ye husbandmen, how happy would ye be, did ye know your own advantages"—it is easy to read such a sentiment as pastoral idealism.[19] But there is a critical difference: the beauty of nature in the georgic tradition and the superiority of the farmer's life are a consequence of human labor and skill; it is the hard-won, human-created beauty of cultivated land and orchards, not the pristine natural beauty of the wild, as in a pastoral scene with its stock tree and stream. Nature in georgic thought can be a lovely locus of peace and leisure, but *only* as the result of hard human work, a work that always is only temporarily set aside. For just as every spring must give way to sterile winter, so every moment of peace and rest must give way to work, for as Virgil says, "The farmer's labour is a treadmill: / All round the year he treads in his own tracks" (II. 400-1). Peace, prosperity, and political stability do not occur naturally; rather, they must be actively created out of human labor, skill and virtue.

SOME VERSIONS OF AMERICAN GEORGIC

The first Europeans who discovered America frequently described its landscape with the tropes and imagery of the literary pastoral. To Christopher Columbus, Amerigo Vespucci, Richard Hakluyt, Arthur Barlow and others, the vast continent appeared to be an untouched paradise of noble savages who "danced away their time / Fresh as their groves and happy as their Climes," as John Dryden put it. The rigors of settlement soon disabused the colonists of such fantasies. Farming before the modern agricultural revolution was hard work in any case, but in America the task of "making land" out of wilderness was much harsher.[20] Most farming took place on the frontier, which meant trees had to be cleared and rocks removed with mostly wooden tools little changed since the ancient Romans. Predators of a type long driven from the European countryside—wolves, foxes, squirrels, crows, blackbirds, caterpillars, grasshoppers, bears, panthers, wildcats—constantly attacked the crops and herds, as did cattle ticks and blackstem rust, a blight affecting wheat. There were noxious weeds like stinkweed, which induced abortion in livestock, and couch grass, which strangled maize. And, of course, the Indians were an ever-present threat.

This harsh existence reinforced the georgic mode's perception of a destructive nature and its corresponding ethic of labor and virtue and self-sufficiency. As Arthur Schlesinger summarized the colonial farming experience, "By necessity the farmer made a religion of work. He might on occasion ignore the Word of God, but the voice of nature brooked no indifference or delay."[21] And from this ethic flowed the ideal of the practical, independent yeoman who owned the small holding that supported his family and guaranteed his freedom and self-sufficiency.

By the eighteenth century, the hard experience of settlement had shifted the American vision of nature from a pastoral to a georgic mode, a shift also reinforced by other cultural and historical changes, especially what Anthony Low calls the "georgic revolution" of the seventeenth century.[22] The aristocratic scorn of physical labor and rural clowns retreated before a rising Protestant middle class that saw work as a "calling" and an expression of God's intentions for humanity in the postlapsarian world.[23] A new science turned to improving agricultural technique and implements, with British innovators like Jethro Tull (1674-1740) and Arthur Young (1741-1820)—the latter a correspondent of George Washington and Thomas Jefferson—improving the productivity and profitability of farming. Farming became fashionable, "the reigning taste of the present time," Young said, and even George III delighted in his hobby farm and his nickname "Farmer George."[24]

Equally important were the political philosophies in which agriculture and the ownership of property took a central role. In the seventeenth century James Harrington, in his utopian *The Commonwealth of Oceana*, had predicated political and social stability on an egalitarian distribution of land that gave full scope to a levelling and improving "Industry."[25] There were the French physiocrats, who saw agriculture as *the* divinely ordained productive occupation, so that whatever benefited agriculture benefited society as a whole.[26] More central to the Founders' philosophy was John Locke's assertion of the importance of private property as the guarantor of individual freedom and the self-sufficiency necessary for what J. G. A. Pocock calls "the full austerity of citizenship in the classical sense."[27] Locke's view is georgic in spirit. Though nature is common to all, human labor applied to land confers title to it: "As much Land as a Man Tills, Plants, Improves, Cultivates and can use the Product of, so much is his *Property*. He by his Labour does, as it were, inclose it from the Common."[28] Moreover, this title is legitimized by the moral virtues typically celebrated in georgic writing: "God gave the World to Men in Common, but...it cannot be supposed he meant it should always remain common and uncultivated. He gave it to the use of the Industrious and Rational (and *Labour* was to be his *Title* to it;) not to the Fancy or Covetousness of the Quarrelsome and Contentious."[29] As James Montmarquet summarizes, "Locke's theory of property...should be seen as a Hesiodic defense of productivity and its rights; of the value of work and the futility of sectarian quarrelling."[30] As well as ensuring the self-sufficiency and freedom of the individual, the possession and improvement of arable land supports the political order by increasing productivity and hence benefiting society as a whole, as well as offering scope to individual merit and initiative. The importance of farming to society both politically and economically was a commonplace in the eighteenth century, as can be seen in Samuel Seabury's address to the farmers of New York in 1774: "Farmers are of the greatest benefit to the state, of any people in it: They furnish food for the merchant, and mechanic; and the raw materials for most manufacturers, the staple exports of the country, are the produce of their industry: be then convinced of your own importance, and think and act accordingly."[31]

Finally, the georgic vision in America found legitimization in the examples of classical agrarian republics like Sparta and Rome, whose defeat of mercantile Athens and Carthage, in the estimation of colonial historians, was owed "as much to their pastoral virtues as to their government forms. Both produced virtue, the agricultural life by fostering frugality, temperance, and independence, the balanced constitution by encouraging moderation, cooperation, and compromise. The plow was both the symbol and the cause of Cincinnatus' 'Roman virtue.'"[32] In addition, the seemingly endless abundance of land in America suggested that the balance of powers could be nourished indefinitely by the virtues inculcated on small farms worked by their owners. As Jefferson put it, "I think our governments will remain virtuous for many centuries; as long as they are chiefly agricultural; and this will be as long as there shall be vacant lands in any part of America."[33]

A survey of some examples of American georgic writing reveals just this emphasis on labor and improving virtues, and the dependence of republican political order on both, typical of classical georgic literature. Frequently we see a disdain for idleness coupled with the imperative to improvement whose roots are both georgic and Christian. As early as 1616, John Rolfe, in his *Description of Virginia* (written for King James), attributes the first settlement's failure to the colonists' refusal to work hard enough and improve the land's limitless potential. As Rolfe describes it, Virginia is "spacious and wide, capable of many hundred thousands of inhabitants," filled with "matter fit for buildings and fortifications, and for building of shipping." With proper cultivation, "the land might yearlie abound with corne" and "buildings, fortifications, and shipping might be reared, wrought and framed." Ultimately this labor could establish "a firme and perfect common weale."[34] Notice that Virginia is described in terms not of its intrinsic beauty but of its potential for development, as a raw material that could be made into a habitable space for humans if skill and labor were applied to it. Hence he focuses on the idleness of the first settlers, their unwillingness simply to work at self-sufficiency: "The vulgar sort looked for supplie out of England—neglected husbandry—some wrote—some said there was want of food, yet sought for none—others that would have sought could not be suffered; in which confusion much confusion yearlie befell them, and in this government happened all the miserie." The settlement now is doing better for "men spent not their tyme idely nor improfitably, for they were daily employed in palazadoing and building of townes, impaling grounds and other

needful business." The result is the peace and order and abundance Virgil attributes to "unrelenting labor": "Everie man sit[s]
under his fig tree in safety, gathering and reaping the fruits of
their labors with much joy and comfort."[35] Human work must
first transform the landscape for it to be a sustaining locus of
leisure and happiness.

Repeatedly in colonial writing what appear to be pastoral
appreciations of the beauty and fertility of the landscape are
ultimately subordinated to the georgic recognition that labor
and virtue create human order out of nature's chaos. Robert
Beverley's *The History and Present State of Virginia* (1705) puts
pastoralesque landscape descriptions in the larger context of
the necessity of labor to improve nature so that it can sustain
civilization, as is apparent in the criticism of the Virginia colonists with which he closes:

> Thus they depend altogether upon the Liberality of Na-
> ture, without endeavouring to improve its Gifts, by
> Art or Industry. They spunge upon the Blessings of a
> warm Sun, and a fruitful Soil, and almost grutch the
> Pains of gathering in the Bounties of the Earth. I should
> be asham'd to publish this slothful Indolence of my
> Countrymen, but that I hope it will rouse them out of
> their Lethargy, and excite them to make the most of all
> those happy Advantages which Nature has given them.[36]

Nature's beauty is appreciated not for its own sake but for its potential—georgic labor and technology, what Beverley calls "Art and Industry," are required to develop that potential and create a self-sufficient community that will benefit the greatest number. Without work the landscape remains a pastoral lotus-land that, given the fickleness of nature, will destroy those who trust its deceptive bounty.

This georgic recognition of the moral rightness of improving nature through labor recurs repeatedly throughout the eighteenth century. It is evident in the rationalizations of some Scotch-Irish squatters in Pennsylvania, who asserted that "it was against the laws of God and nature, that so much land should be idle while so many Christians wanted it to labor on and to raise their bread."[37] This sentiment is georgic as well as Christian: Virgil enjoins farmers to "domesticate / The wild by culture. Do not let your land / Lie idle."[38] A particularly telling example of American georgic thought is found in a poem called *Georgia*, first published anonymously in 1736 and reissued under the name of Reverend Fitzgerald in 1738. The author describes the land as "prolifick" and "rich," yet still a "wide waste Land" because it has not been cultivated with vines and wheat: "all things into wild Luxuriance ran / And burden'd Nature ask'd the Aid of Man."[39] Here an uncontrolled, excessive nature is anthropomorphized into desiring the industry and skill of man so that it can realize its full potential: "He bids the eager

Swain indulge his Toil," and King George seconds this command with his own injunction to the settlers that they pursue their "old wonted Industry" (7, 12). Their charge is "to form for Use what Nature's Bounties yield; / To fix the Staple, or to till the Field; / To Life's essential Arts their Cares confine" (77-80). That is, they are to exploit the rich potential of the land, to apply to it skill and labor so that a cohesive community can arise, one far superior to the wild chaos of unimproved nature: "All with one Voice the needful Task demand, / And long to build the Town, and Clear the Land" (113-14). Like "swarming Bees," the colonists take to their work, clearing the forest and building homes. The result is a joyful vision of future prosperity and abundance:

> A sprightlier Scene succeeds the awful Shade,
> And distant Landskips open thro' the Glade;
> The sunny Hills afar, the prostrate Plains,
> Invite the Labours of the lusty Swains;
> Their Annual Stores already seem possest,
> And future Harvests wave in ev'ry Breast. (123-28)

The sunny views of more untamed lands yet to be improved suggest a continuous civilizing process that will sustain more and more settlers and expand England's empire both politically and economically. This poem illustrates the truth of Anthony Low's observation that georgic "is preeminently the mode suited to the establishment of civilization and the founding of nations."[40]

The georgic ethic to improve nature in order to create civilization can also be found in an anonymous pamphlet called *The Golden Age* (1785), in which an angel gives the American patriot Celadon a vision of the nation's future. From a high mountain Celadon is shown a georgic paradise of "farms, plantations, gardens...laden with every kind of fruit." Then Celadon turns to view the West, "as yet but an uncultivated desert; the haunt of savages; and range of wild beasts. —But the soil in general is much richer than that of the eastern division." Soon it too will be transformed into a "beauteous world rising out of a dreary wilderness," American civilization spreading over the globe.[41] Rather than giving us what Leo Marx calls the "pastoral ideal," this pamphlet presents us with the georgic vision of a wild, savage nature tamed and subdued into a sustaining environment for human civilization.

So far we have seen versions of georgic thought in which the political dimension is limited, the labor of improvement being directed either to the ultimate benefit of the monarch whose kingdom will be enlarged by these efforts, or to the economic well-being of the nation, as in Celadon's vision of future American prosperity. In the period after the revolution, when the form of the new government was being debated, the role of small freeholds in supporting representative government and individual freedom and equality becomes more prominent in agrarian sentiments. Georgic "Art and Industry" are now linked to the work of statecraft, for just as the farmer must control and exploit the forces of nature, so statesmen must politically balance and limit what John Adams called "passions, interests, and power, which can be resisted only by passions, interest and power."[42] And the citizens' political freedom, like that of the Romans during the republic, will be underwritten as well by the self-sufficiency, independence, and other virtues fostered by working their own land. As Meyer Reinhold summarizes, "American agrarianism was, like its classical antecedent, politico-ethical in nature: an agricultural base for the republic with availability of freehold land was deemed by most of the Founding Fathers to be a prime safeguard for liberty and stability. The virtuous farmer, the purity and simplicity of his life, were widely invoked, a model conjured up from a classical past simpler than the English and French present."[43] Political philosophy at the end of the eighteenth century affords numerous examples of this agrarian ideal.

Richard Price, for example, in his *Observations on the Importance of the American Revolution* (1785), after locating political evil in "too great an inequality in the distribution of property," attributes the relative stability of the American states to "the equality which subsists among them." He then launches into a georgic panegyric:

The Happiest state of man is the middle state between the savage and the refined or between the wild and the luxurious state. Such is the state of society in Connecticut and some others of the American provinces where the inhabitants consist, if I am rightly informed, of an independent and hardy yeomanry, all nearly on a level, trained to arms, instructed in their rights, clothed in home-spun, of simple manners, strangers to luxury, drawing plenty from the ground, and that plenty gathered easily by the hand of industry; ...the rich and poor, the haughty grandee and the creeping sycophant, equally unknown, protected by laws which (being of their own will) cannot oppress, and by an equal government which, wanting lucrative places, cannot create corrupt canvassings and ambitious intrigue.[44]

Every georgic note is sounded in this description, from the self-sufficiency guaranteed by labor on private land, to the middling condition contrasted with the pomp and corruption of urban wealth, a frequent theme of georgic writing. Just as in Virgil, small farmers working their own relatively equal plots provide the material and ethical backbone of an "equal government" that guarantees the freedom and independence of the citizenry. This link of labor, independence, and democracy is encapsulated in the following lines written in 1789 by Timothy Dwight:

"Democratick laws afford / No towering title to a tyrant lord, / But peace and pleasure, smiling, bless the soil / And he who sows enjoys the product of his toil."[45]

Agrarian idealism was so pervasive that even a Federalist like James Madison, who saw political stability ultimately residing not so much in rural virtue as in the balancing of different interests and the limiting of factions arising out of "the various and unequal distribution of property,"[46] nonetheless in 1792 praised the life of small farmers in traditional georgic terms:

The life of the husbandman is pre-eminently suited to the comfort and happiness of the individual.... Virtue, the health of the soul, is another part of his patrimony, and no less favored by his situation.... Competency is more universally the lot of those who dwell in the country, where liberty is at the same time their lot. The extremes, both of want and waste, have other abodes.... The classes of citizens who provide at once their own food and their own raiment, may be viewed as the most truly independent and happy. They are more; they are the best basis of public liberty and the strongest bulwark of public safety. It follows that the greater proportion of this class to the whole society, the more free, the more independent, and the more happy must be the society itself.[47]

Likewise the arch-mercantilist Alexander Hamilton agreed that "the cultivation of the earth...has intrinsically a strong claim to pre-eminence over every other form of industry," if only because the farmers' bounty provided exports.[48] Self-sufficiency, independence, freedom, and equality, not to mention economic benefits, all derive from the middling farming life, which undergirds representative government and provides stability in the storms of factional conflict.[49]

Some of the best examples of American georgic sentiments can be found in the writings of J. Hector St. John de Crèvecoeur. The third letter, "What is an American?" from *Letters from an American Farmer* (1783) makes the farming life and its values the essence of Americanism: "We are all tillers of the earth...a people of cultivators...united by the silken bands of mild government, all respecting the laws without dreading their power, because they are equitable. We are all animated with the spirit of an industry which is unfettered and unrestrained, because each person works for himself." Likewise in *Sketches of Eighteenth-Century America*, where labor is given a central role in explaining the American character and its ideal of freedom: "All the praises we at present deserve ought to be bestowed on that strength, fortitude, and perseverance which have been requisite to clear so many fields, to drain so many swamps"; "It is the hands of freemen only that could till this asperous soil" (264, 265). Crèvecoeur explicitly links labor, freedom, and equality, the

latter two resulting from the self-sufficiency and independence
fostered by small farmers and their middling condition.[50]

Ultimately, Crèvecoeur's praises of the civilizing virtues and
labor of small farmers are linked to a larger vision of America's
destiny, a future of peace and prosperity guaranteed by the industry of husbandmen:

> What a care, what an assiduity does this life require!
> Who on contemplating the great and important field
> of action performed every year by a large farmer can
> refrain from valuing and praising as they ought this use-
> ful, this dignified class of men? These are the people
> who, scattered on the edge of this great continent, have
> made it to flourish, and have, without the dangerous
> assistance of mines, gathered, by the sweat of their hon-
> est brows and by the help of their ploughs, such a har-
> vest of commercial emoluments for their country, un-
> contaminated either by spoils or rapine. These are the
> men who in future will replenish this huge continent,
> even to its utmost unknown limits, and render this
> new-found part of the world by far the happiest, the
> most potent as well as the most populous of any. May
> the poor, the wretched of Europe, animated by our
> example, invited by our laws, avoid the fetters of their
> country and come in shoals to partake of our toils as
> well as of our happiness! (237-38)

The old-world feudal chains that limit individual initiative and merit do not exist in America, where "human industry has acquired a boundless field to exert itself in—a field which will not be fully cultivated in many ages,"[51] where abundant land and egalitarian laws give free rein to the improving labor of all. This labor is a civilizing force leading to progress and prosperity, a creator of virtue that transforms a savage wilderness into a garden. Rather than the pastoral view of nature as a harmonious, lovely backdrop for static human leisure, Crèvecoeur instead sees the American land through the georgic lens, as endless potential to be realized by the liberated, dynamic labor and simple virtues of the farmer.

By the turn of the century, such georgic sentiments had become commonplace, and examples could be multiplied. But it is in the writings of Thomas Jefferson, the most famous exemplar of American georgic, that the link between rural labor, republican virtue, and freedom is most firmly established and has its most significant impact on the new nation and its political ideals.

JEFFERSON AND GEORGIC

Thomas Jefferson's fondness for classical culture, especially Virgil, and his love of farming both suggest that he would have been sympathetic to the classical georgic vision. We have already noted his appreciation for his classical education. Virgil appears to have been an especial favorite, second perhaps only to

Homer: numerous editions of Virgil's works in several languages filled his libraries, and in an essay written for the Marquis de Chastellux, he mused, "But as we advance in life...I suspect we are left at last with only Homer and Virgil, perhaps with Homer alone."[52] Jefferson's passion for the farming life was equal to his love of the ancients. Throughout his life and through all the vicissitudes of his political positions, he maintained his deep affection for farming. In his letters he speaks of being "delighted" with farming, of his return to farming "with an ardor which I scarcely knew in my youth," of his attachment to agriculture "by inclination," all summed up in his letter to Charles Wilson Peale in 1811: "I have often thought that if heaven had given me choice of my position and calling, it should have been on a rich spot of earth, well watered, and near a good market for the productions of the garden. No occupation is so delightful to me as the culture of the earth."[53]

Jefferson, moreover, was not just indulging a romantic agrarianism or an idealizing nostalgia. His interest in farming reflected the unpastoral desire for rational improvement that characterized the georgic revolution and goes back to Virgil's emphasis on crafts and technological skills as humanity's response to a fickle environment. In his European travels he constantly inquired into agricultural practices, looking for new and better techniques of cultivation; at Monticello he experimented with crop rotation, and tried to improve old and introduce new crops and livestock species to America.[54] Jefferson was no starry-eyed idealist, but rather a rational improver in what he called "the great workshop of nature,"[55] one who saw increased productivity and prosperity as the material counterpart to the moral advantages farming afforded.

Those moral benefits, and their link to the political order, however, are what interested Jefferson, and they fall squarely into the American georgic tradition we have been tracing. Once more his letters reflect the privileged position he affords farming in promoting virtue and stability. "The moderate and sure income of husbandry," he wrote to Washington in 1787, "begets permanent improvement, quiet life, and orderly conduct, both public and private"; farming "is our wisest pursuit, because it will in the end contribute most to real wealth, good morals and happiness."[56] This link of virtue, farming, and improvement of human civilization—the ethical center of georgic thought—recurs over and over: agriculture is "the most useful of the occupations of man," the "best preservative of morals," the "basis of the subsistence, the comforts and the happiness of man."[57]

The moral value of farming, moreover, is linked to political order.[58] At a most basic level, farmers, literally tied as they are to the land and dependent mainly on their own labor, are natural conservatives who resist political fad and fashion, and who value freedom and self-determination, the virtues most condu-

cive to political independence and freedom, and hence sup-
portive of the nation's interests. As Jefferson wrote to John Jay
in 1785, "Cultivators of the earth are the most valuable citizens. They are the most vigorous, the most independent, the
most virtuous, and they are tied to their country, and wedded
to its liberty and interests, by the most lasting bonds."[59] Twelve
years later he wrote, "Farmers...are the true representatives of
the great American interests, and are alone to be relied on for
expressing proper American sentiments."[60] These "sentiments,"
self-reliance, independence, and a commitment to "liberty," all
are nurtured and reinforced by the conditions of farming, and
they are as well the best guarantors of the "great American interests": the political freedom and independence enshrined in participatory government. Change "American" to "Roman" and
this sentence could have been written by Virgil.

The most representative expression of Jefferson's agrarianism occurs in Query 19 of his *Notes on Virginia*, written in 1781-
82 in response to a request by François Marbois, secretary to
the French minister in Philadelphia, and published in 1787.
The ethical and political benefits of farming are here set out
and linked to the classical georgic distrust of trade and urban-
ism:

But we have an immensity of land courting the industry of the husbandman. Is it best then that all our citi-

zens should be employed in its improvement, or that
one half should be called off from that to exercise manu-
factures and handicraft arts for the other? Those who
labour in the earth are the chosen people of God, if
ever he had a chosen people, whose breasts he has made
his peculiar deposit for substantial and genuine virtue.
It is the focus in which he keeps alive that sacred fire,
which otherwise might escape from the face of the earth.
Corruption of morals in the mass of cultivators is a
phaenomenon of which no age nor nation has furnished
an example. It is the mark set on those, who not looking up to heaven, to their own soil and industry, as
does the husbandman, for their subsistence, depend
for it on the casualties and caprice of customers. Dependence begets subservience and venality, suffocates
the germ of virtue, and prepares fit tools for the designs
of ambition.... The mobs of great cities add just so
much to the support of pure government, as sores do
to the strength of the body.[61]

This passage is a compendium of the georgic themes we have
been tracing: the labor, virtue, and self-sufficiency of the farming
life provide the basis of political freedom, a freedom compromised by the subservience and corruption that follows a life
entangled in the commercial "cash nexus."

Jefferson's agrarianism, of course, was a powerful force in the great debates over the political form and economic direction of the new nation. The famous Manichean division between the democratic champion of the yeoman, Jefferson, and the promoter of capitalism and centralization, Alexander Hamilton, has been overstated. This is partly because the melodramatic pastoral conflict between rural virtue and urban corruption is more interesting than nuanced complexity; and partly because the confusion of agrarianism with pastoral thought has tended to tint Jefferson's views on farming with the rosy hues of pastoral idealism, in which a practical concern with profit is in bad taste.[62] But georgic self-sufficiency, unlike pastoral *otium*, is not a timeless given but a hard-won benefit, and the necessarily utilitarian farmer knows that his freedom and independence depend solely on his ability to turn a profit. "If your work brings you wealth," Hesiod wrote, "you will be envied by the slothful, / because glory and excellence follow riches."[63] Virgil's encomium to Italy's landscape of small farms and their owners praises the richness and abundance that rival India and Arabia, fabled for wealth.[64] So too Jefferson wrote to J. Blair in 1787, "The pursuits of agriculture are the surest road to affluence."[65] Jefferson's worry was not about money per se, but about the political rootlessness of volatile urban mobs, the economic dependence of the wage-slave, and the corrupting effects of excessive luxury promoted by commercial values.[66]

Moreover, Jefferson was not so idealistic as to think that industry and commerce could be completely banished from America. He called his agrarianism a "theory" as early as 1785, in a letter to G. K. von Hagendorp: "Were I to indulge my own theory, I should wish them [Americans] to practise neither commerce nor navigation.... We should thus avoid wars, and all our citizens would be husbandmen.... But this is theory only, & a theory which the servants of America are not at liberty to follow. Our people have a decided taste for navigation & commerce."[67] Commerce and manufacturing were necessary for the American economy, and both were designated by Jefferson as two of the four "pillars," along with agriculture and navigation, equally supporting American independence.[68] Farming should always have moral and economic preeminence—commerce was to be farming's "handmaid," as his first inaugural address put it[69]—because more than any other occupation it reinforced and nourished the values of self-reliance, independence, and equality that protected the freedom of the individual. This concern for political stability and material benefit is anathema to the pastoral sensibility and its timeless, apolitical *otium*; but as we have seen, it follows logically from the georgic ethic of improving nature in order to create a sustaining environment for human civilization. Jefferson's agrarianism is neither a "myth" he cynically manipulated nor an escapist pastoral delusion, but rather a coherent version of the classical georgic tradition.[70]

Jefferson, of course, could not foresee the radical changes
that would challenge the preeminence of the family farm—the
rapid advance of industrialism and the creation of consumer-
ism, the filling of the seemingly endless continent by successive
waves of immigrants, and the modern chemical and technological agricultural revolution which has allowed one person to
feed ninety-nine. The small farmer and the georgic values he
embodies are rapidly disappearing, and the question facing us
today is: how can the values of self-reliance, independence, freedom, and a tragic recognition of the limits nature imposes on
human will and desire—virtues that once were nurtured in the
daily struggle to grow food and that formed the bedrock of
republican government—survive the centrifugal forces of consumer hedonism, therapeutic individualism, and mass-produced
consensus of taste and opinion, not to mention the failure of
our schools to teach the traditions of Western democracy? Or
as one of the last heirs of Hesiod, Victor Hanson, poses the
question, "With more leisure, more bounty and affluence, more
safety, sanitation, and elegance, more spandex between us and
the dirt and grease that are the cost of battling nature, can we,
free of the craggy, unpleasant octogenarian, of the self-employed
skeptic, still maintain a republic founded in another age?"[71]

The Greek georgic tradition has always answered "no."
Without the ballast of the farmer and his tough independence,
the exponentially accelerating forces of mass consumer culture

and its ethic of unbridled appetite threaten to sweep all before them, including perhaps democracy itself, and we may end up like the disintegrating Roman republic whose careening descent into chaos Virgil compared at the end of the first *Georgic* to a chariot "Gathering speed from lap to lap, and a driver / Tugging in vain at the reins is swept along / By his horses and heedless uncontrollable car."[72] If we are to avoid such a disaster, we must turn once more to the insights that shaped the political philosophy of America, the hard questions and tough answers posed by the Greeks—those small farmers who, as all farmers must, looked at life "steadily and whole."

NOTES

1. Bruce E. Johansen, "Debating the Origin of Democracy: Overview of an Annotated Bibliography," *American Indian Culture and Research Journal*, 20.2 (1996): 155-72.

2. Carl J. Richard, *The Founders and the Classics: Greece, Rome, and the American Enlightenment* (Cambridge, MA: Harvard University Press, 1994), 8. See too Meyer Reinhold, *Classica Americana. The Greek and Roman Heritage in the United States* (Detroit, MI: Wayne State University Press, 1984), and Richard M. Gummere, *The American Colonial Mind and the Classical Tradition* (Cambridge, MA: Harvard University Press, 1963), 1-19, 173-90.

3. Russell Kirk, *The Roots of American Order*, 3rd ed. (Washington, DC: Regnery Gateway, 1991), 51; for the Greek influence see 51-96.

4. See Richard, *The Founders and the Classics*, 12-38; Gummere, *The American Colonial Mind*, 55-75; James McLachlan, "Classical Names, American Identities: Some Notes on College Students and the Classical Tradition in the 1770s," in *Classical Traditions in Early America*, ed. John W. Eadie (Ann Arbor, MI: The Center for the Coordination of Ancient and Modern Studies, University of Michigan, 1976), 81-98

5. Jennifer Tolbert Roberts, *Athens on Trial: The Antidemocratic Tradition in Western Thought* (Princeton, NJ: Princeton University Press, 1994), 177.

6. Kirk, *Roots of American Order*, 60.

7. Thomas Jefferson to Dr. Joseph Priestly, 27 January 1800, *Writings*, ed. Merrill D. Peterson (New York: Library of America, 1984), 1072.

8. Arthur M. Schlesinger, *The Birth of the Nation: A Portrait of the American People on the Eve of Independence* (New York: Knopf, 1968), 38.

9. Henry Steele Commager, *The Empire of Reason: How Europe Imagined and America Realized the Enlightenment* (New York: Anchor Press/Doubleday, 1977), 243.

10. Adams and Washington quoted in Schlesinger, *Birth of the Nation*, 41.

11. For example, see Carl J. Richard, "Mixed Government and Classical Pastoralism," in *The Founders and the Classics*, 123-68. This confusion runs throughout an influential work on landscape and American idealism, Leo Marx's *The Machine in the Garden: Technology and the Pastoral Ideal in America* (London and New York: Oxford University Press, 1964).

12. For a more detailed discussion see Bruce S. Thornton, "Rural Dialectic: Pastoral, Georgic, and *The Shepheardes Calender*," *Spenser Studies IX*, ed. Patrick Cullen and Thomas P. Roche, Jr. (New York: AMS Press, 1991), 1-9.

13. Hesiod, *Works and Days* 42, 289-90, 471-72, 299, 309-10, 410-13, 397-400, trans. Apostolos N. Anthanassakis (Baltimore, Md. and London: Johns Hopkins University Press, 1983).

14. See Reinhold, *Classica Americana*, 222, 227-28, for the ubiquity of Virgil in the curriculum and translations of the *Eclogues* and *Georgics*.

15. Virgil, *Georgic* I.199-200, in *Virgil: The Georgics*, trans. L.P. Wilkinson, (Harmondsworth, England: Penguin, 1982). Subsequent references parenthetical.

16. See Victor Davis Hanson, *The Other Greeks: The Family Farm and the Agrarian Roots of Western Civilization* (New York: The Free Press, 1995), 25-126.

17. Hesiod, *Works and Days*, 39, 41.

18. *De Agri Cultura*, trans. William Davis Hooper (Cambridge, MA and London: Harvard University Press, 1934); *Pro Sextus Roscio Amerino* 50; in *Vergil's Georgics: A New Interpretation*, trans. Gary B. Miles (Berkeley and Los Angeles: University of California Press, 1980), 11. See 1-63 for Roman attitudes to farming.

19. Quoted in Gummere, *The American Colonial Mind*, 7.

20. See Stephanie Grauman Wolf, *As Various as Their Land: The Everyday Lives of Eighteenth-Century Americans* (New York: HarperCollins, 1993), 139-74.

21. Schlesinger, *The Birth of the Nation*, 38; Wolf, *As Various as Their Land*, 158.

22. Anthony Low, *The Georgic Revolution* (Princeton, NJ: Princeton University Press,

1985). These changes are briefly summarized in an American context by Reinhold, *Classica Americana*, 99.

23. For the development of a positive view of labor see James A. Montmarquet, *The Idea of Agrarianism: From Hunter-Gatherer to Agrarian Radical in Western Culture* (Moscow, ID: University of Idaho Press, 1989), 105-29.

24. Young quoted in Richard, *The Founders and the Classics*, 161.

25. See Paul A. Rahe, *Republics Ancient and Modern: Classical Republicanism and the American Revolution* (Chapel Hill, NC and London: University of North Carolina Press, 1992), 418-20.

26. See Griswold, *Farming and Democracy* (New York: Harcourt, Brace, 1948), 21-22.

27. J. G. A. Pocock, "Civic Humanism and Its Role in Anglo-American Thought," 1968; reprinted in *Politics, Language and Time: Essays on Political History and Thought* (New York: Atheneum, 1971), 91.

28. From Locke's *Second Treatise of Government*, 5.32, quoted in Montmarquet, *Idea of Agrarianism*, 78. See 76-86 for Locke and agrarianism; also Rahe, *Republics Ancient and Modern*, 500-20.

29. From Locke's *Second Treatise*, 5.34; quoted in Montmarquet, *Idea of Agrarianism*, 79.

30. Montmarquet, *Idea of Agrarianism*, 86.

31. In ed. Wayne D. Rasmussen, *Agriculture in the United States: A Documentary History*, vol. 1 (New York: Random House, 1975), 237.

32. Richard, *The Founders and the Classics*, 159-60. See too Reinhold, *Classica Americana*, 99.

33. Quoted in Richard, *The Founders and the Classics*, 163. Cf. 123: "Most Republicans preferred to rest their hopes for the success of the nation's new representative democracy upon its agricultural lifestyle, a lifestyle deified by classical poets and historians."

34. In Rasmussen, *Agriculture in the United States*, 77.

35. Ibid., 78.

36. Louis B. Wright, ed., *The History and Present State of Virginia*, (Chapel Hill, NC: University of North Carolina Press, 1947), 319.

37. Quoted in Schlesinger, *The Birth of the Nation*, 33.

38. Virgil, *Georgic* II.36-38.

39. Lines 6, 9, 2-4. The text of the poem is quoted in full by Martin D. Snyder, "The Hero in the Garden: Classical Contributions to the Early Images of America," in *Classical Traditions in Early America*, 170-74. Subsequent references parenthetical.

40. Low, *The Georgic Revolution*, 12.

41. Quotes from Marx, *The Machine in the Garden*, 106-7.

42. The phrase of John Adams, from *A Defence of the Constitutions of Government of the United States of America* (1787-88), quoted in Richard, *The Founders and the Classics*, 147.

43. Reinhold, *Classica Americana*, 99.

44. In Bernard Peach, ed., *Richard Price and the Ethical Foundations of the American Revolution* (Durham, NC: Duke University Press, 1979), 208.

45. Quoted by Chester E. Eisinger, "The Freehold Concept in Eighteenth-Century American Letters," *William and Mary Quarterly*, 3rd series, 4.1 (1947), 51. Many other examples of American georgic can be found in Eisinger's survey.

46. Madison, *The Federalist*, no. 10.

47. Quoted in Richard, *The Founders and the Classics*, 165.

48. Hamilton quoted in Richard Hofstadter, *The Age of Reform: From Bryan to F.D.R.* (New York: Knopf, 1955), 27.

49. See Rahe, *Republics Ancient and Modern*, 729-36, for Madison's agrarianism and its relation to Jefferson's.

50. Albert E. Stone, ed., *Letters from an American Farmer and Sketches of Eighteenth-Century America* (Harmondsworth, England: Penguin, 1981), 67-68. Subsequent references parenthetical.

51. Stone, *Letters from an American Farmer*, 165.

52. Reinhold, *Classica Americana*, 232; "Thoughts on English Prosody," quoted in *Jefferson's Literary Commonplace Book*, ed. Douglas L. Wilson (Princeton, NJ: Princeton University Press, 1989), 186.

53. Jefferson to W.B. Giles, 1795; Jefferson to John Adams, 1794; Jefferson to M. Silvestre, 1807; Jefferson to C.W. Peale, 1811. *The Jeffersonian Cyclopedia*, ed. John P. Foley (1900; reprint, New York: Russell and Russell, 1967).

54. Cf. Commager, *The Empire of Reason*, 105: "Of all the American philosophes, it was Jefferson who was most indefatigable in bringing about the transformation from wilderness to cultivation."

55. Letter, 1798, in *The Jeffersonian Cyclopedia*, 323.

56. Jefferson to Washington, *The Jeffersonian Cyclopedia*, 25, 27.

57. Jefferson to M. Silvestre, 1807; Jefferson to J. Blair, 1787; Jefferson to Baron de Moll, 1814; *The Jeffersonian Cyclopedia*, 25, 27.

58. For Jefferson's agrarianism in its political context see Rahe, *Republics Ancient and Modern*, 687-747; more briefly Griswold, *Farming and Democracy*, 18-46.

59. Jefferson to John Jay, *The Jeffersonian Cyclopedia*, 322.

60. Jefferson to Arthur Campbell, 1797, *The Jeffersonian Cyclopedia*, 322.

61. Jefferson, "Notes on the State of Virginia," *Writings*, 290-91.

62. As in Marx, *The Machine in the Garden*, 116-44.

63. Hesiod, *Works and Days* 312-313.

64. Virgil, *Georgics* II.136ff.

65. Jefferson to J. Blair, *The Jeffersonian Cyclopedia*, 25. Not for Jefferson, who never could make Monticello profitable and who died in debt.

66. See Joyce Appleby, "The 'Agrarian Myth' in the Early Republic," 1982; reprinted in *Liberalism and Republicanism in the Historical Imagination* (Cambridge, MA and London: Harvard University Press, 1992), 253-76.

67. Jefferson to G. K. von Hagendorp, 13 October 1785, *Writings*, 836. By 1816 he would say that his desires for agrarianism were "the dreams of an old man," and speculate "that the occasions of realizing them may have passed away without return," Jefferson to William H Crawford, 1816; quoted in Ellis, *American Sphinx*, 259.

68. Cf. Jefferson, "First Annual Message," December 1801; also Jefferson to James Jay, 1809; *The Jeffersonian Cyclopedia*, 23.

69. Jefferson, *Writings*, 495.

70. For the "agrarian myth" in early America see Richard Hofstadter, *The Age of Reform*, 23-37. Hofstadter as well mischaracterizes American agrarianism as pastoral when he writes, "Commercialization had already begun to enter the American Arcadia," 37.

71. Victor Davis Hanson, *Fields without Dreams: Defending the Agrarian Idea* (New York: The Free Press, 1996), 271.

72. Virgil, *Georgic* I.513-15.

OPEN SHUTTERS ON THE PAST: ROME AND THE FOUNDERS

E. Christian Kopff

The American Founders' generation referred to the ancient world, pagan and Christian, again and again. How important, however, were these citations for the American Revolution and the establishment of the American republic?[1] The question is both historical and practical. If direct contact with the classical tradition was essential for the American Founding, it may be equally essential for a contemporary attempt to restore freedom and creativity to the United States. If the classical tags of eighteenth-century political debate were as incidental to the achievements of that age as its powdered wigs and snuffboxes, the classical past will be all the more irrelevant to our age and its dilemmas.

First-rate minds have seen the Founders' use of the classics as a fancy frame around an Anglo-Saxon painting. "The Americans would have believed just as vigorously in public morality had Cato and the Gracchi never lived," wrote Clinton Rossiter.[2] For Bernard Bailyn, "the classics of the ancient world are every-where in the literature of the Revolution, but they are every-where illustrative, not determinative, of thought. They contrib-uted a vivid vocabulary but not the logic or grammar of thought, a universally respected personification but not the source of political and social beliefs. They heightened the colonists' sen-sitivity to ideas and attitudes otherwise derived."[3]

Russell Kirk distinguished between American institutions and the legacy of ancient political thought:

> In truth America's political *institutions* owe next to noth-ing to the ancient world—although American modes of *thinking* about politics indeed were influenced, two cen-turies ago, by Greek and Roman philosophers long dead. One learns much about constitutions from reading Plato and Aristotle and Polybius.... But from such study the American leaders...learned, by their own account, chiefly what political blunders of ancient times ought to be avoided.... The American Framers and the early states-men of the Republic, whether Federalists or Republi-cans, were no admirers of classical political structures.... Nor did ancient political theory, as distinct from insti-tutions, often obtain American approbation.[4]

Hannah Arendt insisted on the centrality of the classics for the leaders of the French and American Revolutions. "Without the classical example shining through the centuries, none of the men of the revolutions on either side of the Atlantic would have possessed the courage for what turned out to be unprecedented action."[5] Gordon Wood agreed. "The Americans' compulsive interest in the ancient republics was in fact crucial to their attempt to understand the moral and social basis of politics."[6] Gilbert Chinard found "that the principles of government so often represented as the birthright of the Anglo-Saxon people were, at least in America, blended with the tradition of Greece and Rome."[7] Similar evaluations have been made by Howard Mumford Jones, J. G. A. Pocock, Meyer Reinhold, and Carl J. Richards in this generation[8] and Carl Becker earlier in the century.[9]

There is more to the creation of the American republic than an imitation or re-creation of classical republicanism. There are, however, some areas where we can see that what Albert Jay Nock called "The Great Tradition" of the Greek and Roman classics was an important factor in the American Founding.

THE CLASSICS AND THE COLONIAL CURRICULUM

The grammar school curriculum of colonial America was classical, like the curriculum which educated the author of Shakespeare's plays two hundred years before.[10] This cultural continuity, imbibed at an early age and reinforced at each level of education, affected every aspect of colonial thought. Bernard

Bailyn found that the classics did not offer the Founders "the logic or grammar of thought." The foundation of logic in the colonial curriculum, however, was the Aristotelian syllogism. It was devalued but not deserted by Ramist logic and was basic for hymn writer Isaac Watts's Lockean *Logic* (1719), a popular colonial text.[11]

As for grammar, those who work through the writings of Thomas Jefferson, who had a classical education, or George Washington, who did not, or their English contemporaries Samuel Johnson, Edward Gibbon and Edmund Burke, will find that the syntax of Greek and Latin had affected the complexity and clarity of their expression and so of their thought. We need to know Latin if we want to think like the Founders. Forrest McDonald saw this clearly. "In thinking in eighteenth-century English,...a rudimentary knowledge of Latin is highly useful; after all, every educated Englishman and American knew Latin, English words were generally closer in meaning to their Latin originals than they are today, and sometimes, as with the use of the subjunctive, it is apparent that an author is accustomed to formulating his thoughts in Latin."[12]

The Founders continue to intrigue us as much for their words as their deeds. Greek and Latin made a significant contribution to the literary quality of documents that still haunt our memory. As Jefferson wrote to John Brazier, August 24, 1819, "The utilities we derive from the remains of the Greek and

Latin languages are, first, as models of pure taste in writing. To these we are certainly indebted for the rational and chaste style of modern composition which so much distinguishes the nations to whom these languages are familiar. Without these models we should probably have continued the inflated style of our northern ancestors, or the hyperbolical and vague one of the east."[13]

Is, however, "contributing a vivid vocabulary" as small a contribution as Bailyn believes? T. S. Eliot's Sweeney admitted, "I gotta use words when I talk to you." Words are instruments to help us understand the world we live in, and after critical examination they may contribute to its renewal. The American Revolution is scarcely imaginable without words like republic and tyranny, without concepts like public virtue and an armed citizenry. This point was seen by Robert Middlekauff. "One way in which boys were affected by what they read is clear. They picked up a vocabulary, a terminology, which they sometimes used to cope with everyday experience. An admired leader became a Cato, an enemy a Cataline, a skilled farmer an American Cincinnatus."[14]

Studying Latin gave the Founding generation access to a rich vocabulary embedded in a complex syntax. Greek and Latin were essential tools for the colonists' conquest of the new world, more important than axe or hoe or musket, because Latin increased the potential of their minds and ultimately all tools are products of the human mind. This is why Thomas Jefferson urged his fellow citizens not to give up the classical curriculum.

> The learning of Greek and Latin, I am told, is going into disuse in Europe. I know not what their manners and occupations may call for: but it would be very ill-judged in us to follow their example in this instance.... I do not pretend that language is science. It is only an instrument for the attainment of science. But that time is not lost which is employed in providing tools for future operation: more especially as in this case the books put into the hands of the youth for this purpose may be such as will at the same time impress their minds with useful facts and good principles.[15]

University professors tend to underestimate the importance of grammar schools. The final pages of Query XIV in *Notes on the State of Virginia* show that Jefferson did not make that mistake. He realized, as the Jesuits did, that what a child learns early on is fundamental for his future achievements. The great traditions of Western civilization depend on the discipline of learning the languages and reading the texts which preserve these traditions. The colonial curriculum disciplined young minds to linguistic complexity and gave them the words and ideas with which to think about theology, politics and science. After running the gauntlet of learning challenging languages, colonial students went on to read great texts. The good principles Jefferson praised were those of Cicero, Sallust, Livy, and Tacitus, the ideals of the good citizen and the honest man, based on a morality of the four virtues and a belief in the immortality of the soul. The classics provided the new nation with its moral and intellectual infrastructure, the ultimate source of its institutional and physical infrastructures.

THE MORAL EXAMPLE: CINCINNATUS

The republican tradition furnished the ideal of the farmer-soldier-citizen.[16] Many colonial Americans lived and worked on their own farms or dreamed of owning one. Their historical model was Cincinnatus in Livy III.24-29. Fifth-century B.C. Rome was a trading village, inhabited by small farmers. Nomadic Italian tribes used to descend from the nearby hills to raid and sack. Every farmer had to be ready to grab his shield and spear and go out under his elected leadership to drive off the raiders. (Americans recognized this way of life from their frontier.) In 458 B.C. a Roman army was lured into the hills and trapped. The Senate named Cincinnatus dictator and asked him to save the troops. He accepted his country's call, rescued the men, and then, instead of using his position and prestige for personal and political aggrandizement, he resigned and returned to his little farm.

As Garry Wills has shown, Cincinnatus haunted the imagination of revolutionary Americans, especially George Washington.[17] Washington resigned his commission at the end of the Revolutionary War. He refused to hold the office of president more than twice, confounding Thomas Jefferson's prediction in his letter to Madison of December 20, 1787: "Experience concurs with reason in concluding that the first magistrate will always be re-elected if the Constitution permits it. He is then an officer for life."[18] Washington's Farewell Address (September 17, 1796) was his testament to the American people. It expounds the principles of free government and is read every year in Congress. The figure of Cincinnatus never left the minds and imaginations of America's leaders. No American president exceeded Washington's two terms until Franklin D. Roosevelt in 1940. After the death of Roosevelt, who fulfilled Jefferson's prediction, men who remembered the ideals of the Old Republic passed the Twenty-second Amendment to enact into law what for Washington and his successors was a moral commitment, based on a classical exemplum.

CLASSICAL THEORY:

BALANCE AND SEPARATION OF POWERS

The classics provided not only moral ideals of restraint and self-sacrifice, but also political lessons. The theory of balance of powers and separation of powers was expounded in the eighteenth century by Bolingbroke and Montesquieu, but the best historical examples were found in the Roman republic as recorded by Livy and theorized by Cicero and Polybius. When the convention called in 1787 to revise the Articles of Confederation decided to ignore its charge and write a new constitution, the delegates debated the structure of the legislative branch. Should it be unicameral, as Benjamin Franklin thought and Turgot had argued in print, or bicameral, like the influential constitution of Massachusetts, whose author, John Adams, was American ambassador in distant London? Adams wrote the first volume of his *Defense of the Constitutions of Government of the United States* to defend the bicameralism of the state constitutions against Turgot and Franklin. He devoted page after page to Polybius VI, the *locus classicus* for the advantages of balance and separation of powers in the Roman Constitution. Published in January 1787, the first volume of the *Defense* crossed the Atlantic by March and was reprinted several times before the Convention opened on May 25. As Gilbert Chinard saw, "Even a casual glance at the records of the Federal Convention will show that Adams's book was used as a sort of repertory by many speakers, who found in it a confirmation of their views, and chiefly convenient historical illustrations and precedents."[19] Russell Kirk summarized clearly Polybius's influence on the Framers: "For the American constitutional delegates at Philadelphia, the most interesting feature of the Roman Republican constitution was its system of checks upon the power of men in high public authority, and its balancing of power among different public offices. The Americans had learned of these

devices from the *History* by Polybius.... The actual forms of
checks and balances that the Americans incorporated into their
Constitution in 1787 were derived from English precedent and
from American colonial experience."[20]

Kirk may be exaggerating the role of English precedent, as
opposed to Whig theorizing. Walter Bagehot's classic *English
Constitution* did not find or praise the separation of powers.
"The efficient secret of the English Constitution may be described as the close union, the nearly complete fusion, of the
executive and legislative powers. No doubt by the traditional
theory, as it exists in all the books, the goodness of our constitution consists in the entire separation of the legislative and
executive authorities, but in truth its merit consists in their
singular approximation."[21] The government of England is run
by small coteries, of noble lords and their henchmen in the
eighteenth century, of party leaders and their henchmen in the
twentieth century. The majority in Parliament is restrained by
no concept of checks and balances or even a written constitution. Bagehot boasts how rapidly and decisively a British government can move, without the constraints that surround an
American President even in times of war.

The situation was not lost on Benjamin Franklin, who saw
his dreams of a highly centralized government and unicameral
legislature disappearing before Adams's arguments and the prestige of the classical tradition. Before the first week was over, on

Thursday, May 31, "The 3d. Resolution, 'that the national Legislature ought to consist of two branches' was agreed to without debate or dissent, except that of Pennsylvania, given probably from complaisance to Docr. Franklin who was understood
to be partial to a single House of Legislation."[22] At last, on
June 28, Franklin had had enough. He rose to protest the constant citation of classical precedent:

> We indeed seem to feel our own want of political wis-
> dom, since we have been running about in search of it.
> We have gone back to ancient history for models of
> Government, and examined the different forms of those
> Republics which having been formed with the seeds of
> their own dissolution now no longer exist. And we
> have viewed Modern States all around Europe, but find
> none of their Constitutions suitable to our circum-
> stances. In this situation of this Assembly, groping as it
> were in the dark to find political truth, and scarce able
> to distinguish it when presented to us, how has it hap-
> pened, Sir, that we have not hitherto once thought of
> humbly applying to the Father of lights to illuminate
> our understanding?

After some pious reflections, Franklin moved that the local clergy be invited to begin each day's proceedings with prayer.
He was asking the delegates to ignore the lessons of history and

fabricate the new constitution from their own lucubrations. For Franklin, the Father of lights had a different lesson to teach than the Author of history, with whom He is sometimes confused. The unquoted proof text for his motion came from Rousseau's *Discours sur l'origine de l'inégalite*: "Commençons donc par écarter tous les faits; car ils ne touchent point à la question." ("Let us begin by putting to one side all the facts, for they are not relevant to the issue.")

Hamilton and several others tried to squelch the resolution. "After several unsuccessful attempts for silently postponing the matter by adjourning, the adjournment was at length carried, without any vote on the motion."[23] When the delegates met again in the afternoon, the first speaker, Luther Martin of Maryland, argued vigorously for equal representation of all states in the Senate, no matter what their population. Madison objected, "There has been much fallacy in the arguments advanced by the gentleman from Maryland." Heated squabbling ensued and finally Franklin rose to speak. "Governor Franklin read some remarks, acknowledging the difficulties of the present subject. Neither ancient nor modern history, (said Gov. Franklin,) can give us light. As a sparrow does not fall without Divine permission, can we suppose that governments can be erected without his will? We shall, I am afraid, be disgraced through little party views. I move that we have prayers every morning." At first no one spoke. Then adjournment was moved and hastily approved. Franklin's motion died without a second.[24]

The power of the classical tradition over the Framers of the United States Constitution was so great that it led them to ignore their most distinguished member, Benjamin Franklin. This is not the whole story, however. Although James Madison's notes on the debate are the fullest, William Paterson's laconic jottings preserve an essential part of Luther Martin's argument: "Amphictyonic Council of Greece represented by two from each town—who were notwithstanding the disproportions of the Towns equal—Rollins *Ancient History* 4 Vol. pa.79."[25] "Who could have thought," wrote Gilbert Chinard, "unless such positive texts were produced, that the limitation of two senators for each State might perhaps be traced to the Amphictyonic Council of Greece?"[26] Rather, who can deny that the documentary record proves that the Amphictyonic League provided the model for the idea of two senators from each state? Who can fail to be impressed that this happened in the face of the vigorous objections of James Madison and the weary protests of Benjamin Franklin? Such was the hold that the classical tradition had on the minds of the Framers.

Classical political thought provided the ideas used by the Framers in their deliberations—for example, that government is best understood as the rule of the one, the few, and the many; that there are good and bad versions of all three; and that the

best government is a mixture of all three, with power balanced
and separated. That this tradition, based on centuries of Greek
and Latin observation and reflection, is irrelevant to America
and should not have influenced the Framers' thought and deliberations has been argued by thinkers from John Taylor of
Caroline to Correa Moylan Walsh. [27] Influence them, however, it did.

TYRANT AND TYRANNY IN THE DECLARATION

Just as classical republicanism saw the best form of government
in a mixed regime with powers balanced and separated, so it had
a vision of the worst regime, tyranny. The concepts of tyranny
and the tyrant were an indispensable contribution of ancient
thought to the Founders. The Declaration of Independence was
written with several goals, but "the longest section in the
Declaration" [28] is devoted to showing that George III was a
tyrant and so had forfeited the loyalty of the colonists. After the
initial Lockean sentiments, it observes that the people rarely
exercise their right to alter or abolish the incumbent form of
government. "But when a long train of abuses & usurpations
pursuing invariably the same object, evinces a design to reduce
them under absolute despotism, it is their right, it is their duty
to throw off such government." The central claim of the
Declaration follows. "The history of the present king of Great
Britain is a history of repeated injuries and usurpations, all
having in direct object the establishment of an absolute tyranny

over these states. To prove this let facts be submitted to a candid world."[29]

More than half the Declaration is devoted to a circumstantial documentation of this assertion. The key concept appears twice in the body of complaints like a bell. "He has refused to pass other laws for the accommodation of large districts of people, unless those people would relinquish the right of representation in the legislature, a right inestimable to them, & formidable to tyrants only." Near the end of the list, we read, "He is at this time transporting large armies of foreign mercenaries to compleat the work of death, desolation & tyranny, already begun with circumstances of cruely and perfidy, scarcely paralleled in the most barbarous ages, & totally unworthy the head of a civilized nation." Finally the argument is summarized: "A prince whose character is thus marked by every act which may define a tyrant is unfit to be the ruler of a free people." In his own draft, Jefferson hammered the point home. "Future ages will scarcely believe that the hardiness of one man adventured, within the short compass of twelve years only, to lay a foundation so broad & so undisguised for tyranny over a people fostered & fixed in principles of freedom." Whatever its preface may mean, the bulk of the Declaration makes a clear assertion: George III fits the traditional picture of a tyrant and therefore revolt from him and a revolution, or return to free rule, is justified and necessary.

The concepts of tyranny and tyrant developed from the Debate on the Constitutions in Herodotus III.80-82, through the history of the Athenian democracy as described by historians such as Herodotus and Thucydides, and were analysed by philosophers such as Plato in *Republic* VIII and Aristotle in the *Politics*. (It should come as no surprise that among the distinctive traits of tyranny in Aristotle's influential discussion in *Politics* V.10-11 are the immiseration of the middle class through heavy taxation and the suppression of a citizen militia.) Polybius, Cicero, Sallust, Livy, and Tacitus continued this tradition of political analysis in their descriptions of Roman history and institutions. The influential introductions Thomas Gordon wrote to his popular translations of Tacitus dwelt on the theme of tyranny.[30] The most popular of Cicero's philosophical works in colonial schools, *De officiis*, returns repeatedly to the figure of the tyrant, often exemplified by Julius Caesar. [31] The Declaration's attempt to prove George III a tyrant was an appeal to a long tradition, which provided a widely understood and accepted standard, derived from the ancient world and developed by Whig writers.

This analysis is confirmed by Jefferson's letter to Henry Lee of May 8, 1825:

This was the object of the Declaration of Independence. Not to find out new principles, or new arguments, never before thought of, not merely to say things which had never been said before; but to place before mankind the common sense of the subject, in terms so plain and firm as to command their assent, and to justify ourselves in the independent stand we are compelled to take. Neither aiming at originality of principle or sentiment, nor yet copied from any particular and previous writing, it was intended to be an expression of the American mind, and to give to that expression the proper tone and spirit called for by the occasion. All its authority rests then on the harmonizing sentiments of the day, whether expressed in conversation, in letters, printed essays, or in the elementary books of public right, as Aristotle, Cicero, Locke, Sidney, &c.[32]

THE CLASSICAL TRADITION AMONG
OTHER TRADITIONS

Jefferson's memory in 1825 of the state of colonial thinking in 1776 is confirmed by John Adams's version in his *Letters of Novanglus* (1774): "These are what are called revolution principles. They are the principles of Aristotle and Plato, of Livy and Cicero, of Sidney, Harrington, and Locke; the principles of nature and eternal reason."[33] These statements, written fifty years apart by two leaders of the Revolution, members of the committee responsible for drafting the Declaration of Independence and presidents of the republic, one a Federalist, the other a Republican, show that the ideas which lay behind the American Founding were understood as a continuous and coherent tradition which had developed from ancient Greek thought through its Roman successors and culminated in seventeenth century English Whig thinking.

Bernard Bailyn's classic analysis of the sources of the colonists' thought found four major strands "dominated and harmonized into a single whole by...one distinctive tradition": the classics, Enlightenment rationalism, covenant theology and the common law were united by modern Whig thought.[34] Bailyn mocks colonial Americans for thinking that English Whigs were continuing an ancient tradition. He exaggerates the Enlightenment element in the colonists' thinking by discussing Locke as an Enlightenment figure. He admits that, among Enlightenment writers, only Locke's influence could be called "decisive" or "determinative." Yet Americans consistently consider Locke a Whig. With Locke transferred to the Whigs, Enlightenment rationalism is reduced to its real but minor role in colonial thought.

We are left with three major influences: the common law, Protestant theology, and classical republicanism, ancient and modern. Americans interpreted all three in a profoundly traditional light. The best laws and customs were those closest to the tradition's source, as Jefferson wrote to Edmund Pendleton on August 13, 1776. "Has not every restitution of the antient Saxon laws had happy effects? Is it not better now that we return at once into that happy system of our ancestors, the wisest & most perfect ever yet devised by the wit of man, as it stood before the 8th century?"[35] Bailyn's comment on the common law concedes this point. "The common lawyers the colonists cited...sought to establish right by appeal to precedent and to an unbroken tradition evolving from time immemorial, and they assumed, if they did not argue, that the accumulation of the ages, the burden of inherited custom, contained within it a greater wisdom than any man or group of men could devise by the power of reason."[36] Bailyn's sentence would be equally true if the words "common lawyers" were replaced by the words, "Colonial preachers," "ancient authors," or "Whig theorists."

The Protestant piety that surrounded the Founders was as traditionalist as their classical republicanism, whether they shared that piety, as George Mason and Patrick Henry did, or questioned it, like Thomas Jefferson and James Madison. Early Protestants were not seeking a new openness to the future, but a return to the Bible. Their battle cry was "*ad fontes!*" Luther, it is true, wrote *De libertate Christiana* but he also wrote *De servo arbitrio,* and in both works he explicates Biblical texts. Colonial Americans read Luther, Calvin, and Wesley, sang Isaac Watts's hymns, and studied the King James' Bible to gain access to the Roman Empire where primitive Christianity was born and to the earlier world of the Old Testament. The Greek entrance requirement for college (abolished at Harvard in 1886) allowed Americans to read Homer, Isocrates, Plato, Aristotle, and Polybius. Its primary purpose, however, was to teach students to read the Greek New Testament so that they could return to the founding texts of the Christian tradition. Protestants judged the Church of Rome on the basis of the New Testament much as Whigs judged the British monarchy on the basis of Cicero and Tacitus. Colonial pulpits thundered out sermon after sermon in support of the cause of freedom, using ancient texts which expounded living traditions that began in the ancient world—Christianity and republicanism. Jonathan Mayhew makes this clear in his sermon on the repeal of the Stamp Act in 1766: "Having been initiated in youth, in the doctrines of civil liberty, as they were taught by such men as Plato, Demosthenes, and Cicero, and other renowned persons among the ancients, and such as Sidney and Milton, Locke and Hoadley among the moderns; I liked them; they seemed rational."[37]

It is only natural that scholars raised after the triumph of Enlightenment rationalism misunderstand the attitudes of men for whom it was axiomatic that the religion and politics they believed and practiced were formed in the ancient world and that direct contact with the sources of these traditions was necessary for them to function effectively and creatively. This misunderstanding or disbelief survives Thomas Jefferson's explicit assertion that the tradition is "the common sense of the matter." As Carl J. Richard writes, "To the founders, there was but one worthy tradition, the tradition of liberty, and they would not have understood the modern historian's need to distinguish between the classical and Whig traditions and to measure the influence of one against the other." [38]

The debate on the importance of Greece and Rome in the early republic is a modern debate among university professors. There was no such debate among the Founders. Some approved of the classical curriculum and its influence, like Thomas Jefferson[39] and John Adams. Adams wrote to Jefferson on July 16, 1814, "Classicks, in spight of our Friend Rush, I must think indispensable."[40] Others, such as Dr. Benjamin Rush and Thomas Paine, deplored the influence of the classics.[41] No one, however, thought to deny that influence.

THE CLASSICAL ENVIRONMENT

The Greek and Latin classics gave to the Founding generation words and ideas with which to frame the great enterprise on which they had embarked. The classical tradition influenced more than thoughts alone, however. It affected the American way of life, to use an old-fashioned expression. The early generations of the American republic wanted to live the classical tradition. This can be seen in the architecture of many private and most public buildings, as Charles and Mary Beard pointed out.

Through the architecture of the republican age, the political note rang with startling intonations. In casting
off monarchy and established church, the patriot Fathers, like their emulative contemporaries, the leaders
of the French republic, returned in their dreams, their
oratory, and their architecture to the glories of republican Greece and Rome—to the simple columns, roofs,
porticoes, and straight lines of early Mediterranean structures. Nothing seemed to them more appropriate. The
ornate elaboration of renaissance Gothic appeared out
of place in a country that was republican in politics,
practical in its interests, and tinged, at least, with democracy. There was of course no strict uniformity of
thought but the stamp of the classics was heavy on the
official buildings and private mansions of the period.

It was with a mind fixed upon the imposing designs of
ancient city planners that Major L'Enfant conceived his
elaborate scheme for the city of Washington.... When,
in 1808, the adopted son of Washington built his man-
sion at Arlington, Virginia, he seemed convinced that
the final triumph of art lay in the achievements of the
Greeks two thousand years in their tombs. It was to
the simplicity, solemnity, and power of Rome, despoiler
of Greece, that Jefferson turned for the design of his

University of Virginia. In the same reverence for classical antiquity, the colonial Georgian style was now pushed aside by architects who built mansions for southern planters, banks, offices for the federal government, and the capitol to house the Congress of the United States. Those who fashioned material structures and those who drafted orations drew their inspiration from the same source.[42]

The classics continued to provide inspiration for public buildings long after the Revolutionary period. In the decades before World War I the architectural firm of McKim, Mead and White used classical models for many public buildings. "Classicism, the firm came to believe, was allied with a national building tradition evolved in the eighteenth and early nineteenth centuries, but, even more, it was part of the rich European architectural traditon to which the United States considered itself heir."[43] Their masterpiece, the old Pennsylvania Station in New York City (1906-1910), was based on the Baths of Caracalla in Rome.[44] The tradition of building banks with classical façades continued until the 1950s. The triumph of globalism in economic policy was heralded by the Kennedy Round of GATT and a modernist bank architecture that proclaimed the new regime of credit, which, like the spirit, bloweth where it listeth, ready to flee one country and community for another at the flick of an interest rate. Modernist architecture houses banks that are national and international institutions, and which no longer measure success with the classical ideal of sustaining stable and productive communities.

THE NECESSITY OF TRADITION

There are a number of reasons why scholars reject the Founders' own evaluation of the importance of the Greek and Latin classics in their thought. Doctoral requirements for American history do not include a reading knowledge of Greek and Latin and so today's scholars have a different education from those they study. Some think that the debate began with Hannah Arendt in the 1960s, forgetting Carl Becker and Gilbert Chinard. Bibliographical quibbles aside, Becker, Chinard and Arendt shared a classical education and so recognized the classical modes of speech and thought that permeated the Founders' writing and thinking. Historians examine the classical tags laboriously collected by Richard M. Gummere[45] and draw the natural conclusion that the classical influence was superficial. Classical ideas and sentiments not marked by explicit citation or Latin tags will be apparent only to someone who knows the relevant classical texts.

There is, however, a deeper reason for our age's rejection of the Founders' opinions. We are children of the Enlightenment. We start from the most recent bibliography and only rarely dig down very deeply. The Founders followed the King's advice in *Alice's Adventures in Wonderland*: "Begin at the beginning, go to the end, then stop." If we find notions in Whig writers, we reach for Ockham's Razor and cut off any connection with the classical past, even against the explicit words of Adams and Jefferson. Our worldview, not just our education, is different.

There is more at stake here than a debate over hermeneutics. If progress and innovation depend on the Enlightenment critique and rejection of tradition, then rejecting the Founders' self-understanding serves a larger social good. Suppose, however, that Adams and Jefferson, or Thomas Gordon and Jonathan Mayhew, or Luther and Calvin, or Aquinas and Dante, are correct—that progress and creativity are available only to those who work within traditions and know the traditions' sources; that the benefits of Christianity and classical republicanism (even for those whose are neither Christians nor republicans) will dry up and disappear if those traditions are not fostered. If so, believing the Founder's self-interpretation is not only important for historical accuracy, but indispensable for society's health.

"I should as soon think of closing all my window shutters to enable me to see as of banishing the Classicks to improve Republican ideas," John Adams wrote to Benjamin Rush on June 19, 1789.[46] Works in Greek and Latin, whether the New Testament and the Fathers, or Homer, Plato and Aristotle, or Virgil, Livy and Tacitus, furnished tested standards with which to judge the world. Hannah Arendt thought the classics gave the Founders the "courage for what turned out to be unprec-

edented action." Their actions, however, were never unprecedented. No one else in their age was doing such things, but
they knew that in the past men had dared them. Today's movie,
television, and computer screens do not say that once upon a
time people existed who valued the spiritual over the material,
the political over the economic, family farms and small busi-
nesses over multinational corporations, family and friends over
"the International Community." The Founders, however, knew
of such men—those who did not despair before overwhelming
odds, whether they faced the Persian Empire or the British
Empire, Hannibal or Cornwallis. The future belongs to those
who know their past. The traditions the Founders knew and
continued are still alive today and available for the future. It is
time to open the shutters.

NOTES

1. Paul A. Rahe, *Republics Ancient and Modern* (Chapel Hill: University of North
   Carolina Press, 1992), esp. pp. 17-27 and the notes on pp. 792-795.
2. Clinton Rossiter, *Seedtime of the Republic* (New York: Harcourt, Brace, 1953),
   357.
3. Bernard Bailyn, *The Ideological Origins of the American Revolution* (Cambridge, MA:
   Harvard University Press, 1967), 26.
4. Russell Kirk, "What Did Americans Inherit from the Ancients?" in *America's
   British Culture* (New Brunswick: Transaction, 1985), 95-106: The quotations are
   found on pp. 96-99.
5. Hannah Arendt, *On Revolution* (New York: Viking, 1963), 197.
6. Gordon S. Wood, *The Creation of the American Republic, 1776-1787* (Chapel Hill:
   University of North Carolina Press, 1969), 50.
7. Gilbert Chinard, *Honest John Adams* (Boston: Little, Brown, 1933), 210.

8. Howard Mumford Jones, *O Strange New World* (New York: Viking, 1964), 227-272; J. G. A. Pocock, *The Machiavellian Moment* (Princeton: Princeton University Press, 1975); Meyer Reinhold, *Classica Americana* (Detroit: Wayne State University Press, 1984); Carl J. Richard, *The Founders and the Classics* (Cambridge MA: Harvard University Press, 1994).

9. Carl Becker, *American Historical Review* 30 (1924-25), 810-812, quoted as the inspiration for Harold Talbot Parker, *The Cult of Antiquity and the French Revolutionaries* (Chicago: University of Chicago Press, 1937), vii.

10. Robert Middlekauff, *Ancients and Axioms: Secondary Education in Eighteenth-Century New England* (New Haven: Yale University Press, 1963); T. W. Baldwin, *William Shakespeare's Smalle Latine and Lesse Greeke* (Urbana: University of Illinois Press, 1944).

11. Middlekauff, *Ancients and Axioms*, 90-91.

12. Forrest McDonald, *Novus Ordo Seclorum: Intellectual Origins of the Constitution* (Lawrence: University Press of Kansas, 1985), xi.

13. *The Writings of Thomas Jefferson*, ed. Andrew A. Lipscomb and Albert Ellery Bergh (Washington, D.C.: Thomas Jefferson Memorial Association, 1905), 15:207.

14. Middlekauff *Ancients and Axioms*, 193. Catiline is the correct spelling.

15. Jefferson, "Notes on the State of Virginia," Query XIV, in *Writings*, ed. Merrill Peterson (New York: Library of America, 1984), 273.

16. Victor Davis Hanson, *The Other Greeks: The Family Farm and the Agrarian Roots of Western Civilization* (New York: Free Press, 1995).

17. Garry Wills, *Cincinnatus: George Washington and the Enlightenment* (Garden City, NY: Doubleday, 1984).

18. Jefferson to James Madison, 20 December 1787, *Writings*, 916. See also Jefferson to John Adams, 13 December 1787, *Writings*, 913.

19. Chinard, *Honest John Adams*, 212.

20. Kirk, "What did Americans Inherit from the Ancients?" 99-100. See also Gilbert Chinard, "Polybius and the American Constitution," *Journal of the History of Ideas* 1 (1940): 38-58.

21. Walter Bagehot, *The English Constitution* (London: Chapman and Hall, 1867), quoted from the World's Classics edition (Oxford: Oxford University Press, 1928), 9. His critique of the American presidential system is found on pp. 14-29, 299-312.

22. *The Records of the Federal Convention of 1787*, ed. Max Farrand (New Haven: Yale University Press, 1966), 1:48.

23. Ibid., 451-452.

24. Ibid., 453-458.

25. Ibid., 459.

26. Chinard, "Polybius," 49.

27. John Taylor, *An Inquiry into the Principles and Policy of the Government of the United States* (Fredericksburg: Green and Cady, 1814); Correa Moylan Walsh, *The Political Science of John Adams* (New York: G. P. Putnam's Sons, 1915). Wood, *Creation of the American Republic*, 567-592, analyzes Adams's classically based thinking as irrelevant and right.

28. Dumas Malone, *Jefferson the Virginian* (Boston: Little, Brown, 1948), 221.

29. Jefferson, *Writings*, 19-24.

30. Meyer Reinhold, *The Classick Pages* (University Park, PA: American Philological Society, 1975), 100-111.

31. Andrew R. Dyck, *A Commentary on Cicero, De Officiis* (Ann Arbor: University of Michigan Press, 1996), 29-33 and index of topics, s.v. "Tyrannicide/tyrant."

32. Jefferson to Henry Lee, 8 May 1825, *Writings*, 1501.

33. *The Works of John Adams*, ed. Charles Francis Adams (Boston: Little, Brown, 1851), 4:15.

34. Bailyn, *Ideological Origins of the American Revolution*, 22-54. The quotation is on p. 23.

35. Jefferson to Edmund Pendleton, 13 August 1776, *Writings*, 752.

36. Bailyn, *Ideological Origins of the American Revolution*, 33.

37. Jonathan Mayhew, *The Snare Broken* (Boston: R. & S. Draper, 1766), 43.

38. Richard, *The Founders and the Classics*, 183.

39. See notes 13 and 15, above.

40. Adams to Jefferson, 16 July 1814, *The Adams-Jefferson Letters*, ed. Lester J. Cappon (Chapel Hill: University of North Carolina Press, 1959), 2:438.

41. Reinhold, "Opponents of Classical Learning in America during the Revolutionary Period,"*Classica Americana*,116-141.

42. Charles A. Beard and Mary R. Beard, *The Rise of American Civilization* (New York: Macmillan, 1927), 1:485-486.

43. Leland M. Roth, *McKim, Mead & White Architects* (New York: Harper & Row, 1983), 115.

44. Lorraine B. Diehl, *The Late, Great Pennsylvania Station* (New York: American Heritage, 1985).

45. Richard M. Gummere, *The American Colonial Mind and the Classical Tradition* (Cambridge, MA: Harvard University Press, 1963); *Seven Wise Men of Colonial America* (Cambridge, MA: Harvard University Press, 1967).

46. Adams to Benjamin Rush, 19 June 1789, *Letters of Benjamin Rush*, ed. L. H. Butterfield (Princeton: Princeton University Press, 1951), 1:518, n. 2, quoted from *Old Family Letters* (Philadelphia: J. P. Lippincott, 1892), Series A, 40.

VIRTUE AND THE CONSTITUTION: AUGUSTINIAN THEOLOGY AND THE FRAME OF AMERICAN COMMON SENSE

Graham Walker

Does the Constitution require the government to promote good moral character in the citizens? Or does the Constitution forbid official efforts to praise virtue and condemn vice?

To millions of Americans today, the answer is easy. They consider virtue a strictly private affair, and they take it as a self-evident truth that "government shouldn't legislate morality." They also believe that the Constitution, and the rights it guarantees, are the bulwark of that truth. Especially among students, these beliefs are not so much convictions as commonplaces, things not argued but taken for granted. To question these beliefs is to risk derision—or worse—on most American university campuses.

But it was not always so. Indeed, it was hardly ever so. The Constitution has been in force for over two hundred years, and for its first hundred and fifty years it apparently did not bar the use of law to promote moral decency. After all, according to the preamble, the Constitution was set up to "establish justice," and most Americans seemed to think that this mandate included more than merely the prohibition of murder and theft or the guarantee of fairness in legal procedures. Not surprisingly, the same Confederation Congress that recommended the Constitution to the states for ratification also enacted the Northwest Ordinance (1787), whose most famous provision states: "Religion, morality and knowledge, being necessary to good government and the happiness of mankind, schools and the means of education shall forever be encouraged." (The first Congress under the Constitution revalidated the Ordinance by adopting an act for its enforcement.) Most of the states at that time had charters announcing in majestic terms their aim to cultivate civic virtue and piety among citizens. Many of the states had official churches and religious tests for officeholders, and these arrangements—explicitly defended as means of promoting moral and civic virtue—remained in place during and after the ratification period; some of them lasted well beyond the Civil War and even into the mid-twentieth century.[1] The vast network of public schools arose from a widespread conviction that schools—especially public, local government-sponsored schools—should act as the training ground of democracy, instilling common habits of piety, honesty and self-control in American school children so that they could become good citizens under the

Constitution.[2]

Obviously, things have changed. All such policies are almost unthinkable today. Most Americans do not support them, and the Supreme Court—since the 1940s—has generally come to regard them as inconsistent with the Constitution, especially when the promotion of virtue is somehow entangled, as it often is, with religion. So great is the change in attitudes that one naturally wonders, how did this change come about? More importantly, is the change good? Was it required by the Constitution? Were earlier generations simply mistaken, while only recently we have managed to get it right? Or is it the other way around?

The Constitution itself is not much help in sorting this out. The text—even including the text of the fateful Fourteenth Amendment—neither explicitly authorizes nor explicitly forbids the public promotion of virtue. The word "virtue" does not appear in the text, and the document creates no obvious institutions for promoting good moral habits among citizens. The Constitution's literal silence on the subject is not in question. The question is what that silence means.

I shall argue here that the Constitution's enigmatic attitude toward virtue requires a two-fold account. First, it can be understood in the light of American federalism, which gave virtue a constitutionally authorized but constitutionally inarticulate public sphere in the states and localities. Second, and more profoundly, it can be understood—and even affirmed—in the light of that strain of biblical theology that received its greatest formulation from St. Augustine. Augustine's theology of original sin, transmitted by Protestant Christianity, was second nature to early Americans. To modern constitutional scholars, however, it is obscure and exotic. Absent such a theology, leading scholars today have a harder time making sense of the matter than early Americans did. Either they portray the Constitution as an ignoble, value-neutral instrument of mere interest-group pluralism, or else they portray it, implausibly, as a shaper of virtuous souls in the civic tradition of ancient republicanism. I shall argue that American common sense has always had access to better, and more homely, foundations.

CONSTITUTIONAL SILENCE

The American Constitution does not praise virtue. It does not even mention it. One looks in vain in the text for any institutional mechanism aimed at the promotion of selflessness, courage, generosity, self-control, piety, or even patriotism. Moreover, this literal silence can look awfully like a hostile silence when you take into account not only what the text *does not* say about virtue but also what it *does* say about other things. For example, the provision in Article VI, forbidding religious tests for federal officeholders, might be taken to imply that the Constitution frowns on the religious promotion of virtue.[3] After all, in the American colonies, which later became the states, such religious tests were widespread, and they were established precisely as an attempt to assure the good character of officeholders. They were supposed to add an eternal incentive for the maintenance of the temporal public trust. Of course religious tests may have been a bad idea, and unlikely to achieve their purpose. But there is no doubt about what that purpose was. Even the English liberal political philosopher John Locke had countenanced such tests on this basis.[4] The tests did not necessarily violate religious freedom; atheists and others failing the tests were denied eligibility to office, not free exercise of their religion (unless, of course, their religion required them to hold public office). Nevertheless, the Supreme Court decided in 1961 that the state of Maryland had been at odds with the values of the Constitution for 173 years, because of the provision of the Maryland Constitution requiring officeholders to declare their "belief in the existence of God."[5]

If the Constitution's ban on religious tests implies hostility to the public promotion of virtue, the language of the First Amendment goes further. The amendment does not explicitly address virtue, of course; it addresses religion, freedom and rights. But it has proved to be the major mechanism by which the Supreme Court has invalidated the public promotion of virtue. Because of this amendment, local schools have had to abandon their attempts to promote reverence for traditional morality (by posting the Ten Commandments on the school wall).[6] Because of this amendment, schools have had to give up on their attempts to make school children feel accountable for their behavior to a higher power (by making them listen to a daily nonsectarian prayer opening the school day, or even by having an opening moment of silence).[7]

The effect of the First Amendment is similar even when the official promotion of virtue does not suffer from a fatal entanglement with religion. Because of this same amendment, local school boards have had to abandon their attempts to promote patriotism (by requiring school children to salute the American flag).[8] Also because of this amendment, legislative efforts to condemn or penalize hateful speech have been thwarted.[9] According to the Supreme Court, the Constitution's First Amendment requires law and public authority at all levels to be "content neutral" in such matters.

Even in recent decisions considered favorable to religion, the constitutional principle established by the Court is hostile to the public promotion of virtue. The reason that high schools must now allow religious films on family life to be shown off-hours on school premises is the same reason that public universities must not eliminate funding to student-run religious newspapers: no public authority may engage in "viewpoint discrimination."[10] "Equal access" to public forums is mandated not only by federal statute,[11] but also, we are told, by the First Amendment's (implied) requirement that public authority always adhere to a posture of neutrality.

In other words, not only is the Constitution itself literally silent about virtue; it also requires silence about virtue from all official public entities.[12] Of course the text does not explicitly require this public silence. Supreme Court rulings do. But the fact that the text says nothing about virtue is highly relevant. It renders these rulings entirely plausible as interpretations of what the text does say—about freedom of speech and freedom of religion and about avoiding laws "respecting an establishment of religion."

Even aside from these rulings—even aside from the long-standing American public practices that have had to be abandoned because of them—the mere textual silence of the Constitution is striking in another way. It is striking in view of the central place that virtue had previously held in the Western tradition of political thought. In every previous era of our civilization, the proposition that "government should not legislate morality" would have seemed either unusual or unintelligible. From Plato and Aristotle to Cicero and on to the medieval scholastics, the cultivation of good character among citizens was considered a central, if not the central, task of political authority. Indeed, to Aristotle, the cultivation of character was as inescapable as it was desirable.[13]

It is true that by the seventeenth and eighteenth centuries early modern political thinkers parted company with Aristotle and company on many points, including the best form of government, the moral and spiritual basis of justice, and the relation of church to state. But on this point, even thinkers like Niccolò Machiavelli, Thomas Hobbes, John Locke and Jean Jacques Rousseau agreed: the promotion of virtue was a crucial public concern. They differed with Aristotle about the reason for this. They typically considered freedom or order to be more integral goals of politics than virtue. Publicly-promoted virtue was desirable because it was useful for securing order and freedom, rather than because of its intrinsic worth. But even as an instrumental rather than a final good, the public cultivation of virtue was considered indispensable.

This multifaceted tradition hardly died when it was borne across the Atlantic. We may even take as an example the one colony known for its lack of an established church, for its multiplicity of religious traditions and for its tolerant attitude toward dissent and nonconformity: Pennsylvania, whose generous course was set by William Penn. As founder, Penn clearly aimed at tolerance and comity. But he aimed to attain them through the cultivation of virtue. His 1682 *Frame of Government* for the new colony begins with a preface which extols "the Great and Wise God," quotes from the New Testament, and declares that government is "a part of Religion itself, a thing Sacred in its Institution and End." Anticipating latter-day skeptics, Penn argues: "I know some say, Let us have good Laws, and no matter for the Men that Execute them; But let them consider, that though good Laws do well, good Men do better; for good Laws may want good Men, and be abolished or evaded by ill Men; but good Men will never want good Laws nor suffer Ill Ones."[14]

Not surprisingly, Penn's founding theory had institutional consequences resembling those of the Northwest Ordinance a hundred years later. The *Frame of Government* created a Provincial Council, whose "Committee of Manners, Education and Arts" was to act as a public censor, "that all Wicked and Scandalous Living may be prevented, and that Youth may be successively trained up in Virtue and useful Knowledge."[15] It established freedom of "Religious Persuasion or Practice," but only for those who "confess and acknowledge the One Almighty and Eternal God." It established a religious test for voting and for office, and laid out a list of vices, including "swearing" and "sodomy," which were to be "discouraged" or "severely punished."[16]

The founder of Pennsylvania illustrates well the early American political theory of virtue because his premises are articulate, but even more because his is one of the *least* stringent regimes of public virtue among the American colonies. If broadminded and tolerant Pennsylvania insisted on the public cultivation of virtue, the others did so with more gusto and less reserve; and they did not stop when they were transformed from colonies into states. As we have seen, some of these practices coexisted with the federal Constitution for roughly a hundred and fifty years.

But there is none of this in the text of that Constitution. How could a nation arising out of such traditions of public virtue—a nation actively practicing such traditions—establish a national Constitution whose text is silent on the subject of virtue?

EXPLAINING THE SILENCE: THE FOUNDING

The Constitution's silence must signal something important about the public status of virtue in America. But what? Silence is not self-explanatory. In the nature of the case, no explanation is mandated by the Constitution itself. Even so, some explanations may be better than others.

The Federalist Papers, written in the heat of controversy over ratification, offer a well-known explanation. Their author, "Publius," explains that the proposed constitution features no mechanism for promoting virtue because it takes a dramatic new approach to politics. Publius concedes that the central problem of popular government is the problem of faction—a group of citizens united by an interested motive against the common good. In this, he is united with Aristotle and company. But according to Publius, the Constitution turns away from the old strategy of dealing with the *causes* of this problem and turns instead to dealing only with its *effects*.[17] This strategy in turn rests on a theory of human nature. As Publius says, "the accumulated experience of ages" teaches us that "men are ambitious, vindictive and rapacious."[18] The "latent causes of faction are thus sown in the nature of man." Even human reasoning is distorted by unruly passion and self-love. This ugly truth about human nature renders "impracticable" any of the traditional institutional efforts to promote virtue and discourage vice, even for the sake of so desirable an end as solving the problem of faction.[19] Instead, Publius claims this Constitution aims to control the effects of faction through devices that will hinder its formation. It does so by a system of representation, by encompassing a large territory with a "multiplicity of interests...parties and sects," and by creating a compound republic, with divisions separating state from national governments and also separating among executive, legislative and judicial branches. Such a system will not rely on virtue to thwart faction. Ambition itself will "counteract ambition" and in so doing it will check faction too.[20]

It is worth nothing parenthetically that Publius' rejection of the public cultivation of virtue is not rooted in a generalized skepticism about moral truth. He assumes, for instance, that there is a common good, even if he speaks of it euphemistically as "the permanent and aggregate interests of the community."[21] He even affirms that "Justice is the end of government."[22] More deeply, Publius's unflattering evaluation of human nature inescapably implies that there are true moral standards in relation to which that negative evaluation makes sense. On this point Publius is dramatically unlike some of his latter-day heirs, who oppose public promotion of virtue on the grounds that there is no moral truth about virtue which could guide such an activity, or no rational justification for calling virtue "virtue" and vice "vice."

By making virtue institutionally unnecessary to justice, Publius clearly means to disengage the as-yet unratified Constitution from the older idea of publicly-promoted virtue. It is especially intriguing, therefore, when the necessity of virtue creeps back into his own institutional argument. Even in *Federalist* 10 he argues that a system of representation—apart from any effort to improve the passions or interests of the electorate—can be justified by the likelihood that it will bring "fit characters" into office, whose "wisdom...patriotism and love of justice" will promote "the public good." Later he defends the executive and the Senate proposed in the Constitution by predicting that they will be staffed by "temperate and respectable" men, whose rationality and wisdom will enable them not only to "intend the public good" but also to maintain it—especially when the electorate at large, which lacks their good qualities of character, is "stimulated by some irregular passion, or some illicit advantage." He defends the proposed judiciary in similar terms, arguing that federal judges will not reflect the "ordinary depravity of human nature" but will instead possess "the requisite integrity."[23] But is there a sufficiently large pool of potential officials who are likely to possess the temperance, wisdom, self-control and self-denial that Publius ascribes to them? If not, his defense of these constitutional institutions falls short.

An adjustment in Publius's view of human nature seems called for, and he supplies it. "The supposition of universal venality in human nature is little less an error in political reasoning than the supposition of universal rectitude." Furthermore, he suggests, there is "a portion of virtue and honor among mankind, which may be a reasonable foundation of confidence.... A man disposed to view human nature as it is, without either flattering its virtues or exaggerating its vices, will see sufficient ground of confidence in the probity of the Senate to be satisfied."[24] In other words, Publius is compelled to take back, at least partly, what he asserted unequivocally in *Federalist* 6. We should not, of course, fault him for correcting his earlier overstatement. But Publius never acknowledges that this correction undercuts the pivotal reasons he had offered in *Federalist* 10 for dismissing the promotion of virtue. If human nature has a politically meaningful potential for virtue, are we not obliged to reopen the possibility that he foreclosed—that is, the possibility that it is a legitimate public concern to address the moral causes of faction and not only its institutional effects?

It is not necessary here to resolve the interpretive difficulties surrounding Publius's reasoning. Even if they were resolved, a larger question would remain: What is the status of *The Federalist Papers?* The American people never ratified *The Federalist Papers.* They ratified the Constitution. If Americans are authoritatively bound, it is the Constitution that binds them, not essays published in the New York newspapers during 1787 and 1788. Still, some say that if we understand Publius, we understand the Constitution. Is this true? Usually, if you want to know what a text means, you ask the author. If the author has later published a definitive explanation, you accept what he says about it. After all, it is his creation. If Jane Austen had published an account of her moral and psychological intentions for the female heroines in *Mansfield Park, Persuasion* and *Emma,* we would today have far fewer essays purporting to reveal exotic meanings of these texts.

But this poses a difficulty. Even if you subscribe to original intent, you cannot reasonably reduce original intent to Madison, Hamilton and Jay (whose conjoint mind became the Publius of *The Federalist Papers*). We often find that advocates of original intent direct our attention to the participants in the Philadelphia Constitutional Convention who drafted the text that was later submitted for ratification. They do not typically refer to all fifty-five of them, however, but to those few who are famous for their historical roles, or especially to the loquacious ones whose writings are admired by latter-day intellectuals. But does being talkative make one's talk authoritative? Does pub-

lishing more things make the things one publishes more representative?

Thomas Pangle handles this difficulty by arguing that the
handful of loquacious founders constituted a "small minority
of geniuses," who alone understood the real nature of the thing
they framed—unlike the majority of nongeniuses who framed a
thing they did not (truly) understand.[25] Pangle perceives the
process of framing and ratification as a kind of covert struggle
between a "pious majority" and a "rationalist and free-thinking
minority."[26] But in this struggle the impious minority had the
upper hand, by Pangle's account, because they inscribed their
notions into the structural logic of the Constitution that they
then persuaded others unknowingly to adopt. The ratifiers did
not know it, but in voting for the Constitution they were voting to invalidate any public concern for virtue or religion. From
this it is supposed to follow that we are now authoritatively
bound to a correct understanding of the thing that most of the
framers and ratifiers misunderstood when they proposed and
ratified it. Something is deeply wrong with this theory.

We might do better to think directly about the ratification
process. By the logic of that process, the "author" of the Constitution is the people at large, expressed through those who
ratified it on their behalf. This would draw our attention not
merely to five loquacious framers, or to fifty-five framers at the
Constitutional Convention, but to the members of the thir-

teen state ratifying conventions, or to the members of the standing state legislatures who selected them, or more compellingly,
to the general public in the thirteen states who elected *them.*
What did these people think they were ratifying? This question
cannot be answered conclusively, because the number of people
involved was large, their records diffuse, and their views apt to
be too varied for any precise generalization. Still, a consideration
of the ratification disputes may offer some insight. Even if we
cannot say conclusively what that whole generation thought,
we may at least shed light on issues that drew their attention,
and may deserve ours. For we live under the document they
ratified.

In this context, the most striking feature of the ratification
debate is that the opponents of ratification—typically derided
as "Anti-Federalist"—were often keenly aware of the very thing
we are exploring, namely the Constitution's silence on the subject of virtue. The Anti-Federalists may have been double-
minded, as Herbert Storing taught us, wanting both the large
union and the small republic, both freedom and commercial
prosperity on the one hand, and virtue and order on the other.[27]
But it was not their double-mindedness, per se, that made them
reluctant about the proposed constitution. What made them
reluctant was the one side of their double mind which saw
clearly the glaring omission in the proposed scheme: the failure
to attend somehow to the cultivation of those human qualities

which make public order decent and stable, and which more than anything else militate against the abuse of public power; that is, to the cultivation of virtue.

It is true that they spoke much of the advantages of a small republic compared to a large one. Among the advantages of the small republic, they pointed out, were a more transparent and direct representation of popular sentiment.[28] (Publius points to this as a disadvantage of a small republic, since the more direct the transmission of popular sentiment, the more public policy would be an expression of unbridled, unreasonable and selfish passions.[29]) But this was not because Anti-Federalists were naive about human nature, as though they failed to notice the rapacious human tendencies identified by Publius in *The Federalist*. It was not that the Anti-Federalists thought man inherently good while the Federalists thought him inherently bad. The Anti-Federalists, too, worried about human nature. They knew as well as Publius that popular passion could be turned to evil ends. They agreed with the Federalists on human nature but disagreed on what to do about it.

Anti-Federalists tended to favor the "small" republic because it was more conducive to promoting virtue among citizens, especially to promoting virtue through religion. As Storing says, "The Constitution and its defenders deliberately turned away from religion as the foundation of civil institutions. Among the Anti-Federalists, on the other hand, there was a great deal of sympathy with views like those of Charles Turner: 'without the prevalence of Christian piety and morals, the best republican Constitution can never save us from slavery and ruin.'"[30] With Mercy Warren, many Anti-Federalists worried that the new Constitution would lead Americans to follow the example of the secularizing enlightenment that had recently triumphed in France: "Bent on gratification, at the expense of every moral tie, they have broken down the barriers of religion, and the spirit of infidelity is nourished at the fount; thence the poisonous streams run through every grade that constitutes the mass of nations."[31] In other words, Warren feared the very thing that Henry Steele Commager later celebrated when he called America "The Empire of Reason."[32] The fact of his celebration underscores the prescience of her fear.

The Anti-Federalists are also known for their demand that a bill of rights be added to the proposed constitution. Before assuming too much on this head, it is worth asking what exactly the Anti-Federalists had in mind. Perhaps inadvertently, we get a fairly clear answer from Publius, who devotes an entire number of *The Federalist Papers* to rebutting their demand. The bulk of Publius's rebuttal is well-known but misses the main point. He cautions that a list of rights runs the risk of implying that individuals do not possess other rights beyond those listed. He also argues that the logic and structure of the proposed constitution obviate the need for a specific enumeration of rights. "Here, in strictness, the people surrender nothing; and as they retain everything they have no need of particular reservations, 'WE, THE PEOPLE of the United States...do ordain and establish this Constitution....'" According to Publius, this is "a better recognition of popular rights than volumes of those *aphorisms* which make the principal figure in several of our State bills of rights and which would sound much better in a *treatise of ethics* than in a constitution of government."[33]

Tucked in at the end of this famous paragraph lies the clue that reveals what Anti-Federalists generally wanted when they talked of a bill of rights. They wanted what they knew. They wanted something like the preambles to the existing state constitutions which, though often called bills of rights, typically featured just what Publius decries: moral aphorisms serving as a kind of public "treatise of ethics." As a leading Anti-Federalist writer put it, "We do not by declarations change the nature of things, or create new truths, but we give existence, or at least establish in the minds of the people truths and principles which they might never have thought of, or soon forgot. If a nation means its systems, religious or political, shall have duration, it ought to recognize the leading principles of them in the front page of every family book."[34] This is why, as Storing comments, bills of rights served, "as they often did in the state constitutions, as preambles, often of an exhortatory kind.... The fundamental case for a bill of rights is that it can be a prime agency of that political and moral education of the people on which free republican government depends."[35] Publius reveals what he decries, but, stunningly, fails to address it.[36] He never takes up the challenge of what Storing calls the "deepest level of the argument over a bill of rights."[37]

The Anti-Federalists' demand for a "bill of rights" seems one of the great ironies of American history. On this principal demand, the Federalists offered a concession: a bill of rights would be added by the first Congress under the Constitution. Anti-Federalists were won over by this concession in sufficient numbers to make ratification possible. But the document they got contains no aphorisms praising virtue. It would hardly be mistaken for a traditional "treatise of ethics." Instead, the first nine amendments ultimately became the mechanism by which the deepest principles of the Anti-Federalists would be permanently driven out of public life. The First Amendment in particular, as we have seen, has proved the death-knell to public virtue in the "small republics" of American states, cities and local school districts.

The only thing the Anti-Federalists got that matched their principles was the Tenth Amendment, which reserved "to the States respectively, or to the people" all governmental powers not delegated to the central government or expressly prohibited to the states. Without saying it in so many words, the Tenth Amendment was long thought to have preserved intact the traditional prerogatives of the states as morally-formative political communities. In legal terminology, these prerogatives were called the "police powers," the powers of a state to police the health, safety, welfare, and morals of the public in that state. The full panoply of state sumptuary laws was jurisdictionally authorized here—laws like William Penn's proscriptions against "swearing" and "sodomy." So thought earlier generations of citizens and judges. But the First Amendment's values are articulate while those of the Tenth are inarticulate; consequently, the Supreme Court has found it easy to overlook the latter for the sake of promoting the former.

These reflections cannot be historically conclusive, but they do suggest a rather plausible hypothesis. Americans of that era may have thought they were agreeing only to add a new top layer above the existing political authority of the colonies or states. That top layer, a central or federal government, would have explicitly enumerated powers, with public virtue pointedly omitted. The enumerated powers of the federal government would effectively preclude its being directly concerned with the promotion of virtue. Far from calling into question the legitimacy of local and state efforts to promote virtue, this arrangement would have the opposite effect. It would preserve the bottom layer—the moral jurisdiction of the states. It would strengthen the local and state promotion of virtue precisely by preventing the new federal government from intruding into the most important matters, which are best controlled closer to home.

If this is plausible, the ratifying generation could well have expected that the new constitution's arrangements for religion would be similar—since the public promotion of virtue was often linked to religion. They might have agreed with contemporary scholars like Akhil Reed Amar and Daniel Dreisbach, who argue that the establishment clause of the First Amendment has more in common with the Tenth Amendment than it has with any other part of the Bill of Rights.[38] If this was the ratifiers' view of the constitutional scheme, they would expect that the legislative branch of the central government would have no jurisdiction to make any laws "respecting an establishment of religion." This would obviously forbid the creation of a central national religion; it would equally obviously forbid any central interference with the states and localities regarding their varying arrangements for the place of religion in public life. Not surprisingly, this understanding of the establishment clause accords with constitutional history until roughly fifty years ago. Before that time, the Supreme Court had never formally claimed that state-endorsed churches or religious tests for office violated the Constitution. Indeed, the long silence of the Court on such matters implied the view of the establishment clause described above.

When the Court did begin making such claims, of course,

it did so on the authority of the Fourteenth Amendment, which was ratified in 1868—although it took the Court seventy-eight more years to discover in this amendment the basis for such claims. I shall return to this later, but it is important to concede here that the Fourteenth Amendment does indeed curtail the jurisdiction of states. It denies them the power to restrict the rights of individual citizens in ways that may previously have been legitimate.[39] According to Amar, this reasonably "incorporates" most of the rights listed in the first nine amendments, obliging the states to respect those rights just as the federal government had always been obliged to do. But it could not reasonably incorporate either the Tenth Amendment or the establishment clause of the First Amendment. It would be nonsensical to do so, Amar argues.[40] How could a state be forced to abide by provisions which prevent the federal government from intruding into a state jurisdiction? By this reasoning, the establishment clause and the Tenth Amendment are in principle "unincorporable." If this were true, it would not follow that state religious establishments would be a good thing if they were once again permitted, rather than forbidden, by the Supreme Court. But it would mean that the moral and religious possibilities of American federalism may be considerably broader than the Court, and most Americans, now see them to be. If even this modest conclusion shocks modern Americans, it is important to keep the main point in view. The point is not that this reading of the Constitution is definitive, but that it is plausible. The Constitution's "silence" on public virtue could reasonably have been—and still reasonably could be—construed in this way.

We have therefore found an answer that fits the question posed earlier. How could a people actively practicing the old traditions of public virtue turn away so dramatically to embrace a new system indifferent or hostile to public virtue? The answer is that they did not. The constitutional silence on virtue is not really as complete as it seemed at first. It is only a half-silence. If the written Constitution of the new federal authority pointedly omitted any mechanism for virtue, or even any explicit concern for it, the constitution of the American polity as a whole still made provision for virtue of a very old-fashioned sort, and for its public promotion—in the states. For the Constitution ratified in 1788 did not eliminate, and did not even delegitimize, the traditional religious and sumptuary jurisdictions of the states. (Indeed, that Constitution did not necessarily have these effects even as amended eighty years later.)

THE FUNDAMENTAL QUESTION

We might stop here, but this answer is too easy. It leaves the original question really only half answered. To see why, we must revisit the question, in ampler form. Given the obvious and widely-acknowledged need for a morally decent citizenry, especially the need for wise and selfless dedication to the common good (a need which even *The Federalist* could not avoid), why should early Americans have agreed to a constitutional order that was even *partly* indifferent to this need? Why should they have agreed to a constitutional order whose top half—the new national or federal part—was silent about virtue, especially when that top half was clearly apt to be the leading half, given its superordinate position and its supremacy clause? Why should they have agreed to it when the top half did not even explicitly endorse the virtue-promoting jurisdiction of the bottom half—the states and localities? (The Tenth Amendment does so, but only implicitly.)

As citizens bound by this Constitution today, we face this as a living question, not merely a historical one. For the deepest question about virtue and the American constitution is not, What did the handful of loquacious founders—like Madison and Jefferson—think? Nor is it, What did *The Federalist Papers* mean? Nor is it, What did the silent majority of the framers think? Nor is it even, How would ordinary Americans at the founding period have understood the Constitution's relation to public virtue? This last question is, of course, a better question than the preceding ones; it may in fact be the question at which judicial interpreters of the Constitution should stop in the course of their official duties. But it is still not the deepest question. The deepest question, and the one we still face, is this: Why should *anyone* affirm this constitutional order which is silent, or half-silent, about human character? I am no longer asking the historian's question, Why is the Constitution silent on virtue? I am asking the philosopher's question, Is the Constitution's silence a good thing?

Jean Yarbrough, a scholar of early American political thought, must have had this question in mind when she referred to virtue as the Constitution's "missing critical provision."[41] But many others laud what she regrets. As we have seen, the celebrated historian Henry Steele Commager chose the title *The Empire of Reason* for his influential book on the American founding. His laudatory subtitle tells all: *How Europe Imagined and America Realized the Enlightenment.*[42]

In fact, of course, there are several different ways to affirm the moral silence of the Constitution. Contemporary scholarship features a number of these ways. But all the choices on the current menu are either implausible, inadequate, or ignoble.

There are a few scholars who argue that the silence of the American Constitution is apparent rather than real, not silence at all. One version of this approach claims that the Constitution continues the great tradition of public virtue in Western political thought from Aristotle to Cicero to Aquinas. As Russell Kirk put it dramatically, "The tap-root of American order runs deep into a Levantine desert," that is, into the historical experience of Judaism and Christianity.[43] This view has a lot of history in its favor. As I have argued, it is compellingly plausible with reference to the unwritten constitution of the American polity as a whole, or more specifically with reference to the almost "invisible" features of the written federal Constitution (which might have protected the religious and moral jurisdictions of the states). But it does not fit, and does not adequately account for, the striking silence of the very visible text. As I will argue below, there are indeed theological premises that make sense of that text, but they are completely unstated in the text itself. If this makes for a Christian commonwealth, it is unlike any previously seen in North America. The claim that the American Constitution is in direct and harmonious continuity with the tradition of public virtue, or with the tradition of Christian commonwealth, may therefore inadvertently approach the truth. But the more complete the claim of unbroken continuity, the less plausible it becomes.

There is also a considerably less plausible version of the argument that the silence of the Constitution is not really silence at all. This version claims to find in the Constitution a modern incarnation of the civic ideals of classical Greek and Roman republicanism, including a stringent public promotion of civic (but not religious) virtues. The historian J. G. A. Pocock has developed this thesis most famously, interpreting the American Constitution as the culmination of an "Atlantic Republic tradition."[44] To put it mildly, this account is historically and textually strained. As a historical matter, it is obliged to ignore or marginalize the overwhelming social and political presence of religion in early American life.[45] As a textual matter, this account finds no warrant at all in the Constitution. Indeed, its account of the centrality of active civic engagement is in tension with the constitutional text's considerable solicitude for private property, private contract, and private commerce.

The "civic republican" account of the American Constitution is also strained theoretically, or at the level of principle. Is it likely that the mass of citizens in a popular republic can have a reliably stable set of virtues if those virtues are pursued entirely apart from religion? Moreover, is the communalism of a continuously engaged citizenry desirable? Would it not crowd out too many important things—not only religious practices but also the private goods of ordinary human life? What George Bernard Shaw said once of socialism might be adapted to the theory offered by Pocock: The trouble with Atlantic republicanism is that it leaves you no free evenings.

What remains is the account which has, in the post-war period, dominated American thinking about virtue and the Constitution. This is more or less the view of Henry Steele Commager, but it was advanced most influentially by Louis Hartz in his 1955 work *The Liberal Tradition in America*.[46] Although devotees of this view sometimes emphasize their secondary differences, they agree that the American Constitution breaks decisively from the older traditions of public virtue. The Constitution, they say, is a liberal one. That is, it stands against any governmental promotion of virtue beyond what is required to coordinate the private pursuits of a variety of individuals. Since it does not seek to judge or shape moral character, the Constitution (and the public order it spawns) can function as a largely value-neutral arbiter of individuals and interest groups in perpetual conflict. (Most of the advocates of this view doubtless possess and perhaps even personally promote good moral character; they simply believe that the Constitution does not permit a public sanction for their private virtues.)

This view has certain textual and historical advantages which account for its success. It obviously has one enormous advantage in its favor: the constitutional text. Strictly speaking, of course, the text is a negative rather than a positive asset, since the point is that the Constitution is just as *silent* on the subject of virtue as a liberal would want it to be. Arguments from silence usually fall short, but it is hard to deny that in this case the textual silence about virtue now looks awfully like institutional indifference toward virtue. Even though it does not have history entirely on its side, the historical advantages of the liberal view are also considerable. Ordinary people may not have embraced the view that virtue was always a private and never a public concern, but some famous Founders did. At least, some of them had views that can plausibly be rendered in a way that fits this view. In particular, the authors of *The Federalist Papers*, as we have seen, provided an account of the Constitution that is largely compatible with what is now called the liberal view. (Liberals may wish to forget the internal tensions in Publius's argument against public virtue, noted above.)

But the textual and historical advantages of the liberal view do not compensate for its theoretical flaws, that is, its flaws at the level of principle. At this level, the liberal interpretation of the Constitution's silence may be no less plausible than the "Christian commonwealth" view, but it renders the Constitution inadequate and ignoble. According to most versions of the liberal story, the reason that the Constitution is silent about virtue is ultimately that there is no authoritative, prepolitical moral truth at which virtue could be aimed. Locke's State of Nature ostensibly contains a Law of Nature, but it is not one that can require self-sacrifice for the good of another or the common good.[47] Hobbes's picture of the State of Nature of course wears no such pretense to begin with.[48] Either way, there is no moral truth to which all owe allegiance. There are natural rights but no natural duties. So individuals cut a deal with one another and with the state; they make promises of self-restraint that can be based on nothing beyond a calculation of private advantage. Consequently, the real glue that binds individuals together as citizens is their instrumental rational calculations; and the state established has as its final purpose nothing greater than to preserve as much of our originally lawless individual autonomy as is possible, given the necessarily social condition.

These philosophic premises of the liberal view make the American Constitution's silence on virtue intelligible but ugly: We do not want public authority to help us become better persons, because there is no such thing as better persons; we only want it to coordinate our desires so we can pursue them with as little interference as possible. If these deeper premises animate the theory of the Constitution adopted by the Supreme Court in the last fifty years or so, it is no wonder that the jurisprudence of individual autonomy has increasingly overpowered other public concerns. This should give us pause. Moreover, the premises of the liberal view make us wonder. Does a prudential treaty—even one among thousands of individuals—really make a nation? Has any nation ever survived with no more social glue than the instrumental calculations of its individual residents? Even more important, can someone who knows and loves a good greater than himself admire a Constitution erected on such grounds? Probably not.

THE AUGUSTINIAN ACCOUNT

But there is a coherent way of thinking, anchored in religion and virtue, that could justify such a constitutional system. This way of thinking is not the fantasy that America is simply one of the old-time Christian commonwealths. But it does depend on the theology that those old commonwealths transmitted to eighteenth-century Americans, and to us. It depends on the theology of creation and fall. This theology received its most influential articulation from St. Augustine, the North African Bishop of Hippo, who died in the fifth century, A.D. Augustine's political theology of sin renders the Constitution's half-silent treatment of virtue intelligible—or even desirable—to stringent and pious public moralists.

Augustine's *City of God* was by many accounts the most widely read book in medieval Europe, after the Bible. In Books XI-XIV of that work, Augustine restates in philosophic terms the basic biblical doctrines of the creation and fall of man. In Book XIX he offers a striking account of the political consequences of these doctrines. Augustine's account begins with the creation, not the fall. Long before Augustine, the Book of Genesis had already announced the central point: *Deus creator omnium*;[49] God is the creator of all things, and he created them *ex nihilo*, out of nothing. Consequently, "no created thing is coeternal with the Creator."[50] But because God is wholly good, "the things which He made are indeed good because from Him, yet mutable because not made out of Him, but out of nothing."[51]

Human nature in particular was "created so excellent, that though it be mutable itself, it can yet secure its blessedness by adhering to the immutable good."[52] Man could have remained "steadfast in the love of that higher and changeless good" by which he was "illumined to intelligence and kindled into love."[53] But our first parents voluntarily defected and so "stripped" themselves of the permeating grace by which their nature had originally cohered.[54] That primordial choice "vitiated and altered" human nature, "and on account of it this nature is subject to the great corruptions we feel and see, and to death, and is distracted and tossed with so many furious and contending emotions, and is certainly far different from what it was before sin."[55] The autonomy man sought turned out to be a kind of freedom contrary to his nature: "by aspiring to be self-sufficing, he fell away from Him who truly suffices him." Thus, "By craving to be more, man becomes less."

Yet "man did not so fall away as to become absolutely nothing; but being turned towards himself, his being became more contracted than it was when he clave to Him who supremely is."[56] This contraction of being afflicts all subsequent human generations.[57] Because of Adam's solidarity with all nature and his regency over it, the entire natural order also suffered a certain contraction of being whose imponderable effects the Bible does not dwell on and Augustine develops only minimally.

More to the point, since man has an associative nature, what he chooses to do with his love has social consequences. Accordingly, "two cities have been formed by two loves, the earthly [*civitas terrena*] by the love of self, even to the contempt of God; the heavenly [*civitas dei*] by the love of God, even to the contempt of self."[58] By Augustine's account, "this whole time or world-age"—this *saeculum*—"In which the dying give place and those who are born succeed, is the career of these two cities."[59] (These "cities" are not geographic city-states but fundamental affinity groups, perhaps better rendered in our terms as "citizenries.")

Augustine fastidiously avoids identifying the *civitas dei* with the institutional church, or the *civitas terrena* with the political state. This is because until the end of time "the two cities are commingled" in every sphere of life.[60] Their commingling will turn out to be the pivotal point for politics. Their commingling is possible because they are not, after all, alien to one another. They differ in their will but not in their essential nature.[61] As this life "is common to both cities, so there is a harmony between them in regard to what belongs to it." However disordered the loves of the earthly city, "the things which this city loves" are hardly evil in themselves. "For it desires earthly peace for the sake of enjoying earthly goods," and such things "are good things, and without doubt the gifts of God." These things are used "by both kinds of men and families alike, but each has its own peculiar and widely different aim in using them."[62] The heavenly city does not become entangled in earthly goods but orders their use to the true and final good of man. The earthly city either becomes fixated on the things themselves, or else orders their use to ephemeral God-surrogates which inflame rather than heal human wounds.

This brings us finally to politics. Politics finds its place within the constraints of the historical interim in which we live, our fallen *saeculum* in which nature remains vitiated by sin. Given the fragmentation of human love in this age, and so of human personality and community, the political state does not rule over one people. The mixed multitude it manages neither possesses nor is capable of approaching consonance. Tragically, its values—that is, its loves—are dissonant. And although Augustine's most fundamental cleavage is between those who love God and those who spurn him, in principle the number of dissonant groups is as large as the number of objects that may attract a false and fragmented love.

Thus it is that, in Gerhart Niemeyer's words, Augustine deserves to be called "the intellectual father of the concept of the limited state," for we note the emergence in Augustine's thought of "an independent political function beyond and besides the mutually exclusive loyalties within the culture, the perception of an autonomous task of political rule."[63] This is so even though Augustine provides no fully developed theory of the political state. What he provides is a reflection on its fundamental tasks. These reduce to the common interest that both its "cities" have in the basic goods of this life, none of which is more basic than a modicum of "earthly peace."[64] The *civitas dei*, for its part, participates in but transcends politics.

"Not scrupling about diversities in the manners, laws, and institutions whereby earthly peace is secured," the heavenly city "desires and maintains a common agreement among men regarding the acquisition of the necessaries of life, and makes this earthly peace bear on the peace of heaven."[65]

Due to "the very great mutability of human affairs," however, earthly peace is chronically unstable. With all their roiling enmities even in peacetime, "the peace of unjust men is not worthy to be called peace in comparison with the peace of the just." Only the peace of heaven can truly be called "the peace of the reasonable creatures, consisting as it does in the perfectly ordered and harmonious enjoyment of God, and of one another in God."[66] Yet because peace is a good of nature, every form of peace, however truncated, partakes somehow of the nature of true peace.[67] Fallen man is still man. He cannot shed the lingering structure of his original nature. He "cannot help loving peace of one kind or another." Despite the inevitable shortfalls of peace in this life, "there is no word we hear with such pleasure, nothing we desire with such zest." "Miserable," says Augustine, is the "people which is alienated from God. Yet even this people has a peace of its own which is not to be lightly esteemed." It is to this peace that politics is ordered— "the temporal peace" which the two cities "together enjoy."[68]

There is of course one department of temporal life where the two cities' interests are irreconcilable. In a way that almost suggests the religious neutrality of the modern liberal state, Augustine notes how "it has come to pass that the two cities could not have common laws of religion."[69]

According to Augustine, political rule would not be necessary according to the true, unfallen order of nature. God "did not intend that his rational creature, who was made in His image, should have dominion over anything but the irrational creature—not man over man, but man over the beasts."[70] Politics is penal and provisional, made necessary by sin. Linking the essence of politics to coercion, Augustine upends classical political science and appears, in the modern sense, acutely realistic— especially in view of his famous adumbration of the *libido dominandi*, the lust of ruling.[71]

Still, such realism does not detach politics from moral parameters. Augustine never suggests that the tasks of politics— the "laws and institutions whereby earthly peace is secured"— should not be informed by truth. For though Augustine develops no full-fledged theory of the functioning of the political state, the moral context he gives it is clear. Politics functions not in a morally blank world but in a fallen one. As long as this condition persists, man can recognize, but never manages to fulfill, the promise of his nature. C. S. Lewis expressed the Augustinian view when he called this "a good world that has gone wrong but still retains the memory of what it ought to have been."[72]

Augustine is happy for political rule to take its bearings from moral truth, or even to promote some virtue and some true piety, to the extent feasible. But feasibility is determined by the fallen condition of nature. As a result, both the tasks and the tools of political rule are limited in scope. For one thing, only the "exterior man" is susceptible of rule, and this but unevenly. A poor means of inculcating virtue, political regulation is more a matter of "intimidating the evil and enabling the good to live more quietly among them." For "the effect of law is to condemn the act, without removing the evil disposition."[73] Only grace can do the latter, and the choice to receive grace can hardly be settled by law.[74] Indeed in man's fallen condition, legal imperatives can have a perverse effect on man's will. In an allusion to the Apostle Paul, Augustine notes that "prohibition increases the desire of illicit action, "unless through spiritual regeneration the good is so "loved that the desire of sin is conquered by that love."[75] But because spiritual regeneration is in fact possible in this life, those who take all this seriously will hardly sit around waiting for the kingdom of God to arrive. Through evangelism, the sacraments, and the church, they will actively inculcate virtue and extol the grace that makes virtue viable. But using the tools of the political state for this effort will have little appeal.

This vision gives politics lower and arguably safer tasks than those imagined by the classical moralism of an Aristotle or a

Cicero. Augustine makes the political task unromantic and unenviable, because it has nothing to do with the central drama of history, nothing to do with bringing the movement of being to fulfillment. Goodness is real enough to those in political life, but the good of human nature is vitiated—and will remain so until the close of any age in which politics might figure. Thus the human material available in this historical interim is, on the whole, not amenable to being formed into a community of true virtue. Of course politics and law are valuable, but the possibilities of inculcating virtue through law are real but narrow. Political rule does what good it can while the central drama proceeds on other levels. Because he recognizes nature as both created and fallen, Augustine's thinking forbids both moral vacuity and moral transformationalism in politics.

Taken as a whole, Augustine's political theology would serve as a kind of substantive and principled justification for a policy of muddling through. It amounts to a principled argument against a politics of principle—not, of course, against a politics that consults principle, but against one that takes the attainment of principle to be its prime task. As we have seen, this is because politics is in essence a provisional palliative for the fallen condition. Coercion is at its heart, virtue at its periphery. History is moving forward with the highest moral stakes for all human beings, requiring the focused and active moral struggle of every soul. God alone can deliver man from his ontic—and moral—instability. Politics and law figure only marginally if at all in this salvific project.

AUGUSTINE AND AMERICA

Taken as a whole, Augustine's political theology would also serve as a justification for the sort of constitutional arrangements ratified in America in 1788, whose mixed and divided system gave a respectful half nod to public virtue.

In its basic features, Augustine's theology would have sounded pretty familiar to most Americans in the late eighteenth century.[76] It certainly matches the doctrine of human nature found in *The Federalist Papers* (as expressed in Numbers 6 and 10 but amended in Number 76): Men are inclined to vice but capable of virtue, and those with political power are not exempt from this condition. People who think this way are obviously not moral cynics or even moral relativists. They simply believe that human sinful inclinations make it necessary to place limiting safeguards around human political powers—including around the power to promote virtue. Even today, this will seem like common sense to a lot of people. I doubt that this is because it is self-evident. More likely it is because most of our grandparents, and their grandparents, absorbed Augustine's theology from the cradle; what is true of many of us was surely even more true of earlier generations of Americans.

I am not a historian, and my argument therefore has hinged more on philosophy than on history. I have demonstrated how

Augustine's theology of creation and fall enables us to appreciate the American Constitution's treatment of virtue. I have not demonstrated that this is how the founding generation thought about these things. Even for a historian, demonstrating historical influences is a hazardous business because actual connections are diffuse; this can be especially true of the most important ones. But since the basic premises of Augustine's political theology resonate so strongly with premises of original American constitutionalism, it seems reasonable to offer some informed speculation.[77] After all, the first of the great Protestant reformers, Martin Luther, was an Augustinian monk. All the reformers, emphatically including John Calvin, drank deeply of Augustine and claimed to be recovering Augustine's central theological insights. A well-known historical theologian once described the Reformation, "inwardly considered," as the triumph of Augustine's theology (of sin and grace) over Augustine's ecclesiology (of church authority).[78] Calvin's theology informed the Puritans. One of the greatest devotees of Calvin, Jonathan Edwards, spawned the Great Awakening in pre-revolutionary America. Edwards was the teacher of John Witherspoon who, as president of Princeton University, was the teacher of James Madison. It seems likely that by Madison's time, the theology of creation and fall would have been so widely shared among Americans of the ratifying generation as to constitute a kind of common sense hardly in need of statement.

THE COURSE OF THEOLOGICAL AMNESIA

Someone unfamiliar with, or alienated from, this theological "common sense" might well find the Constitution's treatment of virtue incomplete. Theological amnesia could make American intellectuals, and the public more generally, receptive to theories that render the Constitution in the terms of some less paradoxical form of political logic. Such an amnesia does not, of course, characterize every scholar whose work I have mentioned. But it could account for the literate public's appetite for the array of polarized interpretations of the moral logic of American constitutionalism, which I described above. It is easy to see how this can occur.

Consider stringent moralists whose solicitude for a virtuous national society is untempered by any encounter with a political theology like Augustine's. The literal text of the Constitution would leave such minds dissatisfied. The response would be predictable: notwithstanding the absence of any federal mechanism for the promotion of virtue, there surely must be some such mechanism; therefore, the Constitution must be construed to contain what it literally does not. They would be quite ready to read the Constitution as the charter of a great national Christian commonwealth. If they are secularists, they would be quite ready to read the Constitution as a national engine of civic republican virtue. Then again, the same moralists could easily reach an opposite conclusion: since it contains no explicit virtue-promoting mechanism, they will be tempted to reject the Constitution as unworthy of their allegiance. Once arrived at that conclusion, there is no telling what such moralists will do in their pursuit of justice.

Consider alternatively those modern, skeptical secularists whose background or predilections keep them safely away from any form of theology. Such minds might be apt to conclude far too much from the Constitution's silence on the subject of virtue. They might be enormously impressed with the channeling mechanisms of numbers 10 and 51 of *The Federalist Papers*, but will pass quickly over the comment in number 51 about justice as the end of government or the invocations of virtue in number 63. They would respond well to a theory that makes the Constitution's silence speak the language of value-neutral interest group competition.

The intellectual absence of Augustinian theology, it seems, would make it likely for the dispute between value-neutral liberalism and classical republicanism to fall out just the way it did. Its absence might also have helped to make that debate so sterile and so inconclusive. Theological amnesia would make it possible for many participants in that debate to think that those two alternatives pretty much exhausted the possible interpretations of the moral logic of American constitutionalism—even though, as a historical matter, both alternatives ignore the demonstrable salience of religious ideas in eighteenth-century America.[79]

It must be added in conclusion that the Supreme Court's doctrine of the Fourteenth Amendment's "incorporation" of the Bill of Rights has gravely complicated all of these matters. Although the doctrine in its current form is relatively young, it has obscured our understanding of both the Constitution's formal terms and its moral rationale. It has done so in two ways. First, by conflating the constitutional prerogatives of the bottom layer with those of the top, the incorporation doctrine has led the Court progressively to deconstruct the institutionally mixed character of the system (which originally gave virtue its formal public sphere in the states and localities). Second, that structural change has in turn abetted a cultural change: the practices and habits once fostered by local civic life and local school boards, which functioned as the seedbeds of theological common sense, have been extinguished—or privatized or perhaps colonized. They have had to give way to the value-neutral requirements of the public order. In consequence, successive generations of students, and thus intellectuals, are either unfamiliar with, or unsympathetic toward, the theology of creation and fall whose terms furnish a more intellectually adequate justification for the original arrangement.

The actual circumstances of American culture and jurisprudence at the end of the twentieth century probably make it impossible for most Americans to escape the vicious circle that this process implies. If my analysis of the process is correct, it will become ever harder for Americans to appreciate the Constitution's original mixed character. The original mixed Constitution was half-opposed, although only half-opposed, to the public promotion of virtue, and it did not ground even its half-opposition in moral relativism or spiritual indifference. As an intellectual matter, it is important not to lose track of the original genius of this design. But it is almost certainly too late for dominant opinion, whether popular or academic, to reconsider. We are going to find out what happens when institutional constraints become metaphysical negations—that is, when millions of people fully embrace the proposition that virtue consists of no more than private whims privately pursued.

NOTES

1. See, for instance, Paul Eidelberg, *The Philosophy of the American Constitution* (New York: Free Press, 1965), esp. appendix 2, "Provisions in state constitutions respecting religion, morality, education and the qualities required of statesmen," 264-271. See also Barry Alan Shain, *The Myth of American Individualism: The Protestant Origins of American Political Thought* (Princeton, N.J.: Princeton University Press, 1994), esp. chap. 2, "A Sketch of 18th-Century American Communalism," 48-83. Until as late as 1961, the State of Maryland required officeholders to declare their "belief in the existence of God"; the Supreme Court struck this down as unconstitutional in *Torasco v. Watkins*, 367 U.S. 488 (1961).

2. Sidney Mead argues that in the absence of a comprehensive religious establishment, schools took over the function exercised by the religious establishment in other countries, namely the promotion of virtue. Sidney E. Mead, *The Lively*

Experiment: The Shaping of Christianity in America (New York: Harper and Row, 1963), 66-68. See also Charles L. Glenn, Jr., The Myth of the Common School (Amherst, Mass.: University of Massachusetts Press, 1988). See also Robert Michaelsen, Piety in the Public School: Trends and Issues in the Relationship Between Religion and the Public Schools in the United States (New York: Macmillan, 1970). See also Michael W. McConnell, "Multiculturalism, Majoritarianism and Educational Choice: What Does Our Constitutional Tradition Have to Say?" University of Chicago Legal Forum 123 (1991): 134-139.

3. "...no religious Test shall ever be required as a Qualification to any Office or public Trust under the United States." U.S. Constitution, art. 6, para. 3.

4. John Locke, Letter Concerning Toleration (Indianapolis: Hackett, 1983), 46-51, where Locke insists that atheists are not to be tolerated because "the bonds of human society can have no hold on atheists." See also John Locke, Some Thoughts Concerning Education, section 70 and section 94. Also, John Locke, Second Treatise on Government, chap. 18, 208.

5. Torasco v. Watkins, 367 U.S. 488 (1961).

6. Stone v. Graham 449 U.S. 39 (1980).

7. Concerning nonsectarian prayer, see Engel v. Vitale, 370 U.S. 421 (1962); concerning a moment of silence, Wallace v. Jafree, 472 U.S. 38 (1985).

8. West Virginia Board of Education v. Barnette, 319 U.S. 624 (1943).

9. For a recent example see R.A.V. v. St. Paul, 112 S.Ct. 2538 (1992), in which the Supreme Court unanimously invalidated a municipal ordinance that made hate speech a crime. For commentary see Edward J. Clearly, "The Fight on Fighting Words. Beyond the Burning Cross: the First Amendment and the Landmark R.A.V. Case," Boston University Law Review 72 (1992), 953 ff.

10. Lamb's Chapel v. Center Moriches Union Free School District, 508 U.S. 384 (1993); Rosenberger v. Rector and Visitors of the University of Virginia, 515 U.S. 817 (1993).

11. Equal Access Act, 20 U.S.C., 4071-74.

12. A notable exception to this rule seems to be in the area of tobacco, where both state and federal authorities actively condemn and discourage the use of cigarettes without running afoul of a constitutional requirement of "content neutrality." This is presumably because harms to the medical health of the community can be identified objectively and rationally, while harms to the moral health of the community—by such things as promiscuity and hate speech—can be identified only subjectively and arbitrarily. This distinction itself clearly begs for some rational scrutiny.

13. Aristotle, The Politics 3-5. According to Aristotle's analysis, even an unjust society inevitably fosters that set of attitudes and moral habits compatible with its unjust

institutions. Until it is crushed by its own faults, such a society simply treats those vices the way a just society treats virtues.

14. William Penn, preface to *The Frame of Government* (1682) in *The Papers of William Penn*, vol. 2, ed. Richard S. Dunn and Mary M. Dunn (Philadelphia: University of Pennsylvania Press, 1982), 211-220.

15. Penn, *The Frame of Government*, § 13, in *Papers*, 217.

16. Penn, *Laws Agreed Upon in England*, §§ 34-35. Section 37 identifies "all such Offences against God, as Swearing, Cursing, Lying, Prophane Talking, Drunkenness, Drinking of Healths, Obscene words, Incest, Sodomy, Rapes, Whoredom, Fornication and other uncleanness (not to be repeated)" as among the crimes eligible to be "discouraged and severely punished." *Papers*, 224-225.

17. *The Federalist Papers*, no. 10.

18. *The Federalist Papers*, no. 6.

19. *The Federalist Papers*, no. 10. He says that human nature renders impracticable the attempt to "give everyone the same opinions, passions and interests." By means of this rhetorical overstatement Publius dismisses the traditional virtue-promoting panoply of politics.

20. See generally *The Federalist Papers*, no. 10 and no. 51.

21. *The Federalist Papers*, no. 10. Sometimes he even calls it by its old-fashioned name, the public good (no. 10), or the general good (no. 51).

22. *The Federalist Papers*, no. 51

23. On the good character of these public officials see generally *The Federalist Papers*, nos. 49, 63, 71, and 78.

24. *The Federalist Papers*, no. 76.

25. Thomas L. Pangle, *The Spirit of Modern Republicanism: The Moral Vision of the American Founders and the Philosophy of Locke* (Chicago: University of Chicago Press, 1988), 2.

26. Ibid., 22.

27. Herbert J. Storing, *What the Anti-Federalists Were For* (Chicago: University of Chicago Press, 1981), 6 and generally.

28. Ibid., 16-19. See directly "Federal Farmer 7" and "Centinel 1," in *The Anti-Federalist: Writings By Opponents of the Constitution*, ed. Herbert J. Storing (Chicago: University of Chicago Press, 1985).

29. *The Federalist Papers*, No. 49; see also no. 63.

30. Storing, *What the Anti-Federalists Were For*, 23.

31. Ibid., 22. Warren also feared that "The federal city provided for would breed monarchical institutions and courtly habits, with their oppressive tendencies and with the effect above all [of] the perpetual ridicule of virtue." Ibid., 20.

32. Henry Steele Commager, *The Empire of Reason: How Europe Imagined and America Realized the Enlightenment* (Garden City, N.Y.: Doubleday, 1977).

33. *The Federalist Papers*, no. 84; emphasis added.

34. "Federal Farmer 16," quoted by Storing, *What The Anti-Federalists Were For*, 70.

35. Ibid., 70. Storing says, "The Anti-Federalists saw, although sometimes only dimly, the insufficiency of a community of mere interest. They saw that the American polity had to be a moral community if it was to be anything, and they saw that the seat of that community must be in the hearts of the people." Ibid., 76.

36. Although he had addressed it indirectly in *Federalist* 10, as we have seen, where he dismissed it as impractical in view of the badness of human nature and the variety of human interests.

37. Storing, *What the Anti-Federalists Were For*, 69.

38. Akhil Reed Amar, "Some Notes on the Establishment Clause," *Roger Williams University Law Review* 2 (1996): 1-14. Daniel Dreisbach argues that "the principal objective of the constitutional framers was to defer to state and local jurisdictions on all matters pertaining to religion." Dreisbach, "Sowing Useful Truths and Principles," *Journal of Church and State* 39 (Summer 1997). See also "The Constitution's Forgotten Religion Clause," *Journal of Church and State* 38 (Spring 1996).

39. The relevant portion of the Fourteenth Amendment reads: "No State shall make or enforce any law which shall abridge the privileges or immunities of citizens of the United States; nor shall any State deprive any person of life, liberty, or property, without due process of law; nor deny to any person within its jurisdiction the equal protection of the laws."

40. Amar, "Some Notes on the Establishment Clause."

41. Jean Yarbrough, "The Constitution and Character: The Missing Critical Provision?" in *To Form a More Perfect Union* (Charlottesville, Va.: University Press of Virginia, 1992), 217-249.

42. Henry Steele Commager may have been guilty of a bit of exaggerated triumphalism, but he must have been on to something.

43. Russell Kirk, *The Roots of American Order* (Malibu, Calif.: Pepperdine University Press, 1978), 11. For something like this view see also Walter Nicgorski, "The Significance of the Non-Lockean Heritage of the Declaration of Independence," *American Journal of Jurisprudence* 21 (1976): 156-177. A somewhat idiosyncratic version of this view is found in John P. Diggins, *The Lost Soul of American Politics: Virtue, Self-Interest, and the Foundations of Liberalism* (New York: Basic Books, 1984).

44. J. G. A. Pocock, *The Machiavellian Moment: Florentine Political Thought and the*

Atlantic Republican Tradition (Princeton N.J.: Princeton University Press, 1975). See also Gordon S. Wood, *The Creation of the American Republic, 1776-1787* (New York: Norton, 1972).

45. The voluminous historical research of both Russell Kirk and Barry Alan Shain (cited above) are, on this point, sufficient antidotes to Pocock's view.

46. Louis Hartz, *The Liberal Tradition in America: An Interpretation of American Political Thought Since the Revolution* (New York: Harcourt, Brace, 1955). Complementary views have been advanced by Commager (as above); by Pangle (as above); by Walter Berns, *Taking the Constitution Seriously* (New York: Simon and Schuster, 1987); and, in modified form, by Martin Diamond, "Ethics and Politics: The American Way," in *The Moral Foundations of the American Republic* (Charlottesville, Va.: University Press of Virginia, 1986), 75-108.

47. Locke, *Second Treatise of Government*, chap. 2 and elsewhere. See also Kirk, *Roots of American Order*, 285-290; also Leo Strauss, *Natural Right and History* (Chicago: University of Chicago Press, 1953), chap. on Locke.

48. Thomas Hobbes, *Leviathan*, part 1, chap. 13.

49. Genesis 1:1. The Latin phrase is from a hymn of Ambrose; see Augustine, *Confessions*, trans. R.S. Pine-Coffin (Middlesex, England: Penguin, 1979), 9.12; also Augustine, *City of God*, 11.4.

50. Augustine, *City of God*, 12.1, 16, 25, and 14.16; see also *Confessions*, 13.2.

51. Augustine, *City of God*, 12.17 and 12.1. But of course the mutable being of creatures is capable—as God's being is not—of dwindling and even of terminating, reverting to the nothingness out of which it was created. Happily, however, God dispatches his unseen "power which pervades all things, and is present in all without being contaminated, which gives being to all that is, and modifies and limits its existence; so that without Him it would not be thus or thus, nor would have any being at all." (Ibid., 12.25) This sustaining permeation of nature is not pantheism. Although nature is not independent of God, God is "independent...of what He makes." For it is "of His own gratuitous goodness He creates, since from eternity He dwelt without creatures in no less perfect a blessedness."

52. Ibid., 12.1. The qualities of reason and will also characterize the angels, according to Augustine.

53. Ibid., 14.13. As Augustine muses in the *Confessions* (7.11), the nature of human nature is such that "unless my being remains in Him, it cannot remain in me."

54. Augustine, *City of God*, 14.1,17; Augustine, *On the Trinity*, 12.11 (16).

55. Augustine, *City of God*, 13.3; 14.12.

56. Ibid., 14.13.

57. Genesis 3:14-19; Romans 8:19-22; Augustine, *City of God*, 14.4 and 13.3,14.

58. Ibid., 14.28. "The former, in a word, glories in itself, the latter in the Lord.... The one lifts up its head in its own glory; the other says to its God, 'Thou art my glory and the lifter up of my head.'" (Ibid., 14.28, quoting Psalms, 3:3). Of course it must be kept in mind that "contempt of self" is only a proximate necessity in view of the fallen condition. In this condition, truly prioritizing the love of God requires denying the autonomous pretensions of the fallen self. In the unfallen order of nature the two loves are not in conflict. Even now, that "contempt of self" which renders love of God preeminent makes not for the demolition of the self, but for the best maintenance of the true self.

59. Ibid., 15.1.

60. Ibid., 18.47 and 19.26.

61. Ibid., 11.33: "the one [is] both by nature good and by will upright, the other also good by nature but by will depraved."

62. Ibid., 19.17; 15.4; 19.17.

63. Gerhart Niemeyer, "Augustine's Political Philosophy?" in *The Christian Vision: Man in Society*, ed. Lynne Morris (Hillsdale, Mich.: Hillsdale College Press, 1984), 67.

64. Augustine, *City of God*, 19.17.

65. Ibid.

66. Ibid., 17.13, 9.12, 17.

67. Since "even what is perverted must of necessity be in harmony with, and in dependence on, and in some part of, the order of things, for otherwise it would have no existence at all." Ibid., 19.12.

68. Ibid., 19.12, 11, 26.

69. Indeed, the heavenly city "has been compelled in this matter to dissent" and thus to face "anger and hatred and persecutions." Ibid., 19.17.

70. Ibid., 19.15.

71. Ibid., and elsewhere.

72. C. S. Lewis, *Mere Christianity* (New York: Macmillan, 1960), 48.

73. Both quotations from Augustine, *Letters*, 153.16; cited by Charles N. Cochrane, *Christianity and Classical Culture* (Oxford: Clarendon, 1940), 509. I am following Cochrane's discussion on this matter of law and virtue. R.A. Markus notes that this is Augustine's mature view of law, developed after a flirtation in his early post-conversion years with a classical and almost Thomistic notion of law's morally ennobling tasks—which notion he later dropped as ill-attuned to the realities of the fallen condition and the central necessity of grace; R. A. Markus,

Saeculum: History and Society in the Theology of St. Augustine (Cambridge: Cambridge University Press, 1970), 87-95.

74. In Augustine's late writings, a call for the persecution of heretics seems to belie this logic of his other mature thinking on this point. Even there, however, his concern might best be interpreted more as a concern for a temporal ecclesiastical and social order than an imagination of forced conversion.

75. Augustine, *City of God*, 13.6; see Romans 7.

76. See *The Myth of American Individualism*, where Barry Alan Shain's historical research demonstrates this more than adequately.

77. This kind of inquiry might also consider more generally the peculiar hospitableness, and susceptibility, of Protestant cultures to modern liberalism. Canadian political scientist George Parkin Grant has explored this problem effectively. Grant has noted that the "believing Protestants were likely to back their constitutional regimes," yet they backed them "without believing that avoidance of violent death was the highest good, or that justice was to be chosen simply as the most convenient contract." By buying into the Hobbesian political scheme, such Protestants tended gradually to lose their faith, while at the same time helping to hide the "fundamental political vacuum" at the heart of liberal regimes. George Parkin Grant, *English-Speaking Justice* (Notre Dame, Ind.: University of Notre Dame Press, 1985), 62. See, in general, part 3, 48-68.

78. Benjamin B. Warfield, *Calvin and Augustine* (Philadelphia: Presbyterian and Reformed Publishing Company, 1956), 322.

79. This salience is demonstrated by Barry Alan Shain in *The Myth of American Individualism*. I must admit that, like Shain, when I first was initiated into the liberal-republican debate over the American Constitution, my initial inclination was to side with the "republicans." They seemed the antidote to the contemporary indifference to virtue. Theirs seemed to be the more noble quest. But it was quixotic. The American Constitution cannot be made to fit it. Their interpretation is not finally congruent either with American history or with the constitutional text. More important, it is not congruent with enduring political wisdom.

NATURAL LAW, THE CONSTITUTION, AND THE THEORY AND PRACTICE OF JUDICIAL REVIEW

Robert P. George

The concept of natural law is central to the Western tradition of thought about morality, politics, and law. Although the Western tradition is not united around a single *theoretical account* of natural law, its principal architects and leading spokesmen—from Aristotle and Thomas Aquinas to Abraham Lincoln and Martin Luther King—have shared a fundamental belief that humanly created "positive" law is morally good or bad, just or unjust, depending on its conformity to the standards of a "natural" (viz., moral) law that is no mere human creation. The natural law is thus a "higher" law, albeit a law that is in principle accessible to human reason and not dependent on (though entirely compatible with, and illumined by) divine revelation.[1] So St. Paul, for example, refers to a law "written on the heart" which informs the consciences even of the Gentiles who do not have the revealed law of Moses to guide them.² And many centuries later, Thomas Jefferson appeals to "the law of nature and nature's God" in justifying the American Revolution.³

Most modern commentators agree that the American founders were firm believers in natural law and sought to craft a Constitution that would conform to its requirements, as they understood them, and embody its basic principles for the design of a just political order. The Framers of the Constitution sought to create institutions and procedures that would afford respect and protection to those basic rights (natural rights) which people possess, not as privileges or opportunities granted by the state, but as principles of natural law, which the state has a moral duty to respect and protect. Throughout the twentieth century, however, a lively debate has existed on the question whether the Constitution incorporates natural law in such a way as to make it a source of judicially enforceable, albeit unwritten, constitutional rights and other guarantees.⁴ In this essay I will discuss two significant moments in this debate: (1) the exchange between majority and dissenting justices in the 1965 Supreme Court case of *Griswold v. Connecticut*;⁵ and (2) an important effort by a distinguished constitutional law scholar, the late Edward S. Corwin of Princeton University, to specify and draw out the implications of the rootedness of American constitutional law in natural law concepts.

THE GRISWOLD PROBLEM

In 1965, the Supreme Court of the United States, by a vote of seven to two, invalidated a Connecticut anti-contraception law on the ground that it violated a fundamental right of marital privacy which, though nowhere mentioned or plainly implied in the constitutional text, was to be found in "penumbras formed by emanations" from various "specific guarantees in the Bill of Rights." Writing in dissent, Justice Hugo Black accused the majority of indulging in "the natural law due process philosophy" of judging. Although critics would later heap ridicule on the majority's metaphysics of "penumbras formed by emanations," Black was content on this score merely to record his view that we "get nowhere in this case by talk about a constitutional 'right of privacy' as an emanation from one or more constitutional provisions." His focus, rather, was on unmasking what he judged to be an implicit revival by the majority of the long discredited natural law doctrine.

As far as Black was concerned, bringing to light the natural law basis of the decision in *Griswold v. Connecticut* was sufficient to establish the incorrectness of the ruling and the unsoundness of the reasoning set forth in Justice William O. Douglas's opinion for the Court. Black assumed that Douglas would not dare to defend the proposition that judges are somehow authorized to enforce an unwritten natural law, or invalidate legislation that allegedly violated unwritten natural rights or substantive due process. In this assumption he was correct. Douglas emphatically denied that the majority was resurrecting the jurisprudential doctrine under which the Court had earlier in the century (beginning with *Lochner v. New York* in 1905) struck down worker protection laws and other forms of economic regulation and social welfare legislation as violations of unwritten natural rights (above all the right to freedom of contract), allegedly protected by the due process clauses of the Fifth and Fourteenth Amendments.[6] Indeed, Douglas did not even mention due process in his long catalog of explicit Bill of Rights guarantees whose penumbral emanations supposedly created a right of married couples to purchase and use contraceptives.[7]

Both Black (in 1937) and Douglas (in 1939) had been appointed by Franklin D. Roosevelt, whose manifest intent was to put onto the Supreme Court jurists who could be counted on to oppose the judicial philosophy that had since at least 1905 impeded the progressive legislative agenda. The most celebrated cases involved freedom of contract and other economic issues,[8] although a small number of cases invalidated restrictions on noneconomic liberties, such as the right of parents to choose private, religiously affiliated schools, rather than public education, for their children,[9] or of teachers to teach foreign languages.[10] Roosevelt and other critics had excoriated the Court for its rulings in cases involving economic regulation and social welfare legislation, suggesting that the justices were, without the slightest constitutional warrant, substituting their personal political and economic opinions for the contrary judgments of the elected representatives of the people.[11] The critics alleged that, under the pretext of giving effect to implied constitutional protections, the "nine old men" were reading the social and economic policies they favored into the Constitution as a means of imposing them on the public.[12] Even twenty years after Roosevelt's death, no self-respecting Roosevelt appointee to the Supreme Court would want to be caught indulging in the practice he had condemned.

In those twenty years, however, much had changed in American social life, and new issues were before the Court. One of these was contraception.[13] The development of the anovulant birth control pill in the early 1960s energized pro-contraception groups, such as Planned Parenthood, and catapulted the issue into the mainstream of public discussion. The practice of contraception, which even fifty years earlier had been condemned not only by the Roman Catholic Church but across the denominational spectrum (and by such esteemed organs of the American social-political establishment as *The Washington Post*), became increasingly respectable among opinion shaping elites and middle and upper class Americans generally. Protestant and Jewish leaders almost unanimously came to endorse the use of contraceptives by married couples to limit the size of their families, and more than a few people predicted—wrongly, as it turned out[14]—that the Vatican would soon revise Catholic teaching to permit contraception for married couples who had legitimate reasons to postpone or avoid pregnancy. People of a liberal social and political persuasion, together with more than a few conservatives, came to view effective contraception as a great boon both for individuals and society alike. The availability of contraceptives would, they supposed, strengthen marriages by relieving the pressures created by couples having more children than they desired or could comfortably afford to raise. It would, moreover, enable sexually active unmarried girls to avoid the ignominy and other burdens of illegitimate pregnancy. Above all, perhaps, it would alleviate welfare costs by reducing out-of-wedlock births to impoverished women.[15]

Many supporters of contraception neither anticipated nor desired a "revolution" in sexual morality. At the same time, most considered the old moral objections to contraception, not to mention legal prohibitions such as the Connecticut statute, to be relics of an unenlightened—even sexually repressive—age.[16] There is every reason to suppose that all nine of the *Griswold* justices shared this view. Black, who was joined in dissent by Potter Stewart, opened his opinion by remarking that Connecticut's law was "every bit as offensive to me as it is to my brethren." Stewart's opinion began with a denunciation of the statute as "uncommonly silly." What distinguished Black and Stewart from their brother justices was not any difference of opinion over the morality of contraception or the undesirability of laws against it; rather, it was their unwillingness to declare that anti-contraception laws, however "offensive" or seven "silly," violated the Constitution.

Black and Stewart reminded their brethren that the judicial invalidation of legislation in the name of rights that lack any foundation in the constitutional text or its historical understanding was precisely what critics had condemned an earlier Court for doing in the cause of conservative economic and social policy. Doing it in the cause of a particular view of sexual morality—even an "enlightened" view—was, they maintained, no more justifiable. Since the Constitution provided no textual or historical basis for a right to contraception (i.e., "marital privacy"), they argued that the only ground on which such a right could be declared is the very ground on which the discredited right to freedom of contract had been declared, namely, the idea of natural law—a law superior to the statutory law, to which judges may appeal in striking down a statute even where the constitutional text provides no warrant for doing so. So, in their view, the majority could not escape the problem merely by declining explicitly to invoke the "natural law due process philosophy" and appealing instead to "penumbras formed by emanations."[17] Natural law jurisprudence by any other name remains natural law jurisprudence; and natural law jurisprudence is, Black insisted, in principle illegitimate.

But, someone may ask, is it not true that the Framers and ratifiers of the Constitution were firm, indeed fervent, believers in natural law and natural rights? Did they not found the United States precisely on the proposition that the institutions of government are justified by the moral imperative that natural rights be protected by civil authority? Did they not design institutions of government with a view to insuring that civil authority would conform itself to the requirements of natural law and not degenerate into tyranny by violating the very rights government is instituted to protect? If so, how could Black and Stewart condemn a jurisprudence of natural rights? Moreover, why would Douglas and those joining his majority in *Griswold* go out of their way to deny, rather implausibly, that theirs was such a jurisprudence?

CORWIN ON NATURAL LAW AND
AMERICAN CONSTITUTIONALISM

In 1949, more than a decade after the effective demise of *Lochner*, and a decade and a half before the Court's decision in *Griswold*, Edward S. Corwin—Woodrow Wilson's successor as McCormick Professor of Jurisprudence at Princeton University and perhaps the nation's preeminent constitutional scholar—delivered an address at the Third Annual Natural Law Institute of the College of Law at the University of Notre Dame. There, Corwin sought to show "how very large a part of its content American constitutional law has always owed, and still owes, to its natural law genesis." He argued that the positive law of the "documentary Constitution is still, in important measure, natural law under the skin."[18]

Corwin's analysis was largely historical. His aim was to show that the legal tradition that shaped the understanding of the Framers of the American Constitution and the early practitioners of American constitutional law was deeply informed by two central natural law concepts (or "juristic connotations of the concept of [natural law]"): "first, that natural law is entitled by its intrinsic excellence to prevail over any law which rests solely on human authority; and second, that natural law may be appealed to by human beings against injustices sanctioned by human authority."[19]

Central to Corwin's account is the idea that the English common law emerged historically as a sort of positive embodiment of the natural law, that is, as a body of law which is the fruit of (juristic) *reason* and enjoys its status as law precisely as such. It differs from statutory law inasmuch as its legal status does not derive, as does, for example, an act of Parliament, from the sheer *will* of a lawmaking authority. "Thus," Corwin concluded, "the common law becomes higher law, without at all losing its quality as positive law."[20]

Indeed, Corwin suggested that an important strand of the English legal tradition conceives the common law as enjoying a certain superiority to acts of Parliament. He gave significant weight to the "famous 'dictum,' so-called [of Lord Coke] in *Dr. Bonham's Case*[21] which reads: 'And it appears in our books, that in many cases, the common law will controul acts of Parliament, and sometimes adjudge them to be utterly void: for when an act of Parliament is against common right and reason, or repugnant, or impossible to be performed, the common law will controul it and adjudge such act to be void....'" In this "dictum," according to Corwin, we have a jursiprudential notion which, when allied later (as it would be) with John Locke's conception of substantive ("inherent and inalienable") rights of the individual, provides the foundation for American-style judicial review.[22] Corwin noted that "the dictum had won repeated recognition in various legal abridgements and digests before the outbreak of the American Revolution," and he cited various invocations of the substance of the dictum by American lawyers and political figures in the years leading up to the Revolution.[23]

A central feature of Corwin's account is his claim that "judicial review initially had nothing to do with a written constitution."[24] He asserted that the idea of judicial review appeared in America some twenty years before the first written constitution, and that judicial review was practiced "in a relationship of semi-independence of the written constitution on the basis of 'common right and reason,' natural law, natural rights, and kindred postulates throughout the first third of the nineteenth century."[25] He argued that the "competing conception of judicial review as something anchored to the written constitution had been in the process of formulation in answer to Blackstone's doctrine that in every state there is a supreme, absolute power, and that this power is vested in the legislature."[26] It was one thing, according to Corwin, for Blackstone to reject the idea of judicial review, as he did, in the context of a system in which the supreme will was embodied in the legislature; it is another thing altogether, however, where the supreme will is understood to be that of the people themselves as expressed in their constitution. In the latter case, as American authorities such as Alexander Hamilton[27] and John Marshall[28] recognized, the duty of courts facing a conflict between legislation (considered as the act of mere agents of the people) and the Constitution (considered as the act of the people themselves) was plainly to give effect to the Constitution.

Corwin viewed these competing conceptions of judicial review as clashing near the beginning of our national history in the case of *Calder v. Bull.*[29] There, in a dispute involving the question whether the Constitution's prohibition *of ex post facto* laws applies only to criminal legislation, Justice Samuel Chase asserted the authority of the Court to invalidate legislative acts on the basis of "certain vital principles in our free republican governments, which will determine and overrule an apparent and flagrant abuse of legislative power...." In reply, Justice James

Iredell, though agreeing with Chase that the constitutional prohibition of *ex post facto* laws did not extend beyond the criminal law, denied the power of courts to act on the basis of the
proposition, advanced by "some speculative jurists...that an act
against natural justice must, in itself, be void."

Who had the better view? Characteristically, Corwin appealed to the authority of history, asserting that while Iredell's
view prevailed as a matter of official doctrine, his victory was
"more in *appearance* than in *reality*."[30] "In the very process of
discarding the doctrine of natural rights and adherent doctrines
as the basis of judicial review," Corwin insisted, "the courts
have contrived to throw about those rights which originally
owed their protection to these doctrines the folds of the documentary Constitution."[31]

NATURAL LAW AND THE *GRISWOLD* PROBLEM

Does Corwin's analysis supply what is needed to vindicate the
natural law jurisprudence Justice Black complained about in
Griswold?

It is possible to read Corwin as supposing that belief in
natural law entails the authority of judges to enforce it where
they judge it to be in conflict with positive law, at least in those
jurisdictions that authorize courts to exercise judicial review of
legislation, and, in particular, where the framers and ratifiers of
a written constitution evidently sought to protect natural rights
and insure the conformity of governmental acts to the require-

ments of natural law. But if this was, in fact, Corwin's view, and his esssentially historical approach to the subject leaves the matter a bit unclear, then I do not believe he was correct. It is certainly true that believers in natural law consider positive law to be legitimate and binding in conscience only where it conforms to natural law and, as such, respects the natural rights of people subject to it. But natural law itself does not settle the question whether it falls ultimately to the legislature or the judiciary in any particular polity to insure that the positive law conforms to natural law and respects natural rights.[32] Nothing in the record suggests that the American Founders believed otherwise. To be sure, there were debates at the margins, such as the debate between Chase and Iredell; but the questions at issue in such debates involved nothing like the *Griswold* problem. They had to do, rather, with such issues as whether the judiciary could, in effect, refuse to enforce laws that were incapable of being complied with, or whether courts could overrule legislative acts which plainly violated "vital principles" that, though not expressly stated, were presupposed by the very institutions of "free republican government."

If we see that natural law does not dictate an answer to the question of its own enforcement, it is clear that authority to enforce the natural law may reasonably be vested primarily, or even virtually exclusively, with the legislature; or, alternatively, a significant measure of such authority may be granted to the judiciary as a check on legislative power. The questions of whether to vest courts with the power of constitutional judicial review at all, and, if so, what the scope of that power should be, are in important ways underdetermined by reason. As such, there are matters to be resolved prudently by the type of authoritative choice among morally acceptable options—what Aquinas called "determinatio" and distinguished from matters that can be resolved "by a process akin to deduction" from the natural law itself.[33] It is a mistake, then, to suppose that believers in natural law will, or necessarily should, embrace expansive judicial review or even "natural law" jurisprudence (of the type criticized by Justice Black in *Griswold*). This is because questions of the existence and content of natural law and natural rights are, as a logical matter, independent of questions of institutional authority to give practical effect to natural law and to protect natural rights.

Let us now return to the *Griswold* case. Imagine that someone, for example Justice Black, accepts the proposition that the framers and ratifiers of the Constitution were fundamentally motivated by a concern to conform governmental acts to natural law and protect natural rights. Suppose further that he agrees that people have a natural right to "marital privacy" which includes the right to use contraceptives. He could, nevertheless, without logical inconsistency, come down on the question of the constitutionality of the Connecticut statute exactly as he did in *Griswold*. Moreover, he could come down that way for precisely the reasons he stated in the case. These reasons do not necessarily involve, and certainly do not logically entail, denial of the existence of natural law or natural rights. Rather, they constitute the denial that judges are authorized under the positive law of the Constitution to invalidate legislation based on their understanding of natural law and natural rights.

As Robert Bork, perhaps the leading contemporary critic of natural law jurisprudence, explains his position: "I am far from denying that there is a natural law, but I do deny both that we have given judges authority to enforce it and that judges have any greater access to that law than do the rest of us."[34] Of course, Bork's view of the scope of judicial authority under the Constitution might or might not be correct. A proposition may be logically sound yet substantively false. Perhaps the Constitution, properly interpreted, does confer upon judges the power to enforce their views of natural law and natural rights, even in the absence of textual or historical warrant for their views. What matters for purposes of the current analysis is that the issue is itself textual and historical. If, as Ronald Dworkin claims, judges do legitimately enjoy the constitutional authority to invalidate legislation precisely on the ground that it violates abstract constitutional principles understood in light of the judges' own best judgments of natural law (viz., moral truth), then, as Dworkin himself acknowledges, that is because this power is conferred on courts by the positive law of the Constitution, not by the natural law itself.[35] So any argument seeking to establish the authority of courts to invalidate legislation by appeal to natural law and natural rights ungrounded in the constitutional text or history will itself have to appeal to the constitutional text and history. This is by no means to suggest that there is anything self-contradictory or necessarily illicit about such arguments. There is no reason in principle why a constitution cannot, expressly or by more or less clear implication, confer such authority on courts. It is merely to indicate that the question of whether a particular constitution in fact confers it is, as I have said, one of positive, not natural, law.

Now I should observe, before concluding, that someone who believes that our own Constitution does, in fact, confer upon judges authority to enforce natural law and natural rights need not come down in favor of the decision in *Griswold*. This is because that decision presupposes not only (a) the authority of courts to enforce natural rights, but also (b) the existence of a substantive natural right to contraception, at least for married couples. Someone who believes in (a) may or may not also believe in (b). Stephen Krason, for example, who relies heavily on Corwin's account of the natural law basis of American constitutionalism to argue for the broad judicial enforcement of natural law principles, at the same time sharply condemns some of the leading decisions in which the Court seems most clearly to have been acting on the justices' understanding of natural law and natural rights (for instance, the establishment of a right to abortion in *Roe v. Wade*).[36] Responding to arguments by Bork and others that acceptance of judicial authority to enforce natural law will likely result in decisions incorporating into our constitutional law the modern liberal view of morality, Krason insists that the answer is to appoint judges who reject liberalism and would enforce "the true natural law."[37] According to Krason, the problem with *Roe* (and he would no doubt add *Griswold*) is not the judicial enforcement of natural law and natural rights, but rather the enforcement of a *false* conception of natural law and natural rights. Challenging the views of Bork and other conservative jurists, including, notably, Justice Antonin Scalia,[38] Krason argues that the correct decision in *Roe* would not have been a form of judicial abstention which would have permitted the question to be resolved legislatively (on the ground, adduced by Bork, Scalia, and others that the Constitution is "silent" on the issue of abortion), but, rather, a decision recognizing the right to life of the unborn and "declar[ing] legalized abortion to be unconstitutional."[39]

I agree with Corwin and his followers that the fabric and theory of our Constitution embody our Founders' belief in natural law and natural rights. While I also share their view that judicial review itself emerged as part of the strategy of the founding generation to insure governmental conformity with natural law and to protect natural rights, I do not draw from this the conclusion that judges have broad authority to go beyond the text, structure, logic, and original understanding of the Constitution to invalidate legislation which, in the opinion of judges, is contrary to natural justice. On the contrary, Black, Bork, Scalia, and other "textualists" and "originalists" are nearer the mark, in my judgment, in calling for judicial restraint in the absence of a clear constitutional warrant for overturning duly enacted legislation. This is because, as I read the document, the Constitution places primary authority for giving effect to natural law and protecting natural rights to the institutions of democratic self-government, not to the courts. It is primarily for the state legislatures, and, where power has been duly delegated under the Constitution, for the Congress, to engage in the practice of making law in harmony with the requirements of morality (natural law), including respect for valuable and honorable liberties (natural rights).

Judicial review is, I believe, constitutionally legitimate, and can, if exercised with proper restraint, help to make the natural law ideal of constitutional government a reality. However, courts can usurp, and I believe often have usurped, legislative authority under the guise of protecting individual rights and liberties from legislative encroachment.[40] Moreover, courts can usurp, and have usurped, legislative authority in good as well as bad causes. Whenever they do so, however, even in good causes,

they violate the rule of law by seizing power authoritatively allocated by the Framers and ratifiers of the Constitution to other
branches of government (even if that power could, rightly, have
been allocated to them). Respect for the rule of law is itself a
requirement of natural justice.[41]

Sometimes courts have no legitimate authority to set right
what they perceive (perhaps rightly) to be a wrong; and where
this is the case, it is wrong—because usurpative—for them to do
so. There is no paradox in this. Fidelity to the rule of law imposes on public officials a duty in justice to respect the constitutional limits of their own authority. To fail in this duty, however noble one's ends, is to behave unconstitutionally, lawlessly,
unjustly. The American Founders were not utopians; they knew
that the maintenance of constitutional government and the rule
of law would limit the power of officials to do good as well as
evil. They also knew, and we must not forget, that to sacrifice
constitutional government and compromise the rule of law in
the hope of rectifying injustices is to strike a bargain with the
devil.

NOTES

1. See Robert P. George, "Natural Law Ethics," *A Companion to Philosophy of Religion*,
   ed. Philip L. Quinn and Charles Taliaferro (Oxford: Blackwell Publishers,
   1997), 453-465.
2. Romans 2:14-15.
3. The Declaration of Independence.

4. For a valuable summary of, and important contribution to, the debate, see Philip A. Hamburger, "Natural Rights, Natural Law, and American Constitutions," *Yale Law Journal* 102 (1993): 907-960.

5. *Griswold v. Connecticut* 381 U.S. 479 (1965).

6. "We do not sit as a super-legislature to determine the wisdom, need, and propriety of laws that touch economic problems, business affairs, and social conditions." Ibid.

7. Douglas listed "the right of association contained in the penumbra of the First Amendment"; the Third Amendment's prohibition of quartering soldiers in private houses in peace time; the Fourth Amendment right against unreasonable searches and seizures; the Fifth Amendment right against self-incrimination; and the Ninth Amendment's concept of "rights retained by the people." In a famous concurring opinion, Justice Arthur Goldberg (a Johnson appointee), joined by Chief Justice Earl Warren and Justice William J. Brennan (both Eisenhower appointees), expounded a due process theory of the case, one buttressed by the invocation of the Ninth Amendment, which, according to Goldberg, "lends strong support to the view that the 'liberty' protected by the Fifth and [Fourteenth] Amendments [is] not restricted to rights specifically mentioned in the first eight amendments." Justice John Marshall Harlan (another Eisenhower appointee), in a separate concurrence, announced his preference for a more straightforward Fourteenth Amendment due process theory.

8. E.g. *Lochner v. New York*, 198 U.S. 45 (1905), invalidating a New York statute limiting the number of hours employees in a bakery could be required or permitted to work; *Adair v. United States*, 208 U.S. 161 (1908), striking down a federal law against "yellow dog contracts" on interstate railroads; *Adkins v. Children's Hospital*, 261 U.S. 525 (1923), citing *Lochner* to invalidate legislation setting minimum wages for women workers in the District of Columbia.

9. *Meyer v. Nebraska*, 262 U.S. 390 (1923).

10. *Pierce v. Society of Sisters*, 268 U.S. 510 (1925).

11. Roosevelt's criticisms of the Court have come to be widely accepted as valid by liberal and conservative constitutional scholars alike. A notable exception is Hadley Arkes, whose recent writings offer a vigorous defense of the "natural rights" approach taken by the justices in *Lochner, Adair, Adkins*, and other leading "Lochner era" cases. See, in particular, Arkes's essay "*Lochner v. New York* and the Cast of Our Laws," in *Great Cases in Constitutional Law*, ed. Robert P. George (Princeton: Princeton University Press, forthcoming), and Arkes's book *The Return of George Sutherland: Restoring a Jurisprudence of Natural Rights* (Princeton:

Princeton University Press, 1994).

12. In his radio address of March 9, 1937, Roosevelt defended his "court packing plan" as necessary to "save the Constitution from the Court and the Court from itself."

13. Pro-contraception groups began challenging anti-contraception statutes in the courts in the 1940s. Prior to *Griswold*, however, these constitutional challenges had ultimately been dismissed on procedural grounds. See *Tileston v. Ullman*, 318 U.S. 44 (1943) and *Poe v. Ullman*, 367 U.S. 497 (1961).

14. See Pope Paul VI, *Humanae Vitae* (1968).

15. The dubiousness of some of these suppositions was not evident in 1965, though opponents of contraception warned that the social consequences of its widespread availability and acceptance would be dire. The *Griswold* court barely considered these warnings. In the end, Douglas's opinion rests on the essentially undefended assertion that the availability of contraceptives is good for the institution of marriage. But that was a debatable proposition even in 1965. Supporters of Connecticut's law argued that access to contraceptives, far from strengthening the institution of marriage, would weaken it by fueling a revolution in sexual mores leading to increased family breakdown, abandonment, divorce, adultery, fornication, and other evils. Some maintained that these social pathologies were predictable consequences of the intrinsically antimarital nature of contraception as a severing of the link between spousal love and openness to procreation that gives marriage its intelligible purpose and specifies its essential requirements (e.g., permanence of commitment, exclusivity (fidelity), obligations of mutual support). If, indeed, the question ultimately turns on empirical and even moral judgments as to whether contraception strengthens or weakens the institution of marriage, it is difficult to see how a court could be justified in displacing a legislative judgment of the matter one way or another. It obviously will not do to say that the invalidation of laws restricting contraception simply leaves the question of the goodness or badness of the practice to the conscientious judgment of individuals and married couples. The question, as Douglas seemed to grasp clearly enough, is whether the *availability* of contraception is good for the *institution* of marriage. The decision is an inherently social one. To recognize this fact is not necessarily to conclude that contraception is bad for marriage or that laws against it will do more good than harm; it is merely to suggest that these questions are unavoidably political. To endorse the political proposition that contraception should be left to individual judgment is to answer the questions in a particular way. Moreover, even if one is prepared to answer them in precisely this way,

the question remains as to whether courts should have the authority to displace contrary legislative judgments. (Thus, Black and Stewart, basing their dissenting opinions solely on the denial of judicial authority, could denounce the Connecticut law as "offensive" and "silly," yet judge it to be constitutionally permissible.)

16. Anti-contraception laws in Connecticut and other states had been enacted by legislatures in the mid-nineteenth century—a time when religious and moral opinion was largely united in opposition to the practice of contraception. The pro-contraception movement, beginning with Margaret Sanger's crusade for birth control and sexual liberation in the early twentieth century, attempted to persuade state legislators to repeal anti-contraception statutes. When, as in Connecticut, their efforts in the legislatures failed or stalled, they turned to the courts in the hope of persuading judges to do what public opinion, still clinging at some level to the older sexual morality, prevented elected representatives from doing. As Justice Douglas's opinion for the majority in *Griswold* makes clear, the pro-contraception parties suggested that a decision invalidating the Connecticut statute could be based explicitly on precisely the doctrine which Black would accuse the majority of surreptitiously reviving, namely, the "natural law substantive due process philosophy" of the "*Lochner* era." After all, *Lochner* itself, though in gross disrepute, had never been *expressly* reversed. Although most commentators were (and are) of the view that *Lochner* had been implicitly overruled in *West Coast Hotel v. Parrish*, 300 U.S. 379 (1937)—a case officially overruling the decision in *Adkins v. Children's Hospital*, which, in turn, had relied on *Lochner*—the *Griswold* majority could, presumably, have invoked the basic principle of *Lochner* while arguing that the court in *Adkins* had misapplied it to the facts in that case. Indeed, they could have argued that the *Lochner* court itself had erroneously applied a perfectly sound principle of constitutional interpretation to the facts before it. However that may be, Douglas plainly wanted no part of such a strategy: "Overtones of some arguments suggest that *Lochner v. New York* should be our guide. But we decline that invitation just as we did in *West Coast Hotel v. Parrish*...." In the very next paragraph he introduced the "penumbras formed by emanations." (Interestingly, Douglas's original proposal was to invalidate the Connecticut statute on the ground that it violated the First Amendment right to freedom of association. He could not, however, put together a majority for that remarkable proposition.)

17. One suspects that the "penumbras-formed-by-emanations" rhetoric was designed to suggest that the alleged marital right to use contraceptives is somehow derivable from the "logic" or "structure" of the Constitution, and does not

depend on any independent moral-political judgment that married couples ought to be free from legal interference in deciding whether to use contraceptives. But this suggestion is dubious. Someone who happens to believe that contraception is morally wrong and damaging to the institution of marriage, and that the legal permission of contraception would harm public morals and exacerbate various social ills, simply has no reason to affirm a constitutional right to contraception. It is only by bringing belief in a right to marital contraception (with all that it presupposes and entails) to the enterprise of constitutional interpretation that one can find such a right in the "logic" or "structure" of the constitution.

18. Edward S. Corwin, "The Debt of American Constitutional Law to Natural Law Concepts," *Notre Dame Lawyer* 25 (1950): 195. Corwin's lecture builds on his famous essay "The 'Higher Law' Background of American Constitutional Law," *Harvard Law Review* 42 (1928): 149-185 (pts. 1-2) and 365-409 (pt. 3).

19. Corwin, "The Debt of American Constitutional Law," 196.

20. Ibid., 197.

21. Cited by Corwin as 8 Rep. 113b, 77 Eng. Rep. 646 (1610).

22. Corwin, "The Debt of American Constitutional Law," 198.

23. Ibid., 199.

24. Ibid., 200 (emphasis in the original).

25. Ibid., 201.

26. Ibid. (emphasis in the original).

27. Corwin cites *Federalist* no. 78.

28. Corwin cites *Marbury v. Madison*, 1 Cranch 137, 2 L. Ed. 60 (1803).

29. 3 Dall. 386, 1 L. Ed. 648 (1798).

30. Corwin, "The Debt of American Constitutional Law," 202.

31. Ibid., 203.

32. See Robert P. George, "Natural Law and Positive Law," in *The Autonomy of Law: Essays on Legal Positivism*, ed. Robert P. George (Oxford: Clarendon Press, 1996).

33. St. Thomas Aquinas, *Summa Theologiae* I-II, q. 95, a. 2c, on which see John Finnis, *Natural Law and Natural Rights* (Oxford: Clarendon Press, 1980), 284-289, and *Aquinas* (Oxford: Oxford University Press, 1998), 266-274.

34. Robert H. Bork, *The Tempting of America: The Political Seduction of the Law* (New York: Free Press, 1990), 66. Of course some people, including, it seems, Chief Justice William H. Rehnquist, reject what Black condemned as natural law jurisprudence precisely on grounds of skepticism about the existence of natural law and natural rights. The statement by Bork that I quote in the text was evidently intended to make clear to those who had interpreted his earlier

writings as grounding his rejection of "judicial activism" in skepticism about natural law and natural rights that he is not of this view.

35. See Ronald Dworkin, Introduction to *Freedom's Law: The Moral Reading of the American Constitution* (Cambridge, Mass.: Harvard University Press, 1996). See also Ronald Dworkin "'Natural' Law Revisited," *University of Florida Law Review* 34 (1982):165-188.

36. See Stephen Krason, "Constitutional Interpretation, Unenumerated Rights, and the Natural Law," *Catholic Social Science Review* 1 (1996): 20-31.

37. Ibid., 25-27.

38. See Antonin Scalia, "Of Democracy, Morality and the Majority," *Origins* 26 (1996): 82-90.

39. Krason, "Constitutional Interpretation," 26.

40. See Robert P. George, "The Tyrant State," *First Things* 67 (November, 1996), reprinted in *The End of Democracy? The Judicial Usurpation of Politics*, ed. Mitchell S. Muncy (Dallas:˙ Spence Publishing Co., 1997), 53-62; and "Justice, Legitimacy, and Allegiance," *Loyola Law Review* 44 (1998): 103-118, reprinted in *The End of Democracy II: A Crisis of Legitimacy*, ed. Mitchell S. Muncy (Dallas: Spence Publishing Co., 1999), 86-104.

41. See Robert P. George, "Free Choice, Practical Reason, and Fitness for the Rule of Law," in *Social Discourse and Moral Judgment*, ed. Daniel N. Robinson (New York: Academic Press, 1992), 123-132.

CHRISTIANITY, THE COMMON LAW, AND THE CONSTITUTION

James R. Stoner, Jr.

On June 5, 1824, Thomas Jefferson wrote a letter to the English radical John Cartwright that was quickly published, and like much that proceeded from his pen, caused quite a stir. The letter reiterated an argument Jefferson had developed in his commonplace book as a young man reading law in Williamsburg, an essay which he had shared with Thomas Cooper in 1814 and which was published shortly after his death as an appendix to his volume of *Virginia Reports*.[1] Jefferson's object in the letters to Cartwright and Cooper, and in the essay on which they were based, was to dispute the maxim that "Christianity is a part of the common law," and he felt he had stumbled upon an elegant proof of his opinion. A case from the reign of Henry VI, in the fifteenth century, concerning who had the right to income set aside for a parish priest, included a line in French (then the language of English courts) which might be translated literally as follows: "As to those laws, which those of holy church have in ancient scripture, it behooves us to give them credence, for this is common law, upon which all manner of laws are founded; and thus, sir, we are obliged to take notice of their law of holy church; and it seems they are obliged to take notice of our law."[2] Although the report is ambiguous, the decision in the case seems to have been that the common law courts, in determining rights of property in such matters, will defer to the judgment of the ecclesiastical courts and the bishop as to who is rightly priest.

Jefferson has no gripe with such a ruling, but he focuses his attention on the subsequent use of the lines just quoted. Henry Finch, in his early seventeenth-century textbook on common law, translates *auncien Scripture* as "Holy Scripture," suggesting that the Bible is the foundation of the laws of England.[3] To Jefferson the translation is bad and the inference false: not Holy Scripture but merely the ancient written law of the Church, ecclesiastical law, is at issue. He supposes that Finch's notion is behind the first declaration of the maxim that "Christianity is parcel of the laws of England," in Chief Justice Matthew Hale's opinion in *Taylor's Case* in the late 1670s (which is later quoted in numerous opinions in the eighteenth century, finding its way even into Blackstone in 1769). Jefferson sees in all this not mere error, but judicial usurpation, like the supposed fraud of including the book of Exodus in the laws of the ninth-century

King Alfred. Jefferson includes evidence for the latter "fraud" in his youthful draft, although it is not generally considered to be such by scholars today.[4] The common law, to Jefferson, is the law inherited from Saxon England, which is older than the introduction of Christianity to England. There is, he thinks, no evidence that Christianity was subsequently adopted as part of the law. Judges, he wrote, were in league with an established Church and were "accomplices in the frauds of the clergy, and even bolder than they."

Jefferson's published letter to Cartwright was quickly answered in 1824 by Supreme Court Justice Joseph Story, first in private correspondence to a third party and subsequently in print.[5] Appointed to the Court by Madison as the only qualified and willing Republican in the largely Federalist New England circuit, a Unitarian by faith, Story disputes Jefferson's critique of Finch's translation and his inference that it is the source of Hale's maxim. On the translation, Story asks how, on Jefferson's narrow reading of *auncien Scripture*, Judge Prisot could have said "that they were common law, *upon which all manner of laws are founded*," since serving as a foundation is more to be expected of the Bible than of church code. Here I think the advantage is probably with Jefferson: Prisot wrote, "*this is* common law," not "*they were* common law," as Story paraphrases; and the antecedent of the singular demonstrative *this* is not "those laws" or even "ancient Scripture" but the phrase "it behooves us to give them credence." For Judge Prisot the common law procedural rule was that the judges were to recognize church law in church property matters. Story's second point, however, has the advantage over Jefferson: Hale does not cite Finch when he coins the maxim that Christianity is part of English law. Story argues that the maxim would have been easily enough inferred from the existence of an ecclesiastical establishment and from the law's own recognition of heresy as a crime. Indeed, Story's interest in the matter went beyond the historical. Despite our lack of ecclesiastical establishment on the English model and the absence here of criminal heresy, he quoted the maxim—as having present force in America—in the speech he delivered at Harvard upon his inauguration as Dane Professor of Law: "One of the beautiful boasts of our municipal jurisprudence is that Christianity is a part of the common law, from which it seeks the sanction of its rights, and by which it endeavors to regulate its doctrines.... There never was a period, in which the common law did not recognize Christianity as lying at its foundation."[6]

The stakes in Jefferson's and Story's disagreement are obviously high. First, what is the meaning of religious liberty in America and its relation to the foundation of our legal order? Second, what is the place of courts in determining these matters? The maxim that Christianity is part of the common law, accepted far beyond Story, would generally be thought incomprehensible if not preposterous if repeated today as a legal maxim rather than a historical proposition. Most of our contemporaries would dismiss it peremptorily as incompatible with the First Amendment's prohibition against religious establishment and its guarantee of religious liberty. But the First Amendment was in place when Justice Story, his contemporaries, and followers decided cases, and they saw no conflict between the maxim and the amendment. My aim, in the pages that follow, is to figure out what nineteenth-century American judges meant when they said that Christianity is a part of the common law, and then consider briefly what it might mean to us today.

COMMON LAW AND THE CONSTITUTION

To begin, we need to consider what "common law" itself meant at the time of the Founding and in the early republic; for if there is one point on which Jefferson and Story would agree, it is that our modern definition of common law as judge-made law is a slander to common law and would, if true, undermine its legitimacy. The modern definition, proclaimed by Justice Holmes and now usually accepted, is based on the assumption that all law originates in human will. Not finding a legislature behind the common law, proponents of the modern definition look for the will responsible and find the judge. However, to minds open to the possibility that law has a source in nature or in the word of God, as the minds of eighteenth- and nineteenth-century Americans surely were, or to a society that can imagine widespread consensus on basic principles of justice, common law is not only a coherent concept but a fact of social life.

Traditionally, common law was the ancient and customary law of England, the basis of decisions in the Court of Common Pleas and the King's Bench. It was not the only law of England—ecclesiastical law and admiralty law, for example, were separate bodies of law administered by separate courts—but in the seventeenth century common law judges succeeded in establishing its claim to being the most comprehensive, most fundamental, and most characteristic form of English law. The common law is in principle unwritten, but written evidence of common law can be found in statutes that declare the common law and in records of the decisions of particular cases, records which enable the decisions to serve as precedent for the decision of subsequent cases. Natural law, of course, is also unwritten; common law is not identical to it, but contains nothing to contradict it.[7] Sir Edward Coke, an early seventeenth-century English judge and authority on common law, called it an "artificial perfection of reason." He meant this term as praise, for he held the traditional opinion that art perfected nature, as the judges, reasoning from case to case, "fined and refined" customs so that they became consistent with one another and with a multitude of maxims held to constitute justice.[8] Common law settled matters of property, especially property in land; in the eighteenth and nineteenth centuries it assimilated and de-

veloped the law merchant or commercial law. It included criminal law as well, and though crimes came increasingly to be defined by statute, with the encouragement of common law judges,
due process remained a part of common law, so that the rights
to habeas corpus, to confront witnesses, to refuse to incrimi-
nate oneself, and above all to be tried by a jury of one's peers
were all common law liberties. As just suggested, statutes could
modify common law, but they might also just declare it—put it
in writing, as we say. Judges typically saw statutes as filling gaps
in the common law, and they subsequently assimilated such
statutes into the common law. It had even been held by English courts that "the common law can control an act of Parliament, and even adjudge them to be altogether void,"[9] though
this seems to have meant chiefly that courts could narrow interpretations of statutes to conform to common law maxims.
After the Glorious Revolution this principle recedes in England,
in the face of new ideas about the sovereignty of Parliament.

Common law was law in England, but it was also thought
to have been carried over to America by the colonists and to
apply here, at least insofar as it was consistent with their circumstances and not contradicted by colonial statutes. In the
early documents of the American Revolution, common law is a
frequent source of appeal against statutes of Parliament that the
colonists thought oppressive.[10] With the Declaration of Independence, appeal is made, of course, to "the laws of Nature,

and of Nature's God," but in the lengthy bill of grievances against the king, his violation of common law liberties is the measure of the "absolute Despotism" he would impose. At the moment of independence, every colony-become-state adopted the common law, with the usual provisos concerning circumstances and contrary statutes, in some cases appointing committees to recommend appropriate revisions in common law for a republican era, such as abolishing primogeniture and entail. Jefferson proposed and served on the revisal committee in Virginia, where he argued against replacing common law with a code, developing instead a series of proposed alterations, the most famous of which was to become, a decade later, the Virginia Statute on Religious Freedom.[11]

While England had not only unwritten common law but an unwritten constitution, one might suppose at first thought that the American insistence on *written* constitutions would work against the transplantation of common law. In the long run perhaps it has, but it is critical to the understanding of our original constitutionalism to grasp why that was not thought to be the case by the Framers of our federal Constitution. In the first place, the common law had a long tradition of written documents declaring what the rights of Englishmen were, if not inventing what they would be. Magna Charta, the Petition of Right, and the English Bill of Rights are only the most famous examples from the metropolis; colonial liberties were included in the colonies' written charters, and the bills of rights in the new states and even the federal Bill of Rights can be seen as belonging to this tradition. To the whole way of thinking that finds fundamental rights to be essentially unwritten, though sometimes declared in writing for safekeeping, the Ninth Amendment to the Constitution of 1787 is perfect testimony, with its promise that "The enumeration in the Constitution of certain rights shall not be construed to deny or disparage others retained by the people." Indeed, when Hamilton writes in *The Federalist Papers* that "the constitution is itself in every rational sense, and to every useful purpose, A BILL OF RIGHTS,"[12] he likewise presumes that the written instrument is not something completely new but the further development of the familiar process of employing written documents to secure unwritten liberties. Everyone agrees, even today, that the technical language of the Constitution must be interpreted with reference to common law.

From the point of view of the common law, then, the Constitution is not a social compact that creates a Hobbesian sovereign out of a state of nature, but a new type of fundamental statute that settles the specific question of political authority within the context of a continuous common law regime. The Constitution, and the state constitutions that were to some extent its model, alter forms of government, but no one thought that titles to land or obligations of marriage were dissolved in the course of their formation. To be sure, the establishment of republican government was understood to have implications for common law. It is the genius of the common law judiciary to seek consistency in the law as a whole—not consistency in the manner of some modern law professors, for whom all law must flow from a one-sentence "theory" or "principle," but a reasonable assimilation that accepts the diversity of human experience and the multiplicity of human endeavors. It was to be expected that arguments would arise, in court but also in legislatures, as to whether certain rules of common law were consonant with republican government. A classic instance of such an argument is James Madison's contention in his *Virginia Report of 1800* that freedom of speech and press must mean more than "no previous restraint" in the context of elected governments, lest an elected government forbid scrutiny of its own actions.[13] Moreover, since cases arising under the Constitution and federal statutes were assigned to a judiciary evidently formed on a common law model, the interpretation of the Constitution fell to judges trained in the common law way. This meant that constitutional precedents would come to have legal status, as precedents do in common law but not under a civil code. Constitutional lawyers take for granted such legal status, but absent the common law, it would not have been so obvious.

Because of the judiciary's common law background, interpretation of the Constitution was apt to follow common law rules for the interpretation of statutes, with such modifications as would be reasonable taking into account the difference between a statute and a constitution. For example, from the common law perspective it makes perfect sense that a chief matter of controversy in the early republic would be whether the powers of Congress should be read strictly, like a criminal statute, or liberally, like a statute against fraud. As Hamilton says in *Federalist* 78, these matters must be settled according to "the nature and reason of the thing," which is to say, in the manner by which common law judges were used to solving legal quandaries. The power of the judiciary under the written Constitution to declare contrary statutes unconstitutional and void rests on precisely this basis, as it is nowhere mentioned explicitly in the text of the Constitution itself.

Like everything in the American constitutional order, the question of the relation of common law to the Constitution is complicated by the fact and the principle of federalism. The original common law judiciaries in America, of course, were in the colonies and so subsequently in the states; naturally enough, divergence in the course of common law developed between the colonies and the mother courts in England, as well as among the colonies and states themselves, so that Madison, in the same *Report*, could deny that there was common law for America as a whole. Perhaps because the establishment of additional states suggested principles of duplication, or because law on the frontier relied on manuals in the absence of established local traditions, there were powerful tendencies in the 1800s towards convergence among the states. It quickly became common for state judges to cite the courts of other states and even of England in the decision of new or difficult cases at common law. The federal judiciary, meanwhile, encountered common law in the exercise of its diversity jurisdiction; and, while it became settled as a result of the early prosecution of seditious libel that there was no federal common law of crimes, a general common law of commercial relations was employed by the federal courts until the "Constitutional Revolution" of the 1930s. Moreover, American federalism itself was judicially mediated in the manner of common law, with issues being settled not abstractly but in the context of particular cases at law, as a result of the choice in the Philadelphia Convention not to establish a congressional veto on state legislation, as Madison wanted, but to rely instead on a Supremacy Clause.

In short, American constitutionalism developed in a common law tradition which gave our constitutional law its specific form. In the common law—unlike Enlightenment theory—tradition and reason worked together, even as jury and judge. The rule of precedent gave traditions legal status, but the counsel of reason that the law remain consistent with itself insured that customs which became unreasonable were bad precedent and could be ignored. The reason of the common law was flexible enough to assimilate some Enlightenment discoveries, concerning, for example, republican government or political economy, without thereby ceding every principle of the traditional order. Common law thus had room for religious liberty without thereby committing to a secular state, indeed without abandoning its claim to include Christianity among its parts.

CHRISTIANITY AND COMMON LAW

As with free speech, a jurisprudence of religious liberty developed in the states in the nineteenth century long before federal constitutional law pre-empted the field in the twentieth. As has often been noted, the federal Constitution is circumspect on the question of religion. The date at the end is given "in the year of our Lord"; Sundays are omitted from the number of days a president has to decide whether to sign or veto a bill in Article I, section 7; and oaths (or, in deference to the Quakers, "affirmations") are mandated of all officeholders. However, the original Constitution mentions religion explicitly only to qualify the requirement of oaths by forbidding a federal religious test.[14] The First Amendment, as many have pointed out, was written to prevent religious establishment and protect free exercise of religion only in reference to the federal government and only in relation to its lawmaking branch. The specific wording that "Congress shall make no law" kept open the question of religious establishments in the states as well as the question of nonstatutory sources of law, and disputes in the nineteenth century courts typically were related to these. The question of whether Christianity remained a part of common law arose primarily in three contexts—blasphemy, Sunday closings, and church property disputes—which I will treat in turn.

BLASPHEMY

The phrase to which Jefferson took such exception, that "Christianity is parcel of the laws of England," appeared in a conviction at common law for blasphemy in England in the 1670s. The full setting of Chief Justice Matthew Hale's remark, albeit in a brief and choppy report, is as follows: "...such kind of wicked blasphemous words were not only an offence to God and religion, but a crime against the laws, State and Government, and therefore punishable in this Court. For to say, religion is a cheat, is to dissolve all those obligations whereby the civil socities are preserved, and that Christianity is parcel of the laws of England; and therefore to reproach the Christian religion is to speak in subversion of the law."[15]

Prosecution for blasphemy at common law was apparently new in Hale's time, the offense having previously been pursued in the ecclesiastical courts, whose jurisdiction was greatly reduced after the English Civil War and Restoration. The justification for prosecution at common law is, naturally, a temporal one, but the claim that the Christian religion is the source of social and legal obligations is indicative of the fundamental status Hale accorded the faith. Subsequent cases confirmed that blasphemy against Christ, his mother's virginity, or the truth of the Gospels could be punished under common law; but the judges insisted in cases like *Dominus Rex v. Woolston* that the law meant only to protect "Christianity in general," because "whatever strikes at the very root of Christianity, tends manifestly to a dissolution of the civil government." Likewise, wrote Lord Chief Justice Raymond in the same case, "to say, an attempt to subvert the establish'd religion is not punishable by those laws upon which it is establish'd, is an absurdity."[16] Still, blasphemy was not heresy, that is, error or difference of opinion in matters of religion, which the common lawyers held to be established only by statute and so repealed through the Toleration Act of 1689. In the words of Lord Mansfield, "The common law of England, which is only common reason or usage, knows of no prosecution for mere opinions."[17] At least by this more tolerant age, it was permitted to dispute particular points of the faith, for the sake of understanding; but the common law protected the basic tenets of Christianity against slander or reviling, since it was the foundation of the law itself.

How does this reasonably stable and coherent account of the common law of blasphemy in England translate to America, where there was neither criminal heresy nor an established church in federal law; where, in the early nineteenth century, such establishments as persisted in some of the states were increasingly on the wane; and where the Declaration of Independence had clearly proclaimed that governments were established by the consent of the people, not by divine decree? The leading case is *The People against Ruggles*, decided by Chancellor James Kent in New York in 1811, which upheld a conviction for blasphemy, the jury having determined that the words "Jesus Christ was a bastard, and his mother must be a whore"—the usual refrain in these cases—"were uttered in a wanton manner, and, as they evidently import, with a wicked and malicious disposition, and not in a serious discussion upon any controverted point in religion."[18] Besides adopting the English judges' implicit distinction between licentious slander and free discussion, Kent addressed both the question of whether the common law of blasphemy could be translated to America and the compatibility of that law with the free exercise clause of the New York Constitution. On the first point, quoting sources as disparate as Cicero and Bacon, he determined that, as blasphemy "tends to corrupt the morals of the people, and to destroy good order," it can be forbidden, despite the change of government occasioned by the Revolution. "We stand equally in need, now as formerly," he wrote, "of all that moral discipline and those principles of virtue, which help to bind society together." On the constitutional question, Kent noted that "free, equal, and undisturbed enjoyment of religious opinion, whatever it may be, and free and decent discussions on any religious subject, is granted and secured," apparently to non-Christians as well as

Christians, and that no religious establishment is allowed in New York, its constitution even including an article that abrogates "such parts of the common law as might be construed to establish or maintain any particular denomination of christians, or their ministers."

Kent also found laws against blasphemy to be of the same mind as the proviso in the religion clause—"the liberty of conscience hereby granted, shall not be so construed as to excuse acts of licentiousness, or justify practices inconsistent with the peace and safety of this state." Moreover, he held that blasphemy was punishable only when directed against the Christian faith, "for this plain reason, that the case assumes that we are a christian people, and the morality of the country is deeply engrafted upon christianity." In Kent's opinion, even though no church had been established and free inquiry was being allowed, the Christian religion was still fundamental to the moral order that underlies the law, and so deserved protection against scurrilous attack. More generally, he added, "Christianity, in its enlarged sense, as a religion revealed and taught in the Bible, is not unknown in our law," as is evident from legislative acts protecting Sunday as holy time and prescribing oaths be taken upon the Gospels.

Kent's argument in *Ruggles* became the starting point for subsequent legal and constitutional discussions, first in New York's constitutional convention of 1821, where an attempt to revise his opinion was defeated by a coalition that included the Jeffersonian Martin Van Buren as well as the Federalist Kent,[19] and later in a series of cases written after the publication of Jefferson's letter and explicitly addressing its claim, though modifying, slightly and by little steps, Kent's confident conclusion. Judge Duncan's able and spirited opinion in *Updegraph v. Commonwealth* reviewed the cases from England, and the special legacy of Pennsylvania, to uphold the principle that Christianity is a part of the common law and thus that blasphemy was a crime. In good common law fashion, however, he found the indictment in the case defective for failing to specify that the words must have been uttered profanely and for failing to cite the exact words employed. On the general point, "the grand objection—the constitutionality of Christianity," Duncan is clear: "Christianity, general Christianity, is and always has been a part of the common law of Pennsylvania; Christianity without the spiritual artillery of European countries; for this Christianity was one of the considerations of the royal charter, and the very basis of its great founder, William Penn; not Christianity founded on any particular religious tenets; not Christianity with an established church, and tithes and spiritual courts; but Christianity with liberty of conscience to all men."[20]

The assimilative spirit of this passage is apparent throughout Duncan's opinion. For example, he cited a colonial statute that said "government in itself is a venerable ordinance of God" without noting its subsequent contradiction by the Declaration of Independence—though he did write that the one exception to "complete liberty of conscience" in colonial times, namely, "the disqualification for office of all who did not profess faith in Jesus Christ," was replaced in the Pennsylvania Constitution of 1776 with the requirement only of belief in God and "in a future state of rewards and punishments."[21] Duncan also introduced in passing an idea that would be increasingly important: blasphemy is not only, "when spoken in a Christian land, and to a Christian audience, the highest offence *contra bonos mores*," but "even if Christianity was not part of the law of the land, it is the popular religion of the country, an insult on which would be indictable, as directly tending to disturb the public peace."[22]

In *The State v. Thomas Jefferson Chandler*, a Delaware case decided in 1837, Chief Justice Clayton reviewed and reiterated the maxim that Christianity is part of the common law, though he quietly edged his argument away from Kent's in the direction just suggested. Noting that "on this subject there may be danger from both licentiousness and bigotry," Clayton upheld a conviction for blasphemy with the caveat that "under our state constitution...the only legitimate end of the prosecution is to preserve the public peace."[23] That Christianity is part of the common law was for him a statement of contingent fact, not a constitutive description. Thus, he wrote, "the people of

Delaware have a full and perfect constitutional right to change their religion as often as they see fit," and if tomorrow they profess "Mahometanism or Judaism, or adopt any other religious creed they please,...all their judges are bound to notice their free choice and religious preference, and to protect them in the exercise of their right" by allowing prosecution for blasphemy, now not of Jesus, but of Mahomet or Moses or any other. The principle at issue for blasphemy is the same as for libel or for the challenge to a duel: what tends to break the peace, or in other words, what will excite a mob, not meaning "that their conduct would be justifiable, but viewing men as they are and not as they should be, looking as we are bound to do, to the motives and feelings which practically regulate and control mankind."[24]

The argument in *Chandler* foreshadows the direction the whole law of free speech would take in the twentieth century, but the traditional emphasis on moral order, rather than empirical effect, could be seen the following year in Chief Justice Shaw's opinion in the Massachusetts case of *Commonwealth v. Abner Kneeland*. Here the indictment was for a printed article and the question of the common law was not explicitly raised, only the question of the constitutionality of the state's statute against blasphemy. Shaw went as far as he could to support free inquiry and even the public announcement of doubt, but he upheld the legislature's determination that a law against blasphemy—even in the form of "wilfully denying" God's existence, without cursing or contumelious reproach—is "essential to preserve the sanction of oaths, prescribed and required in every clause almost of the [state] constitution, and...essential to the peace and safety of society."[25] Shaw's opinion, together with *Updegraph* and *Chandler*, was cited approvingly by a Maine court sustaining the conviction of a visiting lecturer for blasphemy as recently as 1921.[26]

SUNDAY CLOSING

The English common law courts were closed on Sunday, and so in the strictest sense it might be said that the common law recognized the Christian sabbath as a day of rest. We remarked already that the U.S. Constitution presumes no legislative business in Congress will be conducted on that day. Blackstone counted sabbath-breaking among offenses against God and religion, but he stressed rather the value of the uniform day of rest "merely as a civil institution," setting the stage for its principal defense in American courts.[27] In *City Council of Charleston v. S.A. Benjamin*, a Jewish merchant challenged his fine for selling on Sunday in violation of a municipal ordinance on the grounds that it impinged upon the free exercise clause of the South Carolina Constitution. After expressions of respect for the Jewish people and acknowledgment that "it is perhaps not necessary, to the purposes of this case, to rule and hold that the Christian religion is part of the common law of South Caro-

lina," the court proceeded to explain that Christianity "lies at
the foundation" of the very religious liberty clause invoked by
the defendant, as religious toleration arose in Christian lands
out of the Christian spirit. Since the constitutional provision
in question included provisos that freedom of conscience not
"excuse acts of licentiousness, or justify practices inconsistent
with the peace of this State," Judge O'Neall added that licentiousness is defined by the people's morals, so that, while "the
orgies of Bacchus, among the ancients, were not offensive," and
"the Carnivals of Venice went off without note or observation,"
among South Carolinians, whose morals are defined by Christianity, "an open play house or Circus, on Sunday, could not
exist for a day!"[28] Not leaving the matter as an inference from
public opinion, however, O'Neall upheld the ordinance as a
police regulation to maintain good morals, general in applying
to all, but leaving Jews free to observe a second sabbath for
religious purposes. In short, the Christian sabbath is not
established by common law because of its status among the Ten
Commandments, but as the common law supports the morals
of the people, it absorbs, as it were, the precepts by which a
Christian people order their lives.

Similar results were reached in Pennsylvania and in Arkan-
sas, in the former case with the assertion that religious motives
on the part of the legislature did not negate the civil value of
the act, in the latter with explicit mention of the maxim that

Christianity is part of common law.[29] In Ohio, the state supreme court allowed enforcement of a contract made on Sunday, noting that the Ohio Sunday closing statute, in contrast
to statutes in other states, forbade only "common labor," not
"business" generally; in dicta they endorsed the validity of the
act as civil legislation, but explicitly denied that Christianity
was part of the common law of Ohio, since Ohio, unlike England, had no established church.[30] The California Supreme
Court broke with the other states and found the new state's
sabbath law unconstitutional under the state constitution's
clause forbidding religious discrimination, but three years later
two new justices joined with the dissenter in the first case (Justice Stephen Field, later of the United States Supreme Court)
to uphold the reenacted statute as a legitimate exercise of the
police power.[31] In the New York case of *Lindenmuller v. The People*,
decided the same year as the second California case (1861), the
recent Ohio reading of the ancient maxim was pleaded at bar,
but the New York court held rather to Kent's principle in
Ruggles. Christianity is a part of the common law, wrote Judge
Allen, "to the extent that it entitles the christian religion and
its ordinances to respect and protection, as the acknowledged
religion of the people." Consequently,

> every act done maliciously, tending to bring religion
> into contempt, may be punished at common law, and

the christian sabbath, as one of the institutions of that religion, may be protected from desecration by such laws as the legislature, in their wisdom, may deem necessary to secure to the community the privilege of undisturbed worship, and to the day itself that outward respect and observance which may be deemed essential to the peace and good order of society, and to preserve religion and its ordinances from open reviling and contempt—and this not as a duty to God, but as a duty to society and to the state.... In this state the sabbath exists as a day of rest by the common law, and without the necessity of legislative action to establish it; and all that the legislature attempts to do in the "sabbath laws" is to regulate its observance.[32]

The sabbath day is, in other words, a civil institution of the state, in recognition of the Christian religion of the people, and it is so by common law, apart from various statutes. On the other hand, it takes a statute to grant privileges or exemptions to sabbatarians who honor another day.

CHURCH PROPERTY

Among the most unavoidable cases where Christianity and common law intersect are disputes over church property, which typically involve rivals in a divided congregation seeking to establish who controls the disputed church and its grounds.

The leading nineteenth-century English case was *Attorney General v. Pearson*, involving a divided congregation of Dissenting Protestants. At issue was a claim in equity brought by Trinitarians against a controlling faction that had become Unitarian in their worship. Weaving through the complex circumstances of the actual dispute (occasioned by the conversion to Trinitarianism of a minister hired by the Unitarian group), as well as through the changing law of toleration in England, Lord Chancellor Eldon determined that the original purpose of the 1701 trust under which the church's property was held must have been to support Trinitarian worship, Unitarianism then having been illegal in England. He denied "pronouncing any opinion as to any religious doctrine whatever," and even though the maxim that Christianity is part of the common law was pleaded at bar, it was not mentioned in the opinion. He thought that, as with any charitable trust, the original purpose must be established. That required, he thought, inquiry into the religious doctrines of the denomination at hand, as seen in the light of a law where the Church of England was established and Dissenters were tolerated only in some cases and only as far as the law allowed.[33]

Perhaps the most prominent nineteenth-century American case on these matters was *Watson v. Jones*, decided by the Supreme Court in 1872 in the exercise of its diversity jurisdiction.[34] This case arose out of a schism in the Presbyterian Church of the United States in the aftermath of the Civil War, follow-

ing the decision of its General Assembly to count as sin both
giving voluntary aid to the "War of Rebellion" and holding the
doctrine that slavery is a divine institution, and to require the
sinner to repent before admission to the church as a mission-
ary, a member, or a minister. The Louisville, Kentucky,
Presbytery denounced this doctrine as heretical, and within three
years its differences with the General Assembly had caused a
complete break, the Presbytery joining the Presbyterian Church
of the Confederate States. The question before the Court was
whether adherents to the church General Assembly (Jones *et
al.*, with the future Justice Harlan as their lawyer) or adherents
to the Presbytery (Watson *et al.*) have the use of the Walnut
Street Presbyterian Church. Both sides agreed that the civil
courts had to look at the constitution and laws of the Presbyterian Church to settle the issue, but they differed as to the nature of the inquiry. Watson wanted the courts to follow the
English precedent of *Attorney General v. Pearson* and inquire into
the doctrinal question, determining whether the General Assembly obeyed its own laws when it made adherence to the
Union and denunciation of slavery a condition of church mem-
bership. Jones wanted the civil courts to accept the decision of
the General Assembly as to which synod in Kentucky to recognize, look to the constitution and laws of the church only to
determine which body had the final say, and accept its judgment as the authoritative disposition of the church.

The Supreme Court decided for Jones, without mention of the Constitution but with reference to the principles of religious liberty. Distinguishing among religious trusts that condition the grant of property upon a specific doctrine, those that grant rights to a self-governing congregation, and those that make a grant to a church that is part of a larger and more general organization, Justice Miller found the Presbyterian Church to belong clearly to the last sort. Here the *Pearson* case was inapplicable, because, unlike in England, "In this country the full and free right to entertain any religious belief, to practice any religious principle, and to teach any religious doctrine which does not violate the laws of morality and property, and which does not infringe personal rights, is conceded to all. The law knows no heresy, and is committed to the support of no dogma, the establishment of no sect." Miller argued that the right to organize in worship includes the right to govern oneself, and that the judicial tribunals of each denomination are best postioned to understand the "body of constitutional and ecclesiastical law of its own, to be found in their written organic laws, their books of discipline, in their collections of precedents, in their usage and customs, which as to each constitute a system of ecclesiastical law and religious faith." He concluded the following: "the rule of action which should govern the civil courts, founded in a broad and sound view of the relations of church and state under our system of laws, and supported by a preponderating weight of judicial authority, is, that, whenever the questions of discipline or of faith, or ecclesiastical rule, custom or law have been decided by the highest of these church judicatories to which the matter has been carried, the legal tribunals must accept such decisions as final, and as binding on them, in their application to the case before them."[35]

There are several things to note about the decision in *Watson v. Jones* which makes it a fitting conclusion to the discussion of Christianity and common law. First, the Court decided the case without reference to the First Amendment of the Constitution—it was, after all, a diversity case involving state law—but with reference to unwritten principles of religious liberty that it found in the common law as a whole, which it thought sufficient to guide the decision. Second, those unwritten principles were alive to the differences between English and American common law, so that, while English law was consulted, it was ruled inapplicable to the case because of the different institutional structures involved. Third, the decision was consonant with the rule in the Yearbook case which animated Jefferson and Story, decided centuries before, where the common law court deferred to ecclesiastical rulings in settling a property dispute (although of course the Presbyterian organization is different from the Episcopal). The British case, by contrast, involved the court in judging a matter of doctrine in order to decide a church property dispute, something English government after the Act of Supremacy was not shy to do, but which was not acceptable to Americans. Finally, the Court in *Watson v. Jones* was able to recognize, without privileging any particular denomination, that there is something distinctive about church organization and its ecclesiastical law. While property matters concerning congregational churches "must be determined by the ordinary principles which govern voluntary associations,"[36] said the Court, the unique lines of authority that connect a congregation with a larger church are respected and indeed empowered, albeit not on the basis of their own religious claims but as a consequence of the consent of members joining a church to adhere to its rules and judgments. The Court, in other words, found a place for Christian ecclesiology as part of the law, without making churches branches of government. By the actions of individuals in society, Christianity becomes a part of common law.

CHRISTIANITY, COMMON LAW,
AND THE CONSTITUTION

To the Christian, the nineteenth-century American cases in which judges gave legal meaning to the maxim that Christianity is a part of common law, alongside constitutional prohibitions of establishment and guarantees of free exercise, might appear in hindsight as the sounding of the trumpet in retreat before advancing secularism. With the exception perhaps of *Chandler* (the Delaware blasphemy case), however, these decisions represent an important part of the specifically American order on the question of church and state. The common law judges were attempting, in a manner characteristic of common law judges, to find a reasonable median in particular cases where Christianity and liberal republicanism could both be respected—as, in making the Revolution and establishing new governments, the American people (leaving aside a few freethinkers) clearly intended both to be. The judges' aim was not revolutionary, not to impose a secular liberal order on a Christian society; but their own principles seem clearly liberal in the sense of being generous, for all were concerned to maintain free discussion on religious matters in the context of a society that remained anxiously devout. At the same time, without being reactionary and without retrenching on disestablishment, they were conservative, preserving the traditional place of Christianity in law even as the role of organized churches in government was narrowed.

Looking back, it seems clear that they were correct, at least as a matter of history, to assert that Christianity is a part of common law. That theirs was mostly assertion is not to be faulted, for they were judges in a system where precedent was valid law, without a need to start afresh in every case from first principles. The history of the specifically Christian character of common law has yet to be fully written, but it will be an important story.[37] With its origin in Catholic England, common law developed in its early stages under clerical influence. Its emphasis on unwritten customary law has echoes in St. Thomas and in Aristotle, and certain of its characteristic doctrines, such as the presumption of innocence until proof of guilt, have a clear Christian resonance. Its habit of waiting to judge until a case is joined in practice—most clear in a protection of freedom of the press rooted in a regime of "no prior restraint"—depends for its coherence, I think, upon a Christian understanding of free will. Common law is not law that pushes and channels, but law that leaves men free to act on their own best lights and then subjects them to judgment for their choices. The centrality of the particular case in common law, and thus its respect for the individual, recalls the Christian doctrine of the dignity of the individual. The value given to unwrittenness reflects the change from the Old to the New Law. Even the jury, the characteristic institution of common law, is composed of the Apostolic number—though of course this might be accidental, and the requirement of unanimity is beyond what the Disciples themselves achieved.

Looking forward, it is remarkable how little attention the Supreme Court paid to common law when it constitutionalized the law of church and state in the mid-twentieth century. Much of this no doubt is due to the changed understanding of common law to which I alluded at the outset; a common law that is judge-made can hardly count Christianity among its parts, except insofar as a judge illegitimately imposes his own will. In addition, the decision to apply the Bill of Rights to the states through the doctrine of Fourteenth Amendment incorporation, first made in relation to free speech and then extended to religious liberty, created a presumption in the federal courts against the existence of adequate state protection and so set federal judges apart from the common law constitutionalism that had developed in the states. Also at work, but not independently, is a changed understanding of the Constitution, which came to be seen exclusively in terms of liberal principles without attention to the common law tradition in which they were originally embedded—a change that, in the context of religious liberty, upset a balance that, despite secularization and increasing religious diversity, was more or less still intact.

To be sure, the Court, having forgotten common law, sometimes needs to reinvent it, as when, in *Marsh v. Chambers*,[38] the legislative chaplain case, it allows unbroken tradition its say. However, when this is done without a sense of the principles that once informed the American tradition, it seems to run against court precedent and offer no guidance as to when to draw on common law tradition and when to repair to liberal ideals. By calling attention to the forgotten role of common law in religious liberty jurisprudence, I do not mean to suggest that it can be suddenly revived; after all, it was premised on an overwhelmingly Christian society, something we do not have today. Moreover, unwritten law cannot be fashioned like a program or implemented like a plan; it has to take root and grow, little by little, in ways that cannot be altogether foreseen. Still, in the common law as it survives and in the constitutional tradition that grew up in its midst are resources against the nihilism of our present age: a sturdy sense of right and wrong, a manly liberty, a respect for higher order that is not trapped by human words, and an openness to providence and its surprising turns. These make it worth at least a second look.

NOTES

1. Thomas Jefferson to Major John Cartwright, 5 June 1824, *Writings*, ed. Merrill Peterson (New York: Library of America, 1984), 1490-96; Jefferson to Dr. Thomas Cooper, 10 February 1814, *Writings*, 1321-29 (includes the essay from the Commonplace Book).

2. Translated by Joseph Story, in William W. Story, ed., *Life and Letters of Joseph Story* (Boston: Little, Brown, 1851), 432. For the meaning of the term "common law" as it is used in this discussion, see below, p. [3] ff.

3. Henry Finch, *Law, or a Discourse Thereof* (London, 1759 [1613]), 1: 7.

4. For example, see Harold Berman, *Law and Revolution: The Formation of the Western Legal Tradition* (Cambridge: Harvard, 1983), 65, where the preface from Exodus is presumed to be Alfred's; and Stephen C. Perks, *Christianity and Law: An Inquiry into the Influence of Christianity on the Development of English Common Law* (Whitby, England: Avant Books, 1993), which includes a translation of Alfred's Laws in an appendix. For reference to this latter work and many of the cases I discuss, I am indebted to an unpublished paper by Daniel L. Dreisbach, "Christianity and the Common Law" (1997). See also his published essay, "In Search of a Christian Commonwealth: An Examination of Selected Nineteenth-Century Commentaries on References to God and the Christian Religion in the United States Constitution," *Baylor Law Review* 48 (1996): 927, esp. 986-91.

5. Story, *Life and Letters*, 431-33.

6. Joseph Story, *A Discourse Pronounced Upon the Inauguration of the Author as Dane Professor of Law in Harvard University* (Boston: Hilliard, Gray, Little, and Wilkins, 1829), 20-21.

7. For a lovely image of the relation of common law and natural law, see John Wu, *Fountain of Justice: A Study in the Natural Law* (New York: Sheed and Ward, 1955), 63.

8. See my discussion of Coke in *Common Law and Liberal Theory: Coke, Hobbes, and the Origins of American Constitutionalism* (Lawrence: University Press of Kansas, 1992), esp. ch. 1.

9. *Doctor Bonham's Case*, 8 Coke's Reports 118a (1610). For a more complete discussion, see *Common Law and Liberal Theory*, ch. 3.

10. See, for example, the Declaration and Resolves of the First Continental Congress, October 14, 1774.

11. See Jefferson, *Writings*, 37 ff.

12. Jacob E. Cooke, ed., *The Federalist* (Middleton, CT: Wesleyan University Press, 1961 [1787-88]), no. 84, 581.

13. Gaillard Hunt, ed., *The Writings of James Madison* (New York: G.P. Putnam's Sons, 1906), 6:373 ff.

14. U.S. Constitution, art. 6, last clause.

15. *Taylor's Case*, 1 Ventris 293; also reported as *Dominus Rex and Tayler*, 3 Keble 607.

16. *Dominus Rex v. Woolston*, Fitz-Gibbon 64 (94 Eng. Rep. 655, at 656).

17. *Allen Evans v. Chamberlain of London* (1762), in Richard Burn, *Ecclesiastical Law*, 7th ed. (London, 1809), 218.

18. *The People against Ruggles*, 8 Johnson 290 (N.Y. 1811).

19. See the discussion in Jayson L. Spiegel, "Christianity as Part of the Common Law," *North Carolina Central Law Journal* 14 (1984): 494, at 505-06.

20. *Updegraph v. Commonwealth*, 11 Sergeant & Rawle 394 (Pa. 1824), at 400.

21. Ibid., at 402, 403.

22. Ibid., at 399. It is from *Updegraph*, by the way, that the maxim that Christianity is a part of common law finds its way into federal law, in Justice Story's decision in *Vidal v. Girard's Executors*, 2 Howard (43 U.S.) 127 (1844), a case deciding whether the courts could enforce a trust for the establishment of a school for orphans in Philadelphia where one condition was that no clergy be allowed to teach. Despite his acknowledgment of the maxim, or perhaps with respect for its general, nondenominational Christianity, he decided the trust was legal.

23. *The State v. Thomas Jefferson Chandler*, 2 Harrington 553 (Del. 1837), at 574.

24. Ibid., at 567-68, 569-70.

25. *Commonwealth v. Abner Kneeland*, 20 Pickering 206 (Mass. 1838), at 221.

26. *State v. Michael X. Mockus*, 120 Maine 84 (1921).

27. Blackstone, *Commentaries on the Laws of England* (Chicago: University of Chicago Press, 1979 [1769]), 4:63.

28. *City Council of Charleston v. Benjamin*, 2 Strobhart 508 (1846), at 521-23.

29. *Specht v. The Commonwealth*, 8 Pa. 312 (Pa. 1848); *Shrover v. State*, 10 English 259 (Ark. 1850).

30. *Bloom v. Richards*, 2 Ohio St. 387 (Ohio 1853).

31. *Ex parte Newman*, 9 Cal. 502 (Cal. 1858); reversed by *Ex parte Andrews*, 18 Cal. 678 (Cal. 1861).

32. *Lindenmuller v. The People*, 33 Barbour 548 (N.Y. 1861), at 560, 567-69.

33. *Attorney-General v. Pearson*, 3 Merivale 353 (36 Eng. Rep. 135) (1817); the quotation is from 417 (156).

34. 13 Wallace (80 U.S.) 666 (1872). Technically *Watson v. Jones* is a suit in equity, as it involves a trust, but the Court invokes general principles of law in its decision, and even Justice Clifford, who dissents on a point of jurisdiction, refers to the federal courts here as common law courts, at 737.

35. Ibid., at 728, 729, 727.

36. Ibid., at 725.

37. But see the works referred to in note 4, above.

38. 463 U.S. 783 (1983)

LIBERTY AND LICENSE: THE AMERICAN FOUNDING AND THE WESTERN CONCEPTION OF FREEDOM

Barry Alan Shain

Contrary to mythic beliefs widely held by the general public and even most scholars, Americans in the late-eighteenth century were not a people who had founded colonies and then a nation "around a pervasive, indeed, almost monolithic commitment to classic liberal ideas," such as "individualism, freedom, equality," and individual autonomy. Nor is it true that Americans wished to "pursue their individual goals and aspirations in a society dominated by the norm of 'atomistic social freedom.'"[1] Instead, Americans, like their Christian forebears, were more interested in the well-being of their families and communities, local agricultural matters, and the acquisition of Christ's freely given grace, than in securing individual autonomous freedom.[2] They were traditional in their social and political goals and, accordingly, committed to an understanding of freedom that sharply differentiated between liberty and license.

It is easy to forget that in the years 1765-1785, America was a nation of Protestant and communal backwater polities still marked at the beginning of the Revolution by widespread adherence to the principles of a balanced monarchical government and an abiding attachment to England. In this land of largely autonomous Protestant village communities, and townships or counties in the Middle and Southern colonies, the liberal individualism of Thomas Hobbes with its unconstrained understanding of liberty was, at least in speech and writing, thoroughly reviled. Indeed, amid overlapping Western traditions of ideas which can be teased out of American sermons, pamphlets, and newspapers, public-defined limitations on the individual's autonomy and liberty are found throughout. Although each tradition of thought did have a recognizable concern regarding the enduring "true" interests of the individual, not one can be described fairly as defending individual autonomy or liberty unconstrained by a higher moral order. Moreover, each one understood that individual flourishing is best accomplished through a life framed within close corporate boundaries. Thus, eighteenth-century Americans' understanding of liberty did not include autonomous individual freedom; but rather, in all but one of its various forms, it followed the traditional Western understanding of a voluntary submission to a life of righteousness that accorded with universal moral standards and the authoritative interpretive capacity of congregation and community—if you will, an ordered and communal sense of liberty.

One might challenge this view, for is it not widely believed that it was a novel, individualist understanding of liberty for which Americans were prepared to die in their revolutionary struggle with Britain? And is it not the case that when asked today what they are most proud of about America, more than two-thirds of Americans respond, "'our freedom,' or 'liberty,' or some variant"? From this, the author of the poll concludes that "*individual freedom* is the most insistent claim of classical liberalism—and it is the proudest claim of Americans."[3] Such accounts help to create the sense that a powerful continuity exists between Revolutionary Americans and their twentieth-century descendants regarding their understanding and love of liberty. Perhaps, though, it was Abraham Lincoln who had it right when he remarked, "'we all declare for liberty; but in using the same word we do not all mean the same thing.'"[4]

Thus, in what follows, I will attempt to show that when eighteenth-century Americans used the word "liberty," they meant something quite different from the dominant understanding of the term today. Put positively, eighteenth-century Americans continued to adhere to traditional Western patterns of viewing liberty as defensible only when it was constrained, communal deferring, and acting in accord with a higher moral order. Liberty was as much or more about making the right choices as it was the freedom of choosing. And within this enveloping understanding, Americans viewed liberty as having four broad meanings, all of which appear in some way similar to those used today, and eight more specific ones. This means that eighteenth-century Americans understood liberty in at least twelve different ways. We must examine closely, then, how these varying concepts were understood if we are accurately to gauge how the liberty defended by the Founding generation was viewed. In the end, we will find that in viewing liberty as restrained by a defining moral purpose, they understood liberty in a most traditional Western way and refused to embrace a revolutionary new liberal understanding of liberty as a reflection of unconstrained autonomy.

Four Broad Meanings of Liberty

Let us begin by admitting that when examined in a cursory fashion, the broad meanings of liberty discoverable in eighteenth-century English dictionaries seem to be fully familiar. For instance, they offer as the most basic sense of liberty a definition that has not changed in nearly three centuries. Consider this first of several common definitions of liberty which held that liberty was "a being free from obligation, servitude, or constraint" or "liberty in *common Speech*, is freedom of doing anything that is agreeable to a person's disposition, without the controul of another."[5] Surely, this first meaning of liberty is one that has changed little in the intervening centuries.

Yet, all may not be as it seems.

As we look more closely at this first formal sense of liberty, we find in longer narrative descriptions that the actual substantive meaning then attached to liberty was traditional and is separated from modern ones by the radically different intellectual environments within which each century's meanings are embedded. This eighteenth-century understanding of liberty was framed by traditional Anglo-American presuppositions of a divinely ordered universe in which the twin antitheses to liberty were tyranny and licentiousness. As perceived by an anonymous New Englander, liberty was a rationally limited freedom that distinguished men "from the inferior creatures," for: "*Absolutely to follow their own will and pleasures*, what is it, in true sense, but to follow their own corrupt inclinations, to give the reins to their lusts.... Are they whose character this is at *liberty*? So far from it, that instead of being *free*, they are *very slaves*."[6] From this encompassing Anglo-American perspective, man may have been born free but he was bereft of deeply internalized self-control, which could only be gained through rebirth in Christ, communal life, or more likely both; freedom was license, not liberty, and freedom was not fit for a truly human life.

The second of the two most common meanings of liberty offered by early eighteenth-century English dictionaries was legalistic. This meaning of liberty as historically gained exemptions provided by authoritative political leadership is defined in a 1708 dictionary as "a Privilege by which Men enjoy some Benefit or Favour beyond the ordinary Subject." Thirty years later, another dictionary similarly defines liberty as "a privilege by grant or prescription to enjoy some extraordinary benefit."[7] And still later in the century, in the 1773 *Britannica*, liberty, "in a legal sense," continued to be "some privilege that is held by charter or prescription."[8] The widespread English acceptance of this understanding of liberty as a special historic dispensation, normally communal or corporate in character and granted by authoritative political leadership rather than as an innate individual right, should not be surprising. As C. S. Lewis has shown, this is one of the most hallowed Western understandings of liberty, and in this tradition, liberty below the level of the sovereign state almost always referred "to the guaranteed freedoms or immunities (from royal or baronial interference) of a corporate entity."[9]

Thus, in opposition to those who suggest that the American founding generation was committed to a liberal understanding of liberty, we discover that according to the two most common eighteenth-century general English definitions, liberty was understood in a clearly restrictive and communal rather than expansive and individualistic fashion. Liberty was either voluntary submission to rules of behavior tightly constrained by narrow boundaries framed by Holy Scripture and natural law, and authoritatively mediated by congregation or local community, or it was a political gift to a designated group providing a provisional dispensation from normally authoritative central governmental controls. In both instances, it was an opportunity for the community to guide the individual toward self-regulation in the service of God, the public good, and family. Individual autonomy it was not.

A third broad English meaning of liberty that one might believe has remained largely unchanged in modern Western thought is the "liberty of religious conscience." We find a 1737 dictionary describing "liberty [of Conscience, as] a right or power of making profession of any religion a man sincerely believes."[10] Yet, here too the lack of true continuity in meaning between the founding and today is clear since the liberty of conscience no longer carries, as it did throughout the eighteenth century, the grave importance associated with the exercise of religious duties and the search after divinely informed moral precepts. To put the matter simply, freedom of conscience today is applied to a wide range of pursuits where no pretense of serving God or seeking divinely informed moral truth is necessary. No longer, then, does this understanding of liberty revolve around the most important concerns "of life, where whim and fancy have no place."[11] Thus, this particularly Protestant sense of freedom, freedom of religious conscience, is no longer valued in the same way by contemporary shapers of opinion.

Liberty of religious conscience in fact no longer even merits mention in modern dictionaries under the heading of liberty; nonetheless, it importantly continues to provide religious-like legitimacy to those freedoms normally described as civil liberties, those "inalienable liberties guaranteed to the individual by law and by custom; rights of thinking, speaking, and acting as one likes without interference or restraint."[12] Liberty or freedom of religious conscience, indeed, has proved a most valuable tool in the undermining of the very grounds upon which it traditionally stood—the centrality of religion to the lives of its most ardent defenders. Often forgotten today is the eighteenth-century reasoning that legitimated this unchallengeable right. No longer asked is "why should the reason, conscience, or faith of the individual be respected as inviolable?" Nor is the probable answer of eighteenth-century Americans heard, that is, that "the reason in man corresponds to and is part of the reason of the universe. To violate this principle in man is to transgress the universal law."[13] Unlike this earlier liberty of conscience, then, contemporary individual rights do not demand a divine and knowable moral end or *telos* to limit and legitimate it. Again, the apparent similarity between the eighteenth and twentieth centuries' meanings of liberty is delusive.

A fourth important broad Anglo-American understanding of liberty is freedom from enslavement. This is one of its most traditional Western meanings,[14] and the sense that may well have shown the greatest continuity during the previous several centuries. Here again, however, definitions not read in a broader historical context can be deceiving, for slavery's meaning in the eighteenth century did not revolve solely around the experience of bondage in the sense of chattel enslavement. Rather, its meaning broadly reflected ethical thought wherein slavery was fundamentally a disordering of the soul in relation to God's greater moral structuring of a purposeful universe. If one were unable voluntarily to conform (through Christ) to the strictures of the divinely ordered Cosmos, a higher moral order, either because of bondage to another man or because of bondage to sin and Satan, one was a slave. The critical aspect here, then, is the pervasive sense of limitation and structure which liberty (as distinct from license) carried that is absent from the connotations associated with slavery and the contemporary sense of liberty as individual freedom and autonomy.

Accordingly, liberty was understood to be a sought-after voluntary submission to the Divine or rational moral ordering of the universe. In the contemporary world where confidence in such an ordered universe no longer widely exists, particularly among the best educated, neither liberty as freedom from slavery nor slavery itself can be understood in a fashion similar to how those terms were used in the eighteenth century. Today, slavery almost wholly describes the organized use of chattel human labor, and liberty is understood to be the individual freedom to do what one wills unconstrained by a higher moral order. By eighteenth-century lights, what is today described as individual liberty would then have been described as license, and by their standards, contemporary meanings of liberty and slavery would surely seem stunted.

In short, the differences in the conceptions of liberty held by two populations of English speakers, separated by over two centuries, might be particularly well demonstrated by how eighteenth-century Americans would have responded to a query regarding the purpose of liberty. Such a question is surely a recurrent one in Western history and has generally been answered with liberty viewed as "something more formal, rational, and limited than freedom; it concerns rules, and exceptions within a system of rules." Most importantly, liberty has traditionally connoted "firm, rational control of those mysterious depths and of the dangerous passions found there."[15] And Revolutionary-era Americans were, at least in this instance, a people who continued to understand liberty in inherited Western ways. For them, freedom as liberty was only defensible when it was limited by divinely sanctioned transcendent truths in the ultimate service of Christian and corporate purposes. Anything else was simply license.

APPLEBY'S THREE SENSES OF LIBERTY

The four broad Anglo-American meanings of liberty discussed above are not the only ones discoverable in the thought of the

American Founders. And among additional understandings of liberty, are there not many that truly accord with contemporary individualist sensibilities? Indeed, there were many more meanings of liberty that were part of the political, social, and religious conceptual map used by the Founding generation. In fact, Americans understood liberty in as many as eight specific ways: political, philosophical, prescriptive (which overlaps considerably with the second sense discussed above), individualistic, spiritual, familial, natural, and civil. This fact has not gone unnoticed by other scholars.[16] Still what the historical record suggests is that, contrary to expectations and popular perceptions, eighteenth-century Americans continued to distinguish sharply between liberty and license in the restrictive Western tradition and to view and value liberty in ways which would today be viewed as non-individualistic. The historical record is so clear on this point that even mainstream liberal scholars acknowledge that individualistic concepts of liberty were not prevalent during the Founding era. One such scholar is Joyce Appleby, a former president of the American Historical Association and a highly regarded student of the American Founding. The weight of Appleby's scholarly insight here is amplified by her lack of a conservative agenda or an engagement on the morally intrusive side of America's ongoing culture wars.

Appleby, in keeping with a pattern established above, begins her remarks on liberty by drawing attention to the great dissimilarity that exists between the widely accepted senses of liberty current then and today. In particular, she argues that autonomous individual liberty, largely disparaged then, has subsequently come to dominate contemporary thinking about liberty. According to her, the "least familiar concept of liberty used then was the most common to us—that is, liberty as personal freedom." With good reason she further finds that it was political liberty, the right of a corporate body to be autonomously governed by it citizens, that dominated the secular thought of Americans. In its traditional Western formulation, the meaning of political liberty as derived from classical republican sources and defined by Renaissance humanists was corporate "independence and self-government—liberty in the sense of being free from external interference as well as in the sense of being free to take an active part in the running of the commonwealth."[17] This understanding of liberty had a well established Western pedigree that established a people's "right to be free from any outside control of their political life—an assertion of sovereignty," as well as "their corresponding right to govern themselves as they thought fit."[18] A. J. Carlyle further portrayed it as having developed from deep roots in the Hellenistic Mediterranean basin with its principal instantiation having been in classical and Italian-Renaissance republics. He describes it as a political community that "lived by its own laws, and under the terms of the supremacy of the community itself, not only in its law, but in its control over all matters which concerned its life."[19] Certainly, then, this traditional Western sense of liberty shares little in common with contemporary concerns with individual rather than corporate autonomy.

Indeed, Appleby finds that "before the Revolution liberty more often referred to a corporate body's right of self-determination. Within countless communities the ambit of [personal] freedom might well be circumscribed, yet men would speak of sacrificing their lives for liberty—the liberty of the group to have local control."[20] Or as described by an anonymous English pamphleteer, Americans "obey no laws but their own, or in other words they obey no will but their own, and this is the summit of political freedom." For them, he held, "freedom consists in not being subjected to the will and power of another [people]."[21] And it is political liberty that describes "the participation of men in the choice of their government...a sort of collective liberty." Yet, significantly, "a free people in this sense is not necessarily a people of free men."[22] And this is a critical distinction that has been conflated too often. At least, its full implications have gone unrecognized.

Thus, this most important American secular and corporate understanding of liberty, normally depicted as political, described the Western understanding of the citizen's right of political participation in the shaping of the community's destiny and that of this collective body to autonomy, significantly though with no necessary concern with an individual's liberty within that corporate body. Remember that even if such a concern with an individual's freedom did exist, it was framed in terms of true liberty (as described in the first meaning above), which was "a freedom of acting and speaking what is right, a freedom founded in reason, happiness, and security. All licentious freedom, called by whatever specious name, is a savage principle of speaking and doing what a depraved individual thinks fit."[23] Liberty or freedom was bound by the objective standards which made it so valuable. Indeed, an anonymous author held in 1776 that:

> To be free from coercion is a privilege which no man has a right to enjoy. The wild beasts for whom it is best calculated, may perhaps have some right to such liberty, but man can have none. The truest and most complete freedom that man can enjoy, and which best becomes rational creatures who are accountable for their actions, is the liberty to do all the good in his power.... If any citizen were at liberty to do what he pleased, this would be the extinction of liberty.[24]

Accordingly, to the degree individual liberty was countenanced within the gambit of Western political liberty, it placed the needs of the individual subservient to those of the public and delimited the individual's claim to liberty within the constraints of the first broad Anglo-American definition of liberty discussed above.

During the imperial crisis with Britain, however, political liberty was only one of several kinds of liberty that Americans were fearful of losing. Another believed to be in jeopardy was Appleby's second sense of liberty, that of secure possession, also describable as English prescriptive liberties. This meaning of liberty is similar to the second broad meaning discussed above, but in this instance the focus is more on the prescriptive rights awarded to the individual than on those held solely by the community. Accordingly, Appleby characterizes this slowly accumulated collection of historic rights as "negative, private, and limited." Unlike political liberty, "when people talked about these [prescriptive] liberties, they referred to promises between the ruler and the ruled that carried no implications about the kind of rule that prevailed."[25] These established protections or exemptions from certain kinds of governmental activities, invariably historically established, then, had little or nothing to do, at least directly, with a people's ability to govern itself.

One should attend carefully to Appleby's demarcation of the liberties of secure possession as liberties in the plural rather than as liberty abstractly understood, and as promises between the ruler and the ruled. By depicting them in the plural, she captures a critical distinction in the West between them and liberty per se: prescriptive liberties resulted from an inherited

and contested contractual relation between a monarchical government and its subjects. Importantly, this collection of historic rights and exemptions were throughout the eighteenth
century held to be an inheritance that Americans enjoyed not
as men, but as British subjects.[26] As explained in 1765, "when
the powers were conferred upon the colonies, they were conferred too as privileges and immunities...or, to speak more properly, the privileges belonging necessarily to them as British subjects, were solemnly declared and confirmed by their charters."[27]
Before the 1770s these rights were rarely described in America
as abstract, universal human rights. In fact, in keeping with the
second of the broad definitions of liberty, "people of different
sorts had freedoms of different sorts. They enjoyed their particular freedoms as members of particular communities, inher-
iting them through tradition, custom, usage, and prescription."[28]
The necessity of defending the Revolution against Parliament's
claims of sovereignty did, however, force Americans to abandon purely historical grounding of these rights and to "resort
instead to the natural rights of man rather than those peculiar
to Englishmen."[29] For many this was an unwelcomed transi-
tion fraught with great danger and, thus, strenuously opposed.[30]

Unlike liberty when spoken of in the singular, it is quite
common to find this collection of liberties being defended because the "people held it in fee," or because "it had been be-
queathed to them as an inheritance."[31] For instance, a Massachu-

setts Committee of Safety claimed that Americans were "incontestably entitled to all the rights and liberties of Englishmen; that, as we received them from our glorious ancestors without spot or blemish, we are determined to transmit them pure and unsullied to our posterity."[32] These liberties, in effect, were a product of a historical and contractual relationship between the monarch and the American people who had done nothing to abrogate these inherited constraints on the king.[33]

Prescriptive liberties, then, must be understood in their English, if not Western, historical context, which defined the relationship between the individual member of an often nearly autonomous local community and the normally distant but nevertheless sovereign central government. This sense of liberty, more than any other, described "not a right but a congeries of rights—liberties, not liberty—that were derived from civil society and ultimately from the sovereign." In fact, "in England, liberties had been granted by the Crown (usually under duress)."[34] Significantly, local communities, as distinct from the central and sovereign government, were not subject to this "civil rights" contract between the monarch and individuals, nor in England had they historically needed to be, for "when authority came from the king, government was palpably something other, a force against which representatives protected their constituents."[35] And importantly, the corporate power of the local community was historically, in England and in America, not understood to be part of the "governmental other."

It was not until after the Revolution that a few forward-looking Americans, most particularly James Madison, began to consider how a truly free and democratic sovereign people, possessing the full power of the government, might well endanger these heretofore inviolate "civil rights" of securely possessing private property, personal security, and bodily liberty against arbitrary incarceration, that had been slowly negotiated, often in blood, between the Crown and the English nobility, gentry, and commons.[36] But even Hamilton, adhering to the traditional Anglo-American understanding of a declaration or (later) bill of rights, argued against the need for such a document on the traditional grounds that such legal barriers were only necessary to protect a people against the uncontrolled excesses of kings, not against their legitimate democratic representatives. He explained that civil rights "are in their origin, stipulations between kings and their subjects, abridgments of prerogative in favor of privilege," and therefore "they have no application to constitutions, professedly founded upon the power of the people," and that the people "have no need of particular reservations."[37] English "civil" rights, clearly, for many even at the end of the eighteenth century, were protections awarded to a people against an unjust crown, not to an individual against a legitimately constituted sovereign people—however intrusive it might prove to be.

Appleby's third and final sense of liberty is that of individual autonomy. The emergent individualist sense of liberty she notes was "instrumental, utilitarian, individualistic, egalitarian, abstract, and rational." It clearly was a sense of liberty antithetical to others in the eighteenth century and more generally, to the Western understanding of liberty as teleologically ordered and corporate. In fact, Appleby wonders how two understandings of liberty "so at odds" as the individualist and corporate political understandings "could have coexisted in the same political discourse."[38] The answer is that during most of the eighteenth century in America, unlike Britain to which she is surely referring, they did not. In fact, autonomous individual liberty in Revolutionary America was a bastard foundling which few men were willing publicly to claim as their own. Additionally, even though intellectual tides admittedly had begun to change by the last two decades of the century, individual liberty was still seen largely as a personally and socially dangerous form of corruption.

FIVE ADDITIONAL FORMS OF LIBERTY

As helpful as Appleby's innovative typology has shown itself to be in exploring and corroborating the generally illiberal nature of the late-eighteenth-century American understanding of liberty, it is evident that it can only serve as a point of departure, principally because her triad of political and individual liberty, and prescriptive liberties fails to capture adequately the full range of meaning attached to liberty in Revolutionary America. Beyond the three senses of liberty she identifies, and the four described earlier in the chapter, five others must be considered if we are to begin to understand accurately such important seminal documents as the Declaration of Independence and the goals of the subsequent War of Independence. These five other meanings are spiritual or Christian liberty, philosophical liberty or freedom of the will, familial independence, natural liberty, and corporate civil liberty. It might be added that in spite of Appleby's oversight, most of these additional senses of liberty were of far greater importance in the history of the West and the writings of late eighteenth-century Americans than was her third understanding, autonomous individual liberty.

The first of the additional senses is spiritual or Christian liberty. This was the understanding of liberty that a Christian enjoyed through Christ and that freed him from sin and from the necessity of obeying the Mosaic law. As explained by St. Augustine in his *Confessions*, Christian liberty was such that "'whenever God converts a sinner, and translates him into the state of grace, he freeth him from his natural bondage under sin, and by His grace alone inables him freely to will and to do that which is spiritually good.'"[39] Martin Luther had even claimed that the doctrine of Christian liberty "contains the whole of Christian life in a brief form, provided you grasp its meaning."[40]

This understanding of liberty continued to captivate American social and ethical discourse until well into the nineteenth century. Even then, "influential members of the American community stressed that the most valuable form of freedom was a freedom from sin and a freedom to do God's will."[41] This is the meaning that Henry Cumings, delivering a thanksgiving sermon in 1783, attributed to liberty in a manner equally at home in 1630 or in 1850 America. He informed his audience that: "we must exert ourselves to subdue each irregular appetite and passion, to disengage ourselves from the enslaving power of vicious habit, and to acquire the *glorious* internal *liberty of the son of God, which will make us free indeed.*"[42]

Considering the importance of spiritual liberty, both in the first 150 years and the subsequent history of American thought, it is surprising that Appleby fails to mention it. Such an oversight, however, further shows that her understanding of American liberty is not to be faulted for a biased commitment to defending a Christian communalist understanding of liberty.

Appleby also ignores the philosophical sense of liberty—liberty of the will. This, though, is more understandable given that this sense of liberty was viewed as enjoying limited political connotations. The great Scottish philosopher David Hume thus argued that by liberty, "we can only mean *a power of acting or not acting, according to the determination of the will.*" He added that this understanding of liberty was so basic that it was never "the subject of dispute."[43] Yet, he surely exaggerated here, for by his own admission the relationship between sin, freedom of the will, and God's sovereignty is a mystery "which mere natural and unassisted reason is very unfit to handle."[44] Russell Kirk was right in holding that this issue lies at the heart of the theological terrain that divided Western Christendom. He reminds us that "both Martin Luther and John Calvin declared that the most profound difference between Papists and Protestants was the question of freedom of the will.... This controversy over freedom of the will, and over faith and works, was fundamental to the contest between Catholics and Protestants."[45] Nonetheless, by the mid-eighteenth century, Hume's sense that this is a question that was beyond dispute (or more likely, was of such a complex nature that few could address it with any competence) may explain why it rarely entered into the normative political discussions of the time. It was so widely ignored by all sides that it came to have little value in shaping popular moral and political considerations. Philosophical liberty thus was aptly named because it concerned questions that were best left to formal philosophers and theologians, of which America had at most one great representative, Jonathan Edwards; and, of course, it was on exactly this abstruse issue that he was to make his greatest mark in his *Freedom of the Will*.

More striking is the absence in Appleby's typology of an

important understanding of liberty that was possibly even older than spiritual or Christian liberty and certainly deserving of sustained attention. This third neglected sense of liberty was the then still dynamic idea of socially-defined familial independence, that is, the freedom of a householder to be uncontrolled economically, politically, or socially by other private individuals. It must be strongly emphasized, however, that this hallowed Western meaning of liberty had nothing in common with the twentieth-century's ideal of individual autonomy. Indeed, for eighteenth-century Americans, this sense of liberty as personal independence was not a universal human attribute. Rather, it was understood as it had been across Western history by Attic philosophers, republican Romans, and feudal English, as a socially-defined characteristic of self-supporting heads of households, normally males, who were the central ligaments of these largely farming communities.

In particular, one who was designated as independent in eighteenth-century America was deemed to have the economic, political and spiritual resources that enabled him to be his own master, that is, to be independent of another individual such that his will might never be owned or directed by this other private individual. It always was another person against whom one protected oneself in America, as legitimate corporate pressure was judged in an entirely different and salutary light. Familial independence, the liberty of the smallest of communities, for those adhering to this enduring Western understanding of liberty,[46] thus, was not the freedom to do what one liked; neither was it the freedom to ignore God's will, nor the often conflated complement, that of ignoring the legitimate community and its representatives.

When Americans turned to classical sources, they discovered there too a comparable understanding of personal independence.[47] Classicist Richard Mulgan argues from the *Politics* and the *Metaphysics* that for Aristotle the common definition of personal independence was "not belonging to another or as being one's own person." He notes, moreover, that for Aristotle as well as for Plato, this kind of individual liberty was appropriately tempered by the legitimate obedience, even subservience, that they understood the free male (with the possible exception of the philosopher) owed to his community. Mulgan shows that "to Aristotle autonomy is not a pressing problem. Free men are men who have independent interests of their own but will readily and as a matter of course submit to laws and social norms.... Like Plato, Aristotle countenances widespread legal and social compulsion of individual behaviour without any suggestion that compulsion, the overriding of individual choice, involves moral loss or sacrifice, so long as it prevents people from doing wrong."[48] Quentin Skinner finds that the understanding of personal independence envisioned by classical Attic thought was shared by Livy and Cicero, two Roman authors highly regarded by their eighteenth-century American readers.[49] Skinner notes that "Cicero had already laid it down in *De Officiis* (I.10.31) that individual and civic liberty can only be preserved if *communi utilitati serviatur*, if we act 'as slaves to the public interest.' And in Livy there are several echoes of the same astonishing use of the vocabulary of chattel slavery to describe the condition of political liberty."[50] For these authors, then, as for their eighteenth-century American admirers, there was no inconsistency in arguing for personal economic independence, reciprocal dependency, and the need to cede preeminence to the needs of the public.

Familial independence thus described the head of house's "absolute exemption from any degree of subordination, support, or control by any other person." As clarified by Thomas Tucker in 1784, "only in 'an uncivilized State'...did any man have an absolute 'right to consider himself or his family independent of all the world.'"[51] Regardless of his economic independence, the individual male head of house was to be enmeshed in the life of his family, congregation, and polity so that he could aid and be aided in living a life of moral righteousness. This is in keeping with the central moral teaching and understanding of liberty in the Christian and classical West. As a contemporary moral theorist, Alasdair MacIntyre, has written, to be a virtuous man in either of these ethical traditions was to be a bearer of limited rights who filled "a set of roles each of which has its own point and purpose: member of a family, citizen, soldier, philosopher, servant of God."[52] Traditionally, familial independence neither compromised the interdependent relation that existed between the independent male and his family or that which existed between him and the encompassing local community.[53]

Not as yet introduced are natural and (communal) civil liberty, the last two meanings, which are in some sense also the most basic understandings of liberty. In the eighteenth century, they were effectively paired, for as Blackstone explained, "civil liberty...is no other than natural liberty so far restrained by human laws."[54] Natural liberty, accordingly, was that liberty which was legitimately the individual's in a pre-social sense, whereas civil liberty was that which remained of natural liberty after society's expansive needs were fully met. Civil liberty was communal in comparison with the individualist character of the pre-social natural liberty which was to be surrendered upon entering society. Leaving little doubt as to the legitimate limits of this discrimination between pre-social individual freedom and that which is appropriate within society, the polymath jurist, minister, Congressman and inventor, Nathaniel Niles, wrote that "civil Liberty consists, not in any inclinations of the members of a community; but in the being and due administration of such a system of laws, as effectually tends to the greatest felicity of a state."[55] We must above all avoid, then, conflating pre-social "natural" liberty and communal "civil" liberty if we are to understand how late-eighteenth-century Americans understood the concept of liberty. Civil liberty described the residual liberty that belonged to the individual after the needs of society were fulfilled, for "to speak of restraints upon personal freedom and yet call the political condition that was restrained 'liberty' was to speak of what in the eighteenth century was known as 'civil liberty.'"[56]

It should be clear from the foregoing survey of liberty's four broad English meanings and eight more specific eighteenth-century American ones (with one sense overlapping) that in all but one of its various forms, liberty described a voluntary submission to a life of righteousness that accorded with universal moral standards mediated by divine revelation and the authoritative interpretive capacity of congregation and community. Liberty, in keeping with traditional Western perspectives, did not describe an opportunity for individual autonomy or self-expression, but rather one for corporate and individual self-regulation in the service of God, the public good, and family. Again, the most striking finding that follows from this brief introduction to the concept of liberty is that without confidence in a purposeful and ordered universe, and without a community to enforce self-imposed, objectively true ethical standards on citizens, modern-day Americans are incapable of employing meaningfully the late-eighteenth-century comprehensive understanding of liberty. In short, the Western struggle to balance the needs of liberty with those of order,[57] so well captured in the Founders' varying understandings of liberty, has culminated in most contemporary Americans defending an understanding of liberty indistinguishable from license.

NOTES

1. E. C. Ladd, "205 and Going Strong," *Public Opinion* 4 (June-July 1981): 11; and J. David Greenstone, "Political Culture and American Political Development: Liberty, Union, and the Liberal Bipolarity," in *Studies in American Political Development*, ed. Steven Skowrownek, vol. 1 (New Haven: Yale University Press, 1987), 2, 4, 17.

2. See James Lemon, *Best Poor Man's Country: A Geographical Study of Early Southeastern Pennsylvania* (Baltimore: Johns Hopkins University Press, 1972), 43-4. Although he argues to the contrary, his evidence persuasively demonstrates that even in the progressive colony/state of Pennsylvania, these factors shaped the lives of most citizens.

3. Ladd, "205 and Going Strong," 10.

4. Cited by William Linn Westerman, "Between Slavery and Freedom," *American Historical Review* 50 (January 1945): 213-7.

5. Nathan Bailey, ed., *Universal Etymological English Dictionary* (London: Thomas Cox, 1737); and Thomas Dyche and William Pardon, eds., *New General English Dictionary*, 7th ed. (London: Richard Ware, 1752). See also John Kersey, ed., *Dictionarium Anglo-Britannicum: Or, A General English Dictionary* (London: J. Wilde, 1708); and C. Coles, ed., *English Dictionary* (London: F. Collins, 1713).

6. [S. M.], "Letter to the Printer," *Boston Gazette & Country Journal*, 6 April 1778, 2.

7. Kersey, ed., *Dictionarium Anglo-Britannicum*; and Bailey, ed., *Universal Etymological English Dictionary*.

8. Edward and Charles Dilly, eds. *Encyclopedia Britannica, or a Dictionary of Arts and Sciences*, 3 vols. (London: Dilly, 1773), 2:973.

9. C. S. Lewis, *Studies in Words* (Cambridge: Cambridge University Press, 1960), 124.

10. Bailey, ed., *Universal Etymological English Dictionary*, li.

11. Francis Canavan, *Freedom of Expression: Purpose as Limit* (Durham: Carolina Academic Press and the Claremont Institute for the Study of Statesmanship and Political Philosophy, 1984), 68-9.

12. *Webster's New World Dictionary of the American Language*, 2nd College ed., s.v. "liberty."

13. Roland Bainton, "Appeal to Reason and the American Constitution," in *Constitution Reconsidered*, ed. Conyers Read (New York: Columbia University Press, 1938), 124-5.

14. See Hanna Fenichel Pitkin, "Are Freedom and Liberty Twins?" (paper delivered at the Yale Legal Theory Workshop), 20. Later published in *Political Theory* 16 (November 1988): 523-52.

15. Ibid., 28; and see Marsilius of Padua, cited by Brian Tierney, *Idea of Natural Rights: Studies on Natural Rights, Natural Law and Church Law, 1150-1625* (Atlanta: Scholars Press, 1997), 109.

16. See Joyce Appleby, *Capitalism and a New Social Order: The Republican Vision of the 1790s* (New York: New York University Press, 1984); David Hackett Fischer, *Albion's Seed: Four British Folkways in America*, vol. 1 (New York: Oxford University Press, 1989); and J. C. D. Clark, *Language of Liberty 1660-1832: Political Discourse and Social Dynamics in the Anglo-American World* (Cambridge: Cambridge University Press, 1994).

17. Quentin Skinner, *Foundations of Modern Political Thought*, 2 vols. (Cambridge: Cambridge University Press, 1978), 1:77; and Skinner, "Paradoxes of Political Liberty," in *Tanner Lectures on Human Values* (Cambridge: Cambridge University Press, 1986), 242. This paper was originally delivered at Harvard University, 24-25 October 1984. See also J. G. A. Pocock, *Machiavellian Moment: Florentine Political Thought and the Atlantic Republican Tradition* (Princeton: Princeton University Press, 1975), 226-7; and J. H. Hexter, "Review of *The Machiavellian Moment*, by J. Pocock," *History & Theory* 16 (1977): 330.

18. Skinner, *Foundations of Modern Political Thought*, 1:6-7, 155-7.

19. A. J. Carlyle, *Political Liberty: A History of the Conception in the Middle Ages and Modern Times* (Oxford: Clarendon Press, 1941), 21.

20. Appleby, *Capitalism and a New Social Order*, 16.

21. *Prospect of the Consequences of the Present Conduct of Great Britain Towards America* (London: J. Almon, 1776), 14-15.

22. Friedrich A. Hayek, *Constitution of Liberty* (Chicago: University of Chicago, 1960), 13.

23. [Ambrose Serle], *Americans Against Liberty: Or, An Essay on the Nature and Principle*

of True Freedom, 2nd ed. (London: James Mathews, 1776), 19; and see Alexis de Tocqueville, *Democracy in America*, ed. Phillip Bradley (Knopf, 1945; reprint, New York: Vintage Books, 1954), 1:338.

24. *Licentiousness Unmask'd; Or, Liberty Explained. [In Answer to Dr. Price's Pamphlet Upon the Nature of Civil Liberty]* (London: J. Bew, [1776]), 19.

25. Appleby, *Capitalism and a New Social Order*, 16-8.

26. See John Phillip Reid, *Constitutional History of the American Revolution: The Authority To Tax* (Madison: University of Wisconsin Press, 1987), 24.

27. Daniel Dulany, "Considerations on the Propriety of Imposing Taxes in the British Colonies, For the Purpose of Raising a Revenue, by Act of Parliament [1765]," in *Tracts of the American Revolution: 1763-1776*, ed. Merrill Jensen (Indianapolis: Bobbs-Merrill, 1967), 103-4.

28. Edward Countryman, *American Revolution* (New York: Hill and Wang, 1985), 17.

29. Lawrence H. Leder, *Liberty and Authority: Early American Political Ideology, 1689-1763* (Chicago: Quadrangle Books, 1968), 145-6; and see Daniel T. Rodgers, *Contested Truths: Keywords in American Politics Since Independence* (New York: Basic Books, 1987), 52.

30. See the revealing debate of September 8, 1774 in the first Continental Congress, recorded by J. Adams between Richard Henry Lee, John Jay, John Rutledge, William Livingston, Roger Sherman, James Duane, and Joseph Galloway, in *Works of John Adams, Second President of the United States*, ed. Charles Francis Adams (Boston: Little, Brown and Company, 1850-1856), 2:370-3.

31. John Phillip Reid, *Concept of Liberty in the Age of the American Revolution* (Chicago: University of Chicago Press, 1988), 24; and see his *Constitutional History of the American Revolution: The Authority of Rights* (Madison: University of Wisconsin Press, 1986), 67-71.

32. Peter Force, ed., "Resolutions of Worcester County (Maryland) Committee [7 June 1775]," *American Archives*, 5th ser., vol. 2 (Washington: M. St. Clair Clarke and Peter Force, 1839), 924.

33. This understanding was most emphatically contested by William Blackstone who in his 1765 *Commentaries on the Laws of England*, 4 vols. (Chicago: University of Chicago Press, 1979), 1:105, claimed that America was a conquered territory and, thus, "the common law of England, as such, has no allowance or authority there.... They are subject however to the control of the parliament." This, however, did not go unchallenged. See for example, James Wilson, "Considerations on the Nature and Extent of the Legislative Authority of the British Parliament," in the *Works of James Wilson*, ed. Robert Green McCloskey, 2 vols. (Cambridge: Harvard University Press, 1967), 2:738-39.

34. Forrest McDonald, *Novus Ordo Seclorum: The Intellectual Origins of the Constitution* (Lawrence: University Press of Kansas, 1985), 36-7.

35. Edmund S. Morgan, "Government by Fiction: The Idea of Representation," *Yale Review* 72 (Spring 1983): 334-35.

36. See Madison, "Letter to Jefferson, 17 October 1788," in *Essential Bill of Rights: Original Arguments and Fundamental Documents*, ed. Gordon Lloyd and Margie Lloyd (Lanham: University Press of America, 1998), 326; [S. Adams?], "State of the Rights of the Colonists," in *Tracts of the American Revolution 1763-1776*, 239; and J. L. De Lolme, *Constitution of England, Or An Account of the English Government* (London: T. Spilsbury, 1775), 112.

37. Alexander Hamilton, John Jay, and James Madison, "Essay #84," in the *Federalist: A Commentary on the Constitution of the United States*, ed. Edward Mead Earle (Indianapolis: Modern Library Edition, 1937), 558.

38. Appleby, *Capitalism and a New Social Order*, 19-21.

39. Cited by Perry Miller, *New England Mind: From Colony to Province*, vol. 2 (Cambridge: Harvard University Press, 1953), 69.

40. Martin Luther, "Dedication: The Freedom of a Christian," in *Martin Luther: Selections from His Writings*, ed. John Dillenberger (Garden City: Doubleday & Co., Inc., 1961), 52; and see Westminster Assembly, "Westminster Confession of Faith [1646]," in *Creeds of the Churches: A Reader in Christine Doctrine*, ed. John H. Leith (Chicago: Aldine Publishing Co., 1963), 198.

41. J. W. Cooke, *American Tradition of Liberty 1800-1860: From Jefferson to Lincoln* (Lewiston: Edwin Mellen Press, 1986), 100.

42. Henry Cumings, *Thanksgiving Sermon Preached in Billerica* (Boston: T. and J. Fleet, 1784), 35-6.

43. David Hume, *Enquiry Concerning Human Understanding* [1748] (Indianapolis: Hackett Publishing Company, 1977), 63.

44. Ibid., 69; and see H. Shelton Smith, *Changing Conceptions of Original Sin: A Study in American Theology since 1750* (New York: Charles Scribner's Sons, 1955), for his stimulating discussion of these matters.

45. Russell Kirk, *Roots of American Order*, 3rd ed. (Washington, DC: Regnery Gateway, 1991), 232.

46. See William B. Scott, *In Pursuit of Happiness: American Conceptions of Property from the Seventeenth to the Twentieth Century* (Bloomington: Indiana University Press, 1977), 30.

47. See Giovanni Sartori, "Liberty and Law," in *Politicization of Society*, ed. Kenneth S. Templeton, Jr. (Indianapolis: Liberty Press, 1979), 289-90; and Paul A. Rahe, "Primacy of Politics in Classical Greece," *American Historical Review* 89

(April 1984): 278.

48. Richard Mulgan, "Liberty in Ancient Greece," in *Conceptions of Liberty in Political Philosophy*, ed. Zbigniew Pelczynski and John Gray (London: The Athlone Press, 1984), 17-8, 23.

49. See Norman Hampson, *Enlightenment: An Evaluation of its Assumptions, Attitudes and Values* (1968; reprint ed., New York: Penguin Books, 1986), 148.

50. Quentin Skinner, "Idea of Negative Liberty: Philosophical and Historical Perspectives," in *Philosophy in History: Essays on the Historiography of Philosophy*, ed. R. Rorty, J. B. Schneewind, and Q. Skinner (Cambridge: Cambridge University Press, 1984), 214.

51. Jack P. Greene, "'Slavery or Independence': Some Reflections on the Relationship Among Liberty, Black Bondage, and Equality in Revolutionary South Carolina," *South Carolina Historical Magazine* 80 (July 1979): 195-97.

52. Alasdair MacIntyre, *After Virtue: A Study in Moral Theory*, 2nd ed. (Notre Dame: University of Notre Dame Press, 1984), 58-9.

53. See Gregory H. Nobles, "Breaking Into the Backcountry: New Approaches to the Early American Frontier," *William and Mary Quarterly* 46 (October 1989): 648; Rowland Berthoff, "Independence and Attachment, Virtue and Interest: From Republican Citizen to Free Enterpriser, 1787-1837," in *Uprooted Americans: Essays to Honor Oscar Handlin*, ed. R. Bushman et al. (Boston: Little, Brown and Company, 1979), 107; and Lacy K. Ford, Jr., "Ties That Bind," *Reviews in American History* 17 (March 1989): 66.

54. Blackstone, *Commentaries on the Laws of England*, 1:121.

55. Nathaniel Niles, "[First of] Two Discourses on Liberty [1774]," in *American Political Writing During the Founding Era, 1760-1805*, 2 vols., ed. Charles S. Hyneman and Donald S. Lutz (Indianapolis: Liberty Press, 1983), 1:260.

56. Reid, *Concept of Liberty in the Age of the American Revolution*, 32.

57. See Kirk, *Roots of American Order*, 280.

THE FOUNDING AND
THE ENLIGHTENMENT:
TWO THEORIES OF SOVEREIGNTY

Donald W. Livingston

T he Enlightenment is the name given to a certain style of
European thought that originated in the seventeenth
century and, in time, would become the dominant fashion of
intellectual activity, especially in politics. It appeared in the
revolutions of René Descartes and Francis Bacon as the total
transformation of science and metaphysics; but it quickly came
to infect politics—despite Descartes' insistence that his revolution excluded the domains of theology, morals, and politics.
What are the politics of Enlightenment? Did the American
Founders seek to instantiate a regime of Enlightenment politics?

As the one genre of comedy can take on many different
forms, so too can the genre of Enlightenment thought. Enlightenment thinking has intermingled with and modified Christianity, from which it originated; but it has also, in other forms,
been Christianity's most bitter critic. And there have been many

battles fought within the genre of Enlightenment, notably between various liberalisms and Marxisms, but also between countless other *isms*: socialism, Freudianism, structuralism,
deconstructionism, feminism, etc. Today in the academy Enlightenment itself is under attack by postmodernism, which is
its rebellious offspring and inverted mirror image. Rather than
construct a taxonomy of styles of Enlightenment, I shall present
an ideal identity containing what, carried to its pure form, is
most insistent in the politics of Enlightenment.

ENLIGHTENMENT POLITICS

First, Enlightenment politics is the politics of rational autonomy, where reason is conceived as being independent of
tradition. Tradition is the great horror of the Enlightenment,
for tradition is rooted in particularities endowed with special
metaphysical meaning. The Jewish tradition is rooted in God's
call to Abraham; the Christian tradition in the divinity of
Christ as a person in the Trinity. The scandalous particularities
that constitute traditions are for Enlightenment thought the
source of obscurantism, prejudice, and superstition.

Second, there is a universal morality, self-evidently available to all individuals who dare to use their own reason free of
the prejudices of tradition.

Third, political association exists to secure the rational
autonomy of the individual. The enemy of this individual is any
substantial moral community guided by a metaphysical vision of

the good, and any hierarchical authority or form of involuntary subordination legitimated by that vision.

Fourth, to protect the rational autonomy of the individual the state must be endowed with power sufficient to destroy or at least drive to the margin of society those substantial moral communities that pose a threat to the individual's radical self-making. The politics of Enlightenment legitimates the endless expansion of the state in respect to both territory and concentration of power at the center. Ideally this requires world government, for the rights of autonomous individuals are exactly the same everywhere in the world. There must be a single sovereign office to regulate these rights and to protect individuals from the scandalous particularities of moral and theological traditions that spontaneously and constantly form themselves in human society. World government may be impractical, but it is a demand of Enlightenment politics and one that should be approximated as closely as possible.

Fifth, the politics of Enlightenment is an ideological style of politics. Having rejected tradition as the source of wisdom, politics is to be guided by philosophical theory alone. But philosophical principles cut loose from the *sensus communis* of tradition are entirely antinomian. There is no nonarbitrary way to interpret them or apply them. No human activity contains such profound disagreements as does philosophy, which is the purest example of rational autonomy. As Cicero once observed, there is nothing so absurd that some philosopher has not taught it. Instead of being a scene of rational consensus and harmony, a regime that takes seriously its grounding in principles flowing from the autonomy of philosophy, must be a scene of implacable conflict. Whatever stability it exhibits will be due entirely to the remnants of those substantial moral communities which it has rejected and with which it is in constant conflict.[1]

Finally, the politics of Enlightenment is resolutely secular and exhibits a ready disposition to atheism. Theism requires deference to a moral order not of our own making, and one most fully revealed in a sacred tradition. This violates the Enlightenment principle of rational autonomy. Richard Rorty, who defends what he calls American bourgeois liberalism, has said that a truly Enlightened "liberal society...would be one in which no trace of divinity remained."[2]

Not all who profess to be Enlightened may go as far as the six principles stated above, but the inclination of Enlightenment is to up the ante in the direction of these principles; and once on the path, one will feel guilt, or at least be rationally disarmed, about not going all the way.

AN ALTERNATIVE TRADITION: ALTHUSIUS AND HUME

The politics of Enlightenment, however, has not been the only style of thought available in the adventure of modern politics. There is an older idiom which is still with us and from which I would like to take two exponents. One is Johannes Althusius, a continental thinker who flourished in the seventeenth century; and the other is David Hume, who, although speaking some of the language of the Enlightenment, offered the first systematic (and, I think, the most devastating) criticism of Enlightenment politics.[3]

Johannes Althusius (1557-1638) was described by Carl Joachim Friedrich as the "most profound political thinker between Bodin and Hobbes." He was a theorist of federative polities and had an influence on the formation of the Dutch federation, which had successfully seceded from Spain. Eighteenth century Americans greatly admired the Dutch federation, and Hume once called it "the most illustrious government in the world." He modelled his own theory of a federal republic on it—a theory which influenced the Founders.[4] Althusius's most important work was *Politica*, first published in 1603, expanded in 1610, and revised in 1643.[5] In it he begins the story of political legitimation not, as Enlightenment theorists do, with egoistically motivated individuals in an asocial state of nature, but with the family. The family, not the state, is the first political society, and it is political because it contains the relations of authority and subordination. Families form a village and give authority to a village council. Villages form provinces and give authority to a provincial council. Provinces form a commonwealth and give authority to a state council. Althusius does not neglect the rights of individuals to form contracts and associations of all kinds, but individual rights are constrained by the independent social authorities of which one is a part.

Political association is based on consent, but it is not the once and for all consent of Enlightenment contract theorists such as Thomas Hobbes, John Locke, Jean Jacques Rousseau, and John Rawls. Consent for Althusius is continuous, and it may easily be withdrawn. Thus a province or any other political unit may secede and remain independent or join another political unit. Whereas Enlightenment theory rules out independent social authorities, Althusius explicitly recognizes them; and, consequently, conceives of sovereignty as divisible. Each social order has something of its own to celebrate and to defend. Sovereignty is the symbiotic relation between these social units. Accordingly Althusius describes politics as "symbiotics."

The idea of sovereignty and liberty in Althusius is an older notion stretching back into the medieval period with its notion of "subsidiarity"—the idea that as much as possible should be done by the smallest political unit. That sovereignty is divisible was first taught by the early medieval church, which declared itself, its property, and its law independent of the crown. It was in the space opened up by this division of sovereignty into divine and secular authority that the Western idea of liberty first made its appearance. But it was just this space that the politics of Enlightenment would later seek to close with its doctrine of radical individualism and the concomitant doctrine that sovereignty is indivisible.

Similar teachings from this older tradition are to be found in David Hume and the Founders. Hume is famous for his devastating criticism of the contract theory, which is the foundation of Enlightenment politics. But he is hardly known at all for his theory that sovereignty is divisible, for his theory of resistance, and for his vigorous defense of the secession of the American colonies.[6] In the essay "Of Some Remarkable Customs," he argued against the Enlightenment doctrine that sovereignty is indivisible.[7] The Roman republic, he observed, contained two legislatures both of which were sovereign, neither of which was subordinate, and both of which could veto the laws of the other. Hume delighted in showing that, though a contradiction to the rationalist mind, such a regime is not only conceivable, but was in fact one of the most illustrious and energetic regimes in history.

Hume's theory of resistance is internal to his theory of divided sovereignty. Many historians of intellectual history teach that Hume's political theory rules out a doctrine of resistance. In his splendid book *The Enlightenment in America*, Henry May says this of Hume: "It may be as well for his American reputation that he died in 1776, since he had already said, and would doubtless have continued to maintain, that a people never had the right to overthrow their government." May and others come to this mistaken view because they think that in rejecting the

Lockean contract theory (and with it Locke's theory of resistance) Hume must have rejected resistance as such. Their perception of Hume is distorted because it is constrained by the categories of Enlightenment theory. But Hume's notion of resistance (and indeed the older notion of resistance) is more radical than Locke's. Since Hume argues that authority rests on acknowledgement of an opinion of right and not on consent to a contract, resistance will take different forms in different regimes. It is rarely to be expected in absolute monarchies or in democracies. But in what he calls "free government," it is to be expected with frequency. He defines free government as one "which admits of a partition of power among several members, whose united authority is no less, or is commonly greater than that of any monarch; but who, in the usual course of administration, must act by general and equal laws, that are previously know to all the members and to all their subjects."[8]

For Hume the constitutional members of a free government are not an aggregate of individuals but, in the manner of Althusius, distinct social orders endowed with the right of corporate resistance. Here Hume attacks the very root of the Enlightenment state, which is grounded in individualism at the expense of independent social authorities. Hume saw that such a regime must lead to an unprecedented concentration of power at the center and would, in time, he said, create a new kind of tyranny worse than an "oriental despotism."[9] The first regime to attempt the actual destruction of all independent social authority in the name of the natural rights of individuals was the regime of the French Revolution—perversely described as a republic. Tocqueville observed this process of social destruction in horror: "The old localized authorities disappear without either revival or replacement, and everywhere the central government succeeds them in the direction of affairs.... Everywhere men are leaving behind the liberty of the Middle Ages, not to enter into a modern brand of liberty but to return to the ancient despotism; for centralization is nothing else than an up-to-date version of the administration seen in the Roman Empire."[10]

Benjamin Constant, a French liberal, who was a keen contemporary observer of the French Revolution and its Napoleonic aftermath and who gave the first definitive speech on the nature of modern liberty and individualism, nevertheless understood that a flourishing cultural background of independent social authorities is necessary to protect the individual from tyranny at the center. His understanding, like that of Althusius and Hume, was "medieval" and in direct contradiction to the Enlightenment theory of the state. He wrote: "The interests and memories which spring from local customs contain a germ of resistance which is so distasteful to authority that it hastens to uproot it. Authority finds private individuals easier game; its enormous weight can flatten them out effortlessly as if they were so much sand."[11] This is the dark truth hidden in the doctrine of natural rights of individuals and in mantras such as government of the people, by the people, and for the people, when the "people" are conceived as an aggregate of individuals and not as being incorporated into a social order or orders endowed with rights.

Hume's views on the American crisis are buried in the letters written during the last ten years of his life (1766-1776). He supported complete independence for the colonies as early as 1768, before the idea had occurred to most Americans, and he held to that position for the rest of his life. He was virtually alone among major British thinkers in supporting secession of the colonies. The so-called "friends of America"—Edmund Burke, Isaac Barre, and William Pitt—were for compromise, but none favored complete independence. The Edinburgh literati were strongly pro-government, and Hume's position shocked his friends. He refused a request from his oldest friend to write a letter to the King, on behalf of the county of Renfrewshire, asking for strong measures against the Americans. Hume told him: "I am an American in my principles and wish we would let them alone to govern or misgovern themselves as they think proper." Hume held to this position from 1768 until his death on August 25, 1776, five days after the complete text of the Declaration of Independence was published in Edinburgh's *Caledonian Mercury*.[12]

In describing himself as an American in his principles, Hume put into words for the first time an ideology of "Americanism." But it was quite different from the Enlightenment ideology of Americanism that would surface in the late nineteenth century and which characterizes twentieth century liberalism (and most of what today goes by the name of conservatism). Hume's Americanism presupposed the older notion of divided sovereignty, which enabled one to recognize independent social authorities when they emerged out of the flux of history. The Parliament and Crown were already in the grip of the Enlightenment notion of indivisible sovereignty, and so were conceptually blind to seeing a claim to self-government in the colonial societies. Hume was free of these moral blinders, and sometime around the 1730s, he wrote this note to himself: "The Charter Governments in America are almost entirely independent of England."[13] Hume's support of American secession should not be seen as "enlightened" or "progressive"; it was "medieval" in its idiom. It was George III who, in suppressing secession on behalf of a would-be unitary state ruling in the name of the inalienable individual rights of Englishmen, was enlightened and progressive.

It is important to add that the break with Britain was not a Lockean revolution as it is usually described. Secession is completely different from revolution. Lockean revolution is an attempt to overthrow a regime that has violated the original contract. The colonists, however, were not trying to overthrow the British government and replace it with a just one. King, lords, and commons were to remain as before. Indeed Hamilton and many others greatly admired the British government. They wanted simply to limit its jurisdiction over the territory they occupied. That, of course, was a serious matter, but it was not Lockean revolution. Its name is secession, and the reasons that would justify secession are categorically different from those that would justify revolution. Much confusion in American self-understanding has resulted from failure to distinguish secession from revolution and the suppression of secession from civil war.[14] This failure is due in part to the fact that philosophers have had virtually nothing to say about secession. Modern philosophers from Hobbes to Rawls have directed their attention to legitimating the modern unitary state which rules over individuals, and within this form of political association the idea of a people withdrawing to govern themselves is ruled out *a priori*. The Enlightenment state is "one and indivisible."

Further, secession can never be recognized as legitimate unless one accepts the non-Enlightenment conception of divided sovereignty. Since Locke rejected that notion, he could not have consistently supported the secession of the colonies anymore than George III could have. Both were loyal to the Enlightenment state that was beginning to emerge. Indeed Locke goes so far as to argue that one who has given his explicit consent to the regime cannot even immigrate, much less take territory with him. Much conceptual confusion has been generated in American politics and in constitutional law by the thought that there was an American "revolution" and that it was Lockean.

THE FOUNDERS AND
THE SECOND VISION OF AMERICA

I turn now to the Founding. Did the Founders seek to establish an Enlightenment regime? The answer is that they did not, but that their language occasionally contained a youthful Enlightenment idiom, which, like a dormant virus hidden deeply in a cell, would spring to life only many years later when conditions were ripe.[15] Over time America would take on more and more the character of an Enlightenment regime. To appreciate this we must work through two contrary stories Americans have told themselves about what it is the Founders founded. These stories end in two contrary theories of the Constitution. The first I shall call the compact theory, and the second the nationalist theory. It is through the nationalist theory that the politics of Enlightenment enters America. The compact theory articulates that older notion of corporate liberty and divided sovereignty theorized by Althusius and Hume.

The compact theory teaches that each state is a sovereign political society. The states created the central government as their agent, endowing it with only enumerated powers—mainly defense, regulation of commerce, and foreign treaties. The central government (including its supreme court) cannot have the final say as to what powers the states delegated and reserved because the central government is the agent and the states are the principals of the compact. A state may, therefore, as both Thomas Jefferson and James Madison argued, interpose its authority to declare an act of the central government null and void if it goes beyond its delegated powers. This was, of course, nothing more than that legal right of corporate resistance theorized by Hume and Althusius. Indeed any federal system that is serious about protecting the moral communities of its constituent units must allow some form of state, provincial, or cantonal resistance. The Canadian constitution, for instance, allows a province to nullify actions of the central government in the area of civil rights. But further, if states are sovereign, they may withdraw those powers delegated to the central government and secede from the federation.

In sharp contrast to this, the nationalist theory teaches that the states were never sovereign. Upon breaking with Britain, all political jurisdiction vanished, leaving an aggregate of individuals in a state of nature. These individuals spontaneously formed themselves into a sovereign political society and created a central government (the Continental Congress) which authorized the formation of states. The Union created the states; the states did not create the Union.[16] If this were true, then a state could not, as Madison and Jefferson had said, interpose its authority to declare unconstitutional an act of the central government. And a state (being nothing more than an administrative unit of the center) could not legally secede any more than a county could legally secede from a state. The nationalist theory is simply the contract theory of Hobbes applied to America, and so is the theory of an Enlightenment regime. But it was not the constitution of the Founders, and it is grounded in historical claims that are spectacular absurdities.

The former colonies did not lose their character as individual political societies by seceding from Britain. Hume observed in the 1730s that the colonial governments were almost completely independent of England. With the Declaration of Independence, each former colony declared sovereignty for itself; and after the war, each was recognized separately by the British crown as sovereign. The Articles of Confederation declared that "each State retains its sovereignty, freedom, and independence." During and after the war the states exercised the powers of sovereignty: building navies, raising armies, issuing letters of marque, coining money (Massachusetts coined money as early as 1643), and conquering British territory in their own names. New York, Rhode Island, and Virginia asserted their sovereignty in the strongest terms by writing into their ordinances ratifying the Constitution the right to secede. Nothing about the Founding is clearer than that if the nationalist theory had been put to these states, and they had been told that they were not and had never been sovereign states and that once in the Union they could not withdraw, there would have been no Union.

Further evidences for the truth of the compact theory are the many acts of state interposition and threats of secession carried out in every section of the Union for the first seventy years of the polity. In the case of *Chisholm v. Georgia*, Georgia declared a decision of the Supreme Court unconstitutional and ordered the arrest of federal agents that might seek to enforce it. Jefferson and Madison had asserted state interposition in 1798. Connecticut and Massachusetts endorsed nullification in 1808 and in 1814. Vermont nullified fugitive slave laws in 1840, 1843, and 1850. Massachusetts did the same in 1843 and 1850, and declared the Mexican war unconstitutional in 1846. In 1859 Wisconsin asserted the supremacy of its supreme court over that of the U.S. Supreme Court. Northern governors used nullification to block the many unconstitutional centralizing policies of the Lincoln administration.

Secession was also widely considered an option available to an American state. The region that most often considered secession was New England: over the Louisiana Purchase in 1803, the embargo in 1808, over war with England in 1814, and over the annexation of Texas in 1843. From the 1830s to 1861, New England abolitionists argued for the secession of northern states from the union. The American Anti-Slavery Society's declaration was typical: "Resolved, that the abolitionists of this country should make it one of the primary objects of this agitation to dissolve the American Union."[17]

Although Jefferson, as President, had been bitten by the New England secession movements, he admired—in the way Althusius and Hume would have—the regimes of local self-government that were their source; and he based his theory of dividing Virginia into "ward republics" on the New England town meeting model. Regarding the New England secessionist movements, Jefferson declared in 1816 with characteristic liberality: "If any state in the Union will declare that it prefers separation...to a continuance in union...I have no hesitation in saying, 'let us separate.'"[18]

Strong support for the compact theory is to be found in the fact that among the most vigorous advocates of secession were northeastern Federalists who had originally favored a nationalist constitution. Gouvernor Morris of New York had been a nationalist and was a major figure at the Philadelphia Convention. He was disappointed in the Constitution, but he knew it was a compact from which a state could secede. In 1812 he published an essay in the *New York Tribune* calling for the secession of New York and New England to form a high-toned Federalist union. William Rawle was a Pennsylvania Federalist and a friend of George Washington who had preferred a nationalist constitution, but he too knew that the Constitution was a compact between sovereign states. In 1825 he published one of the first commentaries on the Constitution, titled *A View of the Constitution.* In it he lays out the legal steps necessary for the orderly secession of an American state from the Union. His work was widely acclaimed, especially in New England, and was the textbook on constitutional law at West Point from 1825-1840.[19]

No one loved the Union more than John Quincy Adams. But in his famous speech celebrating the Jubilee of the Constitution in 1839, he went out of his way to argue that a state could secede. What holds "the several states of this confederated nation together," he said, is not "in the right" but "in the heart." Should common affection and interest fail, then "far better will it be for the people of the disunited states to part in friendship from each other, than to be held together by constraint. Then will be the time...to form again a more perfect Union by dissolving that which could no longer bind, and to leave the separated parts to be reunited by the law of political gravitation to the center." Four years after this speech, the former president, along with other New England leaders, would sign a document calling for the dissolution of the union over the annexation of Texas.

These and many other examples that could be given show that Americans, from the first, conceived of the Constitution as a compact between sovereign political societies. Indeed, no systematic nationalist theory was formulated at all until 1833 when Joseph Story published his *Commentaries on the Constitution.* Daniel Webster, who began his career as a New England secessionist, became an eloquent defender of the new theory, but it was Abraham Lincoln who seared it into the national consciousness with a writ of fire and sword. It was after Lincoln's presidency that the language of an Enlightenment regime became fully available to Americans.

Although there was no systematic nationalist theory prior to Story's *Commentaries* (1833), there was certainly a nationalist *ambition.* Alexander Hamilton, James Madison, and James Wilson had proposed a nationalist constitution with federal control of the states, but they were soundly defeated. Having just seceded from Britain, the states were not about to consolidate themselves into an American version of a centralized British state. It is even misleading to talk of the compact *theory.* That the Constitution was a compact between the states was a fact of practice more than theory. Even would-be nationalists were compelled to use the language of a compact between sovereign states. In *Federalist* 39, Madison declared that ratification "is to be given by the people, not as individuals composing one entire nation; but as composing the distinct and independent States to which they respectively belong." Each state, he said, "is considered as a sovereign body independent of all others, and only bound by its own voluntary act. In this relation the

new Constitution will...be a federal and not a national Constitution." In *Federalist* 28, Hamilton said that there need be no
worry about federal tyranny since the people of the states had
the authority "to take measures for their own defense with all
the celerity, regularity, and system of independent nations."
And in the New York ratifying convention, Hamilton declared
that no state could be coerced: "To coerce a state would be one
of the maddest projects ever devised. No state would ever suffer
itself to be used as the instrument of coercing another." Even
Wilson was compelled by common understanding to describe
the states as sovereign: "those who can ordain and establish
may certainly repeal or annul the works of the [central] government." These statements extorted from the logic of the popular conception of the Constitution, as a compact between sovereign states, contain all that is necessary for the doctrines of
state interposition and secession.

If the Story-Webster-Lincoln nationalist theory is true—that
sovereignty resides in the American people in the aggregate, that
it was the Union that created the states, and that the Union is
indivisible because sovereignty is indivisible—then there should
have been a solid history of Union continuity. But there was
no such history. It is true that the Articles of Confederation
were said to be "perpetual," but each state is also said to be
"free, sovereign, and independent." According to international
jurists such as Emmeric de Vattel, sovereign states entering into

a treaty of undetermined duration cannot be bound by pious claims of perpetuity. It was recognized by everyone that the Union under the Articles had been dissolved by the individual secession of nine sovereign states. Madison, for instance, declared in *Federalist* 43 that if some states refused to ratify, then "no political relations can subsist between the assenting and dissenting states." He hoped, nevertheless, that a "re-union" would one day occur. The Enlightenment nationalist theory of indivisible sovereignty conceived as an indivisible Union is plainly false. Everyone knew the Union was divisible, which is why no mention was made of indivisibility at the Philadelphia Convention. Having just proposed to dissolve a union explicitly said to be perpetual—a dissolution requiring only nine states, even though the Articles of Confederation required unanimous consent for its alteration—the Framers were in no position to say that the new Union would be indivisible.

Throughout the first seventy years of the polity, most everyone described the Constitution as a compact and the Union as a confederation and an "experiment." This latter term was the idiom set by Washington in his famous farewell address: "Is there doubt whether a common government can embrace so large a sphere? Let experience solve it.... It is well worth a fair and full experiment." In only sixty years after his speech, experience would show conclusively that the Union, as an experiment (having swollen to some ten times its original size) had failed. When Lincoln launched the first modern war against a civilian population to suppress secession, he was not engaged in the conservative act of preserving an indivisible Union, as he claimed. Rather, like the French revolutionaries, Bismarck, and Lenin, he was creating an Enlightenment unitary state on the ruins of a premodern federative polity.[20]

The Founding was not that of an Enlightenment state "one and indivisible," but of a federative polity of divided sovereignty. The idiom of an Enlightenment state did not fully appear in American politics until after the Civil War. American nationalist historians, in order to legitimate a would-be American unitary state, have read the nationalist theory of the Constitution into the Founding, distorting our understanding of the Founding and of the Constitution. British commentators were almost unanimous in interpreting the Civil War as a revolution by the industrial sector to destroy the federative polity and create a unitary state—a process of a piece with the forces of centralization, consolidation, and nationalism that had been sweeping Europe since the French Revolution. The liberal London *Spectator* wrote in December 1866: "The American Revolution marches fast towards its goal—the change of a Federal Commonwealth into a Democratic Republic, one and indivisible." What we call the Civil War they perceived as America's French Revolution. Marx and Mill rejoiced in the revolution as a move to Enlightenment, but Lord Acton did not. Acton was a mod-

ern Catholic defender of that older doctrine of divided sovereignty; and his famous maxim about power tending to corrupt
and absolute power corrupting absolutely was directed explicitly against the Enlightenment unitary states that had grown up
in Europe in imitation of the French republic. He had seen in
the premodern federative polity of the Framers a counterweight
to this European trend, and he wrote to Robert E. Lee on
November 4, 1866: "Secession filled me with hope, not as the
destruction but as the redemption of Democracy...."[21]

The federative polity Acton admired was indeed remarkable. By 1860 the American polity had flourished for seventy
years under the compact theory. By any standard it was a unique
achievement. Whereas the Enlightenment regimes of Europe
were highly centralized and heavily in debt, the central government of the United States had been virtually free of debt since
the 1830s. It imposed no inland taxes but lived off a revenue
from land sales and a tariff on imports. The states had mild
taxes, and the "medieval" principle of subsidiarity flourished.
It was the almost perfect Althusian regime. But this was possible only because of the power the states had to keep the central government confined within the sphere of its ennumerated
powers. It was the reserved powers of the states that kept the
central government tied down by what Jefferson called "the
chains of the Constitution." Once these independent social
authorities were removed, there would be no limit to the con-

centration of power to the center.

This concentration of power in the modern state has proved more destructive than even Lord Acton could have imagined. One need only consider the wars of the Enlightenment state. The French Revolution, by destroying all independent social authority, was able to do what no eighteenth-century monarch could have dreamed of doing, namely, order universal male conscription. Whereas Frederick the Great and Louis XVI had done well to maintain an army of 190,000 men, the French republic could suddenly put in the field an army of a million men. By the end of Napoleon's reign the republic would have employed three million troops. By World War I the Enlightenment state would have the income tax in addition to conscription, and with this vast revenue its wars would be awesome barbarisms. World War I left eight million battle deaths and six million mutilated—more than were killed in the two previous centuries of war in Europe. World War II made no distinction between combatants and civilians, and left approximately fifty million dead. But even this barbarism was dwarfed by the Marxist regimes, which killed well over one hundred million in pursuit of the ideological goal of class struggle in the name of equality. R. J. Rummel has estimated that nearly four times as many people have been killed by modern states in pursuit of ideological goals than have died on the battlefield in all wars fought from 1900 until today. The greatest danger to human life in the twentieth century has not been war but the concentration of power available to modern states. Had Hitler and Stalin been eighteenth-century monarchs, they could not have done what they did simply because they would not have had the *authority* to do so. They would have been hedged in by powerful independent social authorities who could be expected to resist.[22]

What protects liberty is not "democracy" or a doctrine of the "natural rights of individuals," for both of these have been used by totalitarian regimes. The French Revolution instituted "the terror" and the first totalitarian regime, and it ruled in the name of the rights of man. Liberty is best protected by the federative polities defended by Althusius, Hume, the Founders, and Lord Acton, where the federal units are endowed with the right of corporate resistance, including some form of interposition, and—as a last resort—secession.

THE ENLIGHTENMENT AND MODERN AMERICA

Today the United States, under the influence of the nationalist theory, has become the almost perfect Enlightenment regime. Its central government has worked to subvert the independent authority of the states guaranteed by the Tenth Amendment with Alice-in-Wonderland interpretations of the Fourteenth Amendment. There is now no serious obstacle to what the central government can do to the states because it is the central government alone that can define what those obstacles are. The

Supreme Court has long since abandoned its role of policing the bounds of the Constitution and has become the most important social-policy-making body in the Union. Americans are gradually learning how to submit to an entirely new form of tyranny: government by judiciary.[23] The federalist principle of "subsidiarity" has been turned on its head: as much as possible should be done by the largest political unit, not the smallest. Far from being free of debt as the central government was for nearly thirty years under the compact theory, its funded debt is approximately six trillion dollars, and its unfunded liability is approximately seventeen trillion dollars, which includes such things as federal health care and social security. For these committments to be honored, the next generation must be taxed at over 80 percent of income or new sources of revenue must be found, perhaps in plundering private annuity funds or in denying churches tax exempt status, which will only further weaken independent social authorities.[24]

The sheer size of the American regime is out of scale with any version of politics the Founders could understand.[25] In 1997 the central government spent approximately 1.6 trillion dollars, more than it spent (even adjusting for inflation) from the revolutionary period to 1940. Its notion of representation bears no relation to the conception the Founders had nor even to the best parliamentary regimes of Europe. The Constitution was made for three million citizens incorporated into thirteen sovereign states. Today California has a population of thirty-three million and is not treated by the central government as a sovereign state. There are 270 million Americans, but only 535 representatives, including senators. England, with less than a quarter of our population, has 636 representatives; and Switzerland, with six million citizens, has 247 representatives. If the proportion of representatives to population that exists today had existed in 1790, there would have been only five representatives in the House. Even this would not be so bad if the central government could be kept within the bounds of its enumerated powers.

Another way the United States has become an Enlightenment regime is by allowing itself to be captured by an ideological style of politics. It is said that America is unique in not being a culture with substantial traditions like other countries. America is an idea; a set of abstract principles; a "proposition country"; a culture of individual rights. This, of course, is absurd. No country is or could be an idea. America is a substantial culture, or better, an order of substantial cultures like any other country.[26] It is just that the Enlightenment thinker cannot acknowledge the authority of these cultures anymore than he can acknowledge *any* independent social authority. Nationalists such as Story, Webster, and Lincoln, for instance, could not bring themselves to acknowledge that the political societies of the colonies had each declared its own sovereignty and that each had become an independent state. For the nationalist, post-secessionist colonial Americans were nothing more than an aggregate of individuals under the power of a new central authority thought of as the Union. This Enlightenment ideology has legitimated the constant hollowing out of the remnants of traditional American society. The former Soviet Union was also an Enlightenment regime that claimed to be an idea, but the idea vanished like morning mist when fifteen republics reasserted their sovereignty and in an act of un-Enlightenment peacefully seceded from the union. This and secessions in eastern Europe, as well as the spectacular devolution and secession movements in western Europe brought on by the European Union, have weakened the legitimacy of the Enlightenment state.[27] Even the French are finally beginning to come to terms with their broken memory brought on by the French Revolution, which gave us the first true Enlightenment state.

But Americans too have a broken memory, for we have inherited the legacies of two incompatible theories of the Constitution: the compact theory and the nationalist theory. From the 1830s on, both theories would be woven into the contradictory texture of American politics. But it is the nature of traditions to be dialectical and to contain discordant elements. And what is often seen as a fresh and novel reform is usually a reaching back to pick up something that had been lost in a moment of distraction. If the nationalist theory has barbarized itself into a bureaucratic consolidationism, an ideological style of politics, the hollowing out of traditional American society, and political ossification, it is time to revive the compact theory of the Founders and to restore genuine American federalism—which is something considerably deeper than the currently fashionable talk of block grants to the states.

In his message to Congress in July 1861, Lincoln justified coercing the seceding states back into the Union with a sophistical nationalist theory not thirty years old. He flatly stated that "the Union is older than the States and in fact created them as States." But the federative understanding of the American polity survived long after Lincoln, even though his eloquence introduced a French-revolutionary, nationalist idiom into American political speech. Over a century later President Reagan, in his first inaugural address, could still assert the compact theory: "the States," he said, "created the central government, the central government did not create the States." The Constitution of the Founders is still available, and the people of the sovereign states may, whenever they choose, reclaim jurisdiction over that vast domain of unenumerated powers reserved to them by the Ninth and Tenth Amendments, which they have allowed, in a fit of absent-mindedness, to slip out of their hands.

NOTES

1. See my *Philosophical Melancholy and Delirium* (Chicago:University of Chicago Press, 1998) for a systematic critique of Enlightenment thought as that critique is to be found in the philosophy of David Hume. See also Alasdair MacIntyre's *After Virtue* (Notre Dame: Notre Dame University Press, 1981) and *Whose Justice? Which Rationality?* (Notre Dame: Notre Dame University Press, 1988). For a post-modern critique of Enlightenment liberalism that, nevertheless, retains much of the spirit of liberal *practice*, see John Gray, *Liberalisms: Essays in Political Philosophy* (New York: Routledge, 1989); *Post-Liberalism: Studies in Political Thought* (New York: Routledge, 1993); and *Enlightenment's Wake* (New York: Routledge, 1995).

2. Richard Rorty, *Contingency, Irony, and Solidarity* (Cambridge: Cambridge University Press, 1989), 44-45.

3. See *Philosophical Melancholy and Delirium*, chapters 12-15.

4. Ibid., 199-216, 317-332.

5. *Politica* is now available from Liberty Classics, Indianapolis, 1995.

6. Ibid., chapters 13 and 14.

7. David Hume, *Essays Moral, Literary, and Political* (Indianapolis: Liberty Classics, 1987), 366-376.

8. Henry May, *The Enlightenment in America* (New York: Oxford University Press, 1976), 120.

9. Ibid., 40-41.

10. Ibid., 359.

11. Quoted in Bertrand de Jouvenel, *On Power* (Indianapolis: Liberty Classics, 1993), 285n. This remarkable study of the way in which state power naturally grows and expands is necessary reading for all those who value liberty. On the question of what sovereignty is see de Jouvenel, *Sovereignty* (Indianapolis: Liberty Classics, 1998).

12. Ibid., 253. See also *The Political Writings of Benjamin Constant*, trans. and ed. Biancamaria Fontana (Cambridge: Cambridge University Press, 1988). This volume contains the important essay "Liberty of the Ancients Compared with that of the Moderns."

13. For an extended discussion of Hume and America see *Philosophical Melancholy and Delirium*, chapters 10-13.

14. Ernest Campbell Mossner, "Hume's Early Memoranda, 1729-40: The Complete Text," *Journal of the History of Ideas* 9 (1948): 504.

15. See my "The Secession Tradition in America" in *Secession, State, and Liberty*, ed.

by David Gordon (New Brunswick: Transaction Publishers, 1998), 1-33.

16. For more on the idea that the Declaration of Independence frames a doctrine of corporate liberty rather than a doctrine of radical individualism with a conception of rights capable of trumping the claims of a legitimately established sovereign majority, see Willmoore Kendall and George Carey, *The Basic Symbols of the American Political Tradition* (Baton Rouge: Louisiana State University Press, 1970); Barry Shain, *The Myth of American Individualism* (Princeton: Princeton University Press, 1994); Donald Lutz, *The Origins of American Constitutionalism* (Baton Rouge: Louisiana State University Press, 1988); and M. E. Bradford, *A Better Guide Than Reason* (New Brunswick: Transaction Publishers, 1994), 185-203.

17. For a defense of the nationalist theory, see Samuel Beer, *To Make a Nation: The Rediscovery of American Federalism* (Cambridge: Harvard University Press, 1993).

18. Quoted in Albert Taylor Bledsoe, *Is Davis a Traitor? or Was Secession a Constitutional Right Previous to the War of 1861?* (Richmond, VA: The Hermitage Press, 1907), 149. This work was first published in 1866 and is a systematic and formidable defense of the thesis that secession was a right under the Constitution. For a contemporary defense of the abolitionist thesis that secession was the best way to handle slavery, see Jeffrey Hummel, *Emancipating Slaves and Enslaving Freemen* (Chicago: Open Court, 1996).

19. Letter to William Crawford (20 January 1816).

20. A new edition of Rawle's *A View of the Constitution* is available, edited by Walter D. Kennedy and James R. Kennedy (Baton Rouge: Land and Land Publishing Division, 1993), see especially the last chapter, "Of the Union."

21. On the idea that the barbarism of modern total war begins with the war to consolidate the American union, see B.H. Liddell Hart, *The Revolution in Warfare* (Westport: Greenwood Press, 1947), 45.

22. John E. Acton, *Selected Writings of Lord Acton*, ed. Rufus Fears, 2 vols. (Indianapolis: Liberty Classics, 1985), 1:363, 277-78, and 216-62.

23. The mass killings made possible by the concentration of power in modern states are documented by R. J. Rummel, *Death by Government* (New Brunswick: Transaction, 1994).

24. The destruction of American federalism and the rise of radical individualism has been effected in large part by arbitrary readings of the Fourteenth Amendment. For a definitive study of what that amendment says and was intended to say, and how it has been corrupted by the Supreme Court, see Raoul Berger, *Government by Judiciary* (Indianapolis: Liberty Classics, 1997), and *The Fourteenth Amendment and the Bill of Rights* (Norman: Oklahoma University Press,

1989). It is perhaps a fitting irony that this amendment, which has been arbitrarily manipulated by the Supreme Court to effect a massive transfer of power to the center was not constitutionally passed by Congress and was not ratified by the states. See Forrest McDonald, "Was the Fourteenth Amendment Constitutionally Adopted?" *The Georgia Journal of Southern Legal History* l, no. 1 (Spring/Summer, 1991).

25. On the cost to future generations of the unfunded liability and public debt of the central government, see Laurence J. Katlikoff, "Generational Accounting," *NBER Reporter* (Winter, 1995/6), 8-14; and "Working Paper #9103," Federal Bank of Cleveland (March 1991), 34.

26. Concerning the relation between liberty, human flourishing, and the size of a polity, see Leopold Kohr, *The Breakdown of Nations* (New York: E. P. Dutton, 1978); for a plan to institute the human scale polity of the Founders in contemporary Vermont, see Frank Bryan and John McClaughry, *The Vermont Papers* (Chelsea: Chelsea Greem Publishing Co., 1989). For a recent argument that the American regime is too large and too centralized, and that peaceful secession through referendum is the only remedy, see Thomas Naylor and William Willimon, *Downsizing the USA* (Grand Rapids, MI: Eerdmans, 1997).

27. I discuss the question of whether America is a philosophical abstraction in *Philosophical Melancholy and Delirium*, 375-82.

28. The future direction of the European Union is not at all clear. It could end by destroying the sovereignty of the states in the interest of a powerful section which would dominate an empire on the model of the contemporary United States, or it could devolve further into a Europe of small states. Belgium has devolved power to four states, and the other big states of Europe (which are nothing other than artifacts of monarchy) are under pressure to devolve power to their smaller and more natural units such as Scotland, Wales, Normandy, Catalonia, Bavaria, etc. This would, in effect, be a return to the Europe of the high Middle Ages and a reenactment, in modern form, of that remarkable federative polity known as the Holy Roman Empire—a form of political association that lasted for nearly a thousand years. The system of vast scale unitary states begins with the French Revolution, but, in the case of most states, is hardly a century old.

REVOLUTIONS, NOT MADE, BUT PREVENTED: 1776, 1688, AND THE TRIUMPH OF THE OLD WHIGS

Bruce Frohnen

Edmund Burke, eighteenth-century founder of modern conservatism, member of Parliament, and agent for the colony of New York, was often accused of betraying his principles by opposing the French Revolution set in motion in 1789. Burke was accused of inconsistency or worse because he had argued persuasively for the American cause during the years leading up to the War for Independence, yet set his face against the revolution in France. This charge is worth mentioning because Burke's answer to it provides the key to understanding the politics of American independence. Burke pointed out that, whereas French revolutionaries sought to destroy civilization and remake it in a brutal, heartless mold, Americans had sought merely to preserve their accustomed liberties against an overreaching Parliament.[1]

The roots of English liberty and limited government lay in

the distant past even in 1776. But their full expression, in Burke's view and in the view of most Englishmen in Britain and America, lay in the settlement of the constitutional conflict known as the Glorious Revolution of 1688. Burke called this conflict "a revolution, not made, but prevented."[2]

In this essay I will argue that the conflict of 1776 was, to American minds, a defense of the settlement of 1688-1689 and that Americans were right to see it in this way. Rather than a political and cultural revolution like France's in 1789, the War for Independence was a fundamentally conservative war of secession. Like the enemies of James II in 1688, Americans in 1776 sought to protect their English constitutional heritage from those who would subvert it in the name of absolute sovereignty. It was to maintain local control, inherited rights, and limited government that Americans declared their independence, as it was to protect this inheritance that they formed "a more perfect union" under the Constitution.[3]

I will refer to the inheritance over which the conflicts of 1688 and 1776 were waged as a set of Old Whig principles. In this I follow Burke, whose *Appeal from the New to the Old Whigs* reasserted these principles' importance in the face of French revolutionary extremism. While I discuss the Old Whig view of politics as consisting of three separate principles—of local control, inherited rights, and limited government—it is important to note that these principles are merely shorthand attempts to capture the essence of interdependent practices making up a unified political life. Thus, there will be seeming repetition and overlap between principles. (For example, local control was seen as an inherited right.) Further, the Old Whig label is somewhat anachronistic because neither Whigs nor Tories constituted philosophically coherent political parties much before the nineteenth century.[4] But Burke was far from alone in seeking to defend mixed, limited government against absolutism, whether monarchical or democratic. Indeed, Burke's Old Whig orthodoxy was the orthodoxy of many powerful figures in British politics, and of the mainstream of American thought during the eighteenth century.

I will begin with a summary of the English Constitution, to which Old Whigs in particular were attached. Next I will review the causes and consequences of the Glorious Revolution, first in Britain, then in America. I will then discuss Americans' attempts to defend their patrimony against an increasingly absolutist Parliament and to make safe the limited, mixed government to which they looked for protection of their liberties and way of life.

THE ENGLISH CONSTITUTION

Whether in England or America, Englishmen in the seventeenth and eighteenth centuries judged their rulers according to their adherence to a constitutional order stretching into the distant past.[5] Not wholly immune to the social contract theories put forth most famously by John Locke (and in fact dating back to medieval canonist arguments justifying rebellion against tyrants),[6] Englishmen nonetheless preferred not to detail any specific origins for their traditions. Instead they derived standards of conduct from concrete historical examples combined with long-standing usage.

Prior to the adoption of Magna Charta, Englishmen had looked to customary practices, regularized by judges into a common law, for protection against arbitrary rule. Rather than an abstract ideology, common law provided specific rights, such as the right to be tried for crimes by one's peers and the right not to be taxed without the consent of one's representatives in Parliament. Long accepted rights and the institutions that grew out of them formed the English Constitution. As such they molded the ruler's behavior and provided Englishmen with justification to challenge any ruler who sought arbitrary power.

The English Constitution still provided standards for judging political conduct in the England of 1688 and in America during the period leading up to the War for Independence. It also anchored political arguments in a vision of the past in which local control and tradition played a dominant role. Writing in 1776, an American using the pseudonym "Demophilus" provided a typical explication of the ancient roots of the English Constitution through his interpretation of Saxon social and political organization. According to Demophilus, the Saxons were organized into small, local townships or tithings, allied with one another through mutual defense agreements. The Saxons occasionally formed larger units whose size and character depended on the reasons for their formation. Only if the interest involved was that of the people at large—primarily in cases of military need—would all of the tribes join to serve it.[7] Thus the rightful powers of any central government were limited in scope and purpose and derived from the needs of the localities. There was no "state" in the modern sense of a central regime acting for the entire people on all matters.

Englishmen in 1688 and Americans in 1776 shared the same goal: retention of their ancient and rightful inheritance. They sought to maintain a political structure based on local rule and providing only limited, derivative authority to central political institutions. The freedom of local communities to arrange their lives in common with relatively little interference from the central government was considered crucial, important enough to spark rebellion when violated by either King or Parliament.

Historically, rebellions tended to succeed more often in England than on the continent. A principal reason for this relative success was the traditional strength of English localities. Many of the common law rights Englishmen held dear belonged, not to individuals, but to corporations, towns, and counties. Local charters (including colonial charters in America) were considered sacred by the English, unlike their continental counterparts who saw them as grants from the king, revocable at his will. The customary right to engage in local politics and commerce, along with national dependence on local militia, provided nobility and commons with the motivation and the means to resist royal attempts to undermine their ancient constitution.

THE GLORIOUS REVOLUTION

Britain's Charles I attempted to undermine his kingdom's ancient constitution by claiming arbitrary power for himself. This led to his loss of the crown and of his head. Decades of turmoil in the mid-seventeenth century—civil wars, Charles I's execution, and military dictatorship—finally seemed at an end with the restoration of the monarchy under Charles's son, Charles II in 1660. However, Charles II built a large standing army and mercilessly persecuted his enemies. Then, after Charles II's death in 1685, came the reign of his younger brother, James II. James II had converted to Catholicism (itself seen as a threat to liberty in Protestant England), but it was James II's actions that eventually cost him the throne.

Like his father, James II sought to concentrate all political power in himself. In attempting this subversion of the English Constitution, James sought to take away the powers of English localities, cutting back inherited English rights and counterattempts by Parliament to limit his use of his prerogative (extra-legal) powers. In opposing these actions and in reestablishing constitutional authority after James II's flight, the British aristocracy formulated the Old Whig principles Burke would defend against French revolutionaries at the end of the eighteenth century and Americans would defend against the British Parliament in 1776.

LOCAL CONTROL

Lois Schwoerer relates the story of "Sir Edward Seymour, a staunch Tory who, it has been said, was 'prouder of ruling Devon than controlling England.'" Despite being a Tory, and thus supposedly a friend to royal power, Seymour declared "I had rather pay double to [the militia] from whom I fear nothing, than half so much to those [the army] of whom I must ever be afraid."[8] Like the bulk of his peers, Seymour feared the army because it was the king's. It had no real connection or loyalty to any particular town or county—or to inherited, local rights.

Time out of mind, English politics had derived from the local power of nobles and members of Parliament. Whether noblemen on their estates or successful merchants in their incorporated towns, prominent Englishmen sought to attain prominence in their own localities, rather than abandoning them for the capital. Members of Parliament sought to use contacts made at Westminster mainly to enhance their positions back home. A vibrant and active local life was made possible by charters granting political and economic rights to local corporations. These charters fostered, as they depended in part upon, a frame of mind protective of inherited rights. It was the militia, however, that gave teeth to attempts to protect this inheritance.

Until the middle of the seventeenth century, England had no standing army. Military needs, whether in foreign wars or local rebellions, were filled by troops raised by local lords and primarily loyal to them, and by the local, nonprofessional militia. Oliver Cromwell built the first real, professional standing army in England, and used it to execute a king and rule with an iron fist. At the restoration, Charles II established royal guards constituting a standing army. Resistance was both immediate and energetic, spawning persistent calls for a reformed militia to replace the guards because they endangered English liberty.[9]

As late as 1685 the local militia was used to put down rebellion; but by that time James had inherited Charles's throne and his large standing army. James's augmented army threatened to eliminate or at least overawe the militia. Through his army he also threatened to undermine the local authority of nobles who traditionally enjoyed the role of military as well as economic and political leaders in their towns and counties.

Thus James sought to weaken not just local military defenses, but the very fabric of local life. He also attacked the economic and political lives of towns and counties by revoking local charters. He escalated Charles II's use of *quo warranto* proceedings, whereby the king's lawyers and judges sought, and invariably found, some legal technicality or inconsistency by which to void these charters, and with them all local rights and liberties. Scores of cities, towns, and local corporations (such as universities), along with American colonies, lost their charters. They were deprived of ancient rights to levy their own local taxes, regulate local commerce, run local affairs through elected councils, and in England to elect members of Parliament.

INHERITED RIGHTS

Representation in Parliament was a long-standing right of Englishmen. Although the voting franchise was severely restricted and never standardized, it often was established in the charters of local towns and corporations. Rooted in historical practice and in Magna Charta's declaration of the right not to be taxed without consent, this representation served as a significant check on James's powers for two reasons. First, Parliament could refuse to grant the king's requests for taxes (old and new) if it disagreed strongly with royal policies or found them dangerous to English liberties. Second, through its power of withholding consent, Parliament over time had become the primary lawmaking body in England. James could not simply declare, for example, that his fellow Catholics in England would no longer be banned from public office and public worship. He had prorogued Parliament and initiated *quo warranto* proceedings in earnest after Parliament refused his demand that the Test and Penal Acts, which so burdened Catholics, be repealed.

Determined to have his way on these and other issues, James sought to pack Parliament. Revoking local charters, he sent representatives to the localities to determine who should be allowed to vote and hold office under the new charters he planned to issue. His representatives were instructed to ask potential voters and members of Parliament whether they would support repeal of the Test and Penal Acts.

As Maurice Ashley has pointed out, James's strategy backfired. Prominent Englishmen from all walks of life and parts of the country opposed his methods as violating the traditional right of free and honest representation.[10] Moreover, because James sought a Parliament dominated by Protestant Dissenters (believing that Dissenters would support his policies in exchange for greater religious toleration for themselves), his goal was a Parliament that would be not only servile, but unrepresentative. Dissenters made up too small and too poor a portion of the people to be representative.[11]

LIMITED GOVERNMENT

An unrepresentative Parliament could not protect the people's interests because it would neither know nor value these interests. Moreover, a Dissenter Parliament would be dependent on the king for its power and legitimacy and so fail to check his ambitions. Like the common law, a representative Parliament was necessary to limit the central government to its proper role of serving the common good in accordance with established custom.

The English believed they had the best, freest government on earth. Political powers were separated and elements within the realm, principally the king, the nobility in the House of Lords, and the gentry in the House of Commons, kept a watchful eye to see that no others acted beyond their rightful powers, "lest the extraordinary power intrusted in the crown should lean towards arbitrary government, or the tumultuary licentiousness of the people should incline towards a democracy."[12]

James rejected this vision of England's Constitution. He sought to eliminate the power of either nobility or commons to limit his power. Unable to bend Parliament to his will, he dismissed it and ruled alone for three years. Such long periods without the holding of a Parliament were considered grievances by many Englishmen. But James's rule was considered particularly egregious because he sought to assume Parliament's role in its absence.

Most unpopular was James's use of his dispensing and suspending powers to essentially repeal the Test and Penal Acts. Historically, the king's dispensing power had been a tool by which he could protect individuals from a valid law that in the specific circumstances would produce injustice. Kings had used the suspending power to keep clearly unjust or unwise laws from being enforced until Parliament could reconvene to formally revoke them. But James used his dispensing and suspending powers in direct opposition to the clear desires of his Parliament. Rather than dispensing a small number of Catholics in special circumstances from the Test Act, for example, he openly flouted the act by appointing dozens of Catholics to high positions. He suspended the Penal Acts, which, for example, confined Catholics to their towns and villages, even though Parliament clearly did not consider such laws unjust or unwise. James even made a "Declaration of Indulgence," in effect revoking both acts (that is, legislating) without Parliamentary approval. James's actions led one prominent jurist to note that, if the dispensing power were "once allowed of, there will need no parliament. All the legislature will be in the king."[13]

James's subjects were afraid that his Catholicism, his standing army, and his attempts to undermine all checks on his powers meant that he was attempting to build the kind of absolute monarchy constructed by the French King Louis XIV.[14] In fact, the English had, since the time of Henry VIII, been fighting theories of absolute sovereignty which denied the sanctity of inherited rights. This conflict had become heated during the reign of Charles I, with both King and Parliament claiming sovereignty and warring over it. As one of Charles's opponents, Henry Parker, put the argument, "two supreames cannot bee in the same sence and respect.... There is an Arbitrary power in every State somewhere."[15] The men of 1688 refused to accept this rationalistic formulation. Instead they looked to William of Orange for re-establishment of a free Parliament and protection of their inherited rights. William's army, ostensibly brought to England solely to ensure free elections, frightened James into abandoning his throne.[16] This made possible a peaceful settlement that re-established the traditional, mixed and limited British Constitution, with William as the new king. Thus the revolution was a success, not for radical Whigs or commonwealthmen, but for a combination of Whigs and Tories thrown together to prevent the overthrow of government in potentially revolutionary times.

THE CONSTITUTIONAL SETTLEMENT

Unwilling to simply assume the throne after James fled the country, William called a convention to determine Britain's future. He called to London all living nobles and local gentry who had served in any of the former Parliaments. They met in a special convention and, after debate among themselves and negotiations with William, drew up a Declaration of Rights indicting James for his trespasses on the English Constitution and reasserting their inherited rights. Their job was made easier, however, by James's last, desperate attempts to regain his subjects' loyalty.

Particularly important was James's decision to give back to the localities, though not the colonies, their charters. Thus,

while James's *quo warranto* proceedings were mentioned as grievances in William's manifesto, many pamphlets of the period,
the convention's debates over free elections, and early drafts of
the Declaration, they were not mentioned in the Declaration's
final draft.[17] Even looking to a new and presumably less dangerous King William, however, the convention saw fit to endorse
the old militia by reasserting the right of English Protestants to
bear arms. In addition, persistent Parliamentary pressure kept
William from maintaining a large peacetime standing army.

The central concern at the convention was to make clear
England's attachment and adherence to custom and historical
precedent. Thus the Declaration of Rights, as its name suggested
at the time, put into explicit language rights that had long been
accepted in practice, rather than seeking to create any universal,
abstract rights. In debate the Declaration's drafters cited older
declaratory acts including Magna Charta and the Petition of
Right. In the document itself they justified their actions as declaring their rights "as their Ancestors, in like Case, have usually done."[18] Accordingly, royal attempts to suspend and dispense laws, and to levy taxes without Parliament's consent were
declared illegal, as were the keeping of a peacetime standing
army and a number of judicial practices violating common law
rights.

The convention deemed the Declaration crucial to protecting inherited rights—so crucial that it pushed successfully for

passage of a statutory Bill of Rights in the next Parliament. Perhaps the most powerful check on subsequent kings' powers was Parliament's control of the purse strings. This made it necessary for monarchs to call Parliament more frequently and show greater respect for its acts (which they could no longer suspend or dispense). Parliament thus took greater control in making laws and levying taxes, as well as in protecting local interests and inherited rights from overreaching royal ambitions.[19]

THE GLORIOUS REVOLUTION IN AMERICA

At the end of the seventeenth century, American colonies remained sparsely settled outposts of the mother country. But their inhabitants did not see themselves as mere appendages. Rather, they sought to lead lives even more locally based than those in England, and they were encouraged in this by geographic isolation and a loosely constructed empire.

Donald Lutz captures well the substance and roots of American localism in colonial charters and circumstances:

The typical colonial charter, beginning with the first, ...left the design for local government to the settlers, so long as local law was not contrary to the laws of England... [T]he grant of local control, the impossibility of running any colony from London given the distance involved, and the preoccupation in England with the English Civil War gave the settlers considerable latitude

in running their own affairs. The legal situation, geogra-
phy, and the perilous circumstances led each colony to
move quickly to secure the cooperation of everyone in
the community, and this was naturally accomplished in
small communities by meeting together regularly to plan
and make collective decisions. Town or colony meetings
were often a regular event before any foundation document was written and approved.[20]

Not all colonies were founded on the basis of charters, but
the distances involved generally meant that their early days were
characterized by similar independence from England and vital
local lives. Colonies developed their own assemblies and courts,
which limited the powers of governors sent from England and
saw to it that taxes were raised only with colonial consent. As
he sought to undermine local vitality in England to enhance
his own power, so James II sought to undermine it in America
to achieve "dependence, uniformity, centralization, and profit."
Charters were revoked; assemblies were dismissed; taxes were
raised without consent; and administration was handled by
governors acting directly under orders from England.[21] James
even sought to eliminate colonial boundaries, forming in the
north the "Dominion of New England" and making similar
moves in the middle and southern colonies in an attempt to
wipe out local autonomy.

James's actions upset the delicate balance in America between local rights and the demands of empire. By revoking charters and ruling directly he violated the English Constitution in America in the same way he had in England, and produced a similarly hostile response. Indeed, James's insistence that English rights did not extend to the colonies or their settlers fueled a natural rights argument not seen since Henry VIII's conquest of Ireland.

James claimed absolute sovereignty over the colonies by right of conquest. Settlers countered that they had gone to a new land in a state of nature, thereupon gaining the right to form a new government, which they did through charters and other means that granted the mother country only limited rights to rule over them.[22] It is important to note that colonists used this "natural rights" argument specifically to establish the validity and binding, inviolable character of their charters and other inherited rights. Natural law thinking was very much alive in England and America. However, it remained within its traditional mode, deeming every man entitled to government by some kind of consent and rulers who would pursue the common good and adhere to the limits established by custom and the law of the land. Limited government was required, but not any particular form of government.

Americans sought the rights of Englishmen. They were not yet in a position to press to the breaking point their arguments for local autonomy. In the late seventeenth century, as David Lovejoy puts it, "Virginians felt themselves equal to the people who stayed at home...as far as treatment from government was concerned."[23] Already Americans were claiming that they were the equal of their English counterparts, and therefore entitled to the same rights.

Americans' attachment to their inherited way of life was shown by their almost universal reversion to older forms of government. Soon after news of the revolution reached America, rebellions spread throughout the colonies. Well-nigh bloodless, these rebellions re-established charters where they had existed (New York returned to a charter James had rejected), and restored colonial assemblies. The colonies also sought to reassert more ancient rights of the English Constitution. More than six years after the revolution, Maryland sought from King William an explicit grant of Magna Charta and full rights of Englishmen. New York reasserted the rights of Magna Charta and the Petition of Right. And, as Jack Greene notes, "Between 1688 and 1696, the legislatures of at least seven colonies tried to pass measures in imitation of Parliament's 1689 Declaration of Rights."[24]

THE WAR FOR INDEPENDENCE

Neither King nor Parliament ever officially recognized colonists' claims to the rights of Englishmen.[25] This did not cause great unrest in the colonies principally because Parliament only infrequently put into practice its theoretical absolute sovereignty there. English troops, for example, were not considered a grievance in America before the 1750s because their primary purpose was to provide needed military defense for the colonies. It was when the English Parliament, increasingly acting as an absolute sovereign in England, began exercising what it saw as its rightful power to tax the colonies without their consent that the place of rights in the empire again came into the open.

The story is familiar. Parliament's attempts to impose direct taxes provoked strong protest in the colonies. Taxes were repealed by the Rockingham faction of the Whig party. (It was to this faction that Burke, the Old Whig defender of American rights, belonged.) However, Parliament also passed The Declaratory Act, asserting its right to govern the colonies as it saw fit. It was this assertion—that American colonists had no inherited English rights—that sparked conflict and eventual rebellion.

Bernard Bailyn has insisted that the colonists rebelled, not because English actions were truly dangerous to their liberties, but because they were caught in the grips of an ideology based in delusions of a grand conspiracy to take them away.[26] J. G. A. Pocock, intent on finding revolutionary change in Americans' thinking, claims events in the mid-eighteenth century forced development of an ultimately unworkable theory of confederation, where no such theory had before existed in Anglo-Scottish thought.[27] However, the real changes during the mid-eighteenth century were made by an increasingly powerful and arbitrary Parliament. In opposition, Americans explicitly defended the principles laid down in 1688-1689. John Dickinson referred to English claims of absolute sovereignty over the colonies as "a total contradiction to every principle laid down at the time of the [Glorious] Revolution, as the rules by which the rights and privileges of every branch of our legislature were to be governed for ever." Parliament's arbitrary actions rested on the same "high prerogative doctrine" put forward by James II, and had to be resisted.[28]

Parliament denied Americans the rights of Englishmen, echoing James's assertion that there can never be two sovereigns in one political body.[29] In response Americans denied that Parliament had the right to legislate for the colonies, reserving that right to their own mixed governments of local assemblies and governors, restricted only by Parliamentary acts necessary to regulate the empire, particularly in matters of trade.[30] Colonists like Dickinson argued that the legislature of an empire, unlike that of a particular nation, had legitimate power only in regard to issues that concerned the empire as a whole, and where specifically granted, for example in colonial charters.

Many on the American side, from Samuel Adams to James Wilson to Thomas Jefferson, put forward once again the argument that their ancestors had found America in a state of nature and settled it for themselves, free to form their own governments, binding themselves to England only where charters and other agreements said so.[31] The colonists held that they had the capacity and even the duty to form separate peoples when dictated by circumstances such as isolation or oppression. For Americans, as for the Saxons, the "people" might be a very small group. A number of American writers defined "people" as the inhabitants of a given colony with whom George III either had broken faith or over whom he had never had legitimate dominion.[32] In 1767 John Dickinson wrote, in what he apparently thought to be a moderate tone, that Americans were "as much dependent on Great Britain as one perfectly free people can be on another."

Americans were insisting on the right to be ruled only by their own consent. As James Wilson put it, "the only reason why a free and independent man was bound by human laws was this—that he bound himself." The American Tory counterargument was put forward, for example, by Samuel Seabury: "The position, that we are bound by no laws to which we have not consented either by ourselves or our representatives is a novel position unsupported by any authoritative record of the British constitution, ancient or modern. It is republican in its very nature, and tends to the utter subversion of the English monarchy."[34]

The majority in Parliament, though they officially might have called themselves Whigs, agreed with Seabury. When their re-imposition of direct taxes brought renewed unrest, they imposed punitive acts destroying local rule and in many ways tried to erase distinctions among colonies. The local assemblies that once limited the power of the crown in America were shut down. Inherited rights were ignored as even habeas corpus and the right to trial by one's peers were revoked, with American defendants being sent to England for trial. Old Whig principles were violated with the intention of bringing Americans to heel.

War was the result. However, one should not lose sight of the war's nature. The English Constitution was demanded, not abandoned, by most literate men on the American side. Even in the supposedly radical Declaration of Independence, universal rights are seen as being fulfilled through inherited institutions and practices. Thus, while it is asserted that "all men" are endowed with inalienable rights, the list of grievances that makes up the bulk of the document heavily emphasizes inherited, customary English rights. All men may have the natural right to ordered liberty and rule by the accustomed law of the land, but their particular rights are defined historically, through the growth of traditions.

The sins of King George were depicted in the Declaration as "all having in direct object the establishment of an absolute Tyranny over these states." Parliament took the lead in the colonies, but Americans had long relied on a system in which the English crown, personified by the king, acted on them only

through their own legislatures. Thus George was unjust to allow Parliament's "pretended" legislation to take effect directly
on the colonists. He also was wrong in allowing Parliament to
interfere with and dissolve their legislatures, house a standing
army among them, take away rights such as trial by jury, and
revoke local laws and charters.

Americans fought the War for Independence to re-establish
their accustomed way of life. This was not primarily a political
life. It was frequently represented in speeches and sermons of
the time with the passage from the Book of Kings wherein "Judah
and Israel dwelt safely, every man under his vine and under his
fig tree." It was a local life, in Americans' views best protected
by the mixed constitution and traditions of their ancestors—
culminating in the Settlement of 1688-1689. Americans fought
a war to defend for themselves the constitution established in
England by this settlement, so that they might continue living
as they had for generations.

CONCLUSION

It has become almost commonplace for historians and political
theorists to decry our Constitution as a betrayal of revolutionary radicalism. But if one examines the War for Independence
in the context of English history—the history to which Americans colonists believed they belonged and to which they looked
for standards of political conduct—one can see the continuity of
the American founding. The American Constitution was in-

tended to create only a "more perfect" union, to solidify and preserve the local control, inherited rights, and mixed government for which the war of 1776, and the revolution of 1688, had been fought.

Our Constitution's framers recognized that the people were most loyal to their own communities and states rather than to what James Wilson called the newly created "system of republicks." John Adams and Thomas Jefferson shared Wilson's view and his concern to protect what Jefferson called America's "little republics."[35] The question, as Herbert Storing noted, was whether the new structure strengthened federal authority so much that it destroyed the federal principle. Both sides argued for a federal form of government—one in which the states would delegate certain powers to a national government.[36] The debate concerned whether the Constitution gave the central government so much power that the states would no longer be able to defend themselves against the encroachments of federal politicians intent on extending their power beyond its proper bounds.[37]

States were to remain the people's primary governments. The more distant and artificial federal government would simply tend a limited set of issues, as Parliament once had, or ought to have done. The federal government would maintain internal peace, the sanctity of inherited rights like that to enter into free and binding contracts, and free interstate commerce. The Constitution in effect set up a limited central government to limit some of the powers of local governments. The goal remained locally-based, mixed government respectful of inherited rights. Accordingly, the Constitution's central articles and the later-attached Bill of Rights amendments contain the sum and substance, and often the exact language, of earlier common law declarations.[38]

Convinced that "the accumulation of all powers, legislative, executive, and judiciary, in the same hands, whether one, a few, or many, and whether hereditary, self-appointed, or elective, may justly be pronounced the very definition of tyranny," the Framers set up a system of separated powers, checking and balancing one another so as to defeat any attempt to rule in an arbitrary fashion.[39] The Constitution, like the War for Independence, was intended to preserve an Old Whig constitution, which itself had the limited purpose of protecting well ordered political liberty. These limited political goals were sought, in turn, so that the people and their communities could go about their lives relatively unmolested. It was an old-fashioned vision, perhaps, but then it was a very old constitution that had for centuries been the touchstone looked to by men opposing the rise and spread of arbitrary rule.

NOTES

1. See, for example, Edmund Burke, "Speech on Conciliation with America," in *Works* (London: John C. Nimmo, 1899), 2:127.

2. Burke, "Speech on the Army Estimates," *Works*, 1:454.

3. Jack Greene refers to the principles for which Americans fought as "limited government, government by consent, and local control." See Green, "The Glorious Revolution and the British Empire," in *The Revolution of 1688-1689: Changing Perspectives*, ed. Lois G. Schwoerer (Cambridge: Cambridge University Press, 1992), 268. My analysis owes much to his, but I place greater emphasis on the inherited rights of the common law tradition from which grew the notion of rule by consent.

4. Lois G. Schwoerer, *No Standing Armies* (Baltimore: Johns Hopkins University Press, 1974), 161. See also John Miller, *The Glorious Revolution* (London: Longman, 1983), 83-84. Miller points out that the much-emphasized "country/court" distinction is more illusory that real, given the local nature of British politics and the shifting nature of national coalitions.

5. Here I am not following Pocock's *Ancient Constitution and the Feudal Law*. For an insightful critique of Pocock see Donald R. Kelley, "Elizabethan Political Thought," in *The Varieties of British Political Thought, 1500-1800*, ed. J. G. A. Pocock (Cambridge: Cambridge University Press, 1993), 67-69.

6. Ironically, Sir Robert Filmer, in his *Patriarcha*, accused Catholics of fostering what he deemed the treasonous view that man is born free, at liberty to form government to his liking. See Maurice Ashley, *The Glorious Revolution of 1688* (New York: Scribner's, 1966), 100. See also Lois G. Schwoerer, *The Declaration of Rights, 1689* (Baltimore: Johns Hopkins University Press, 1981), 159-60, where she points out that social contract language goes back to the Middle Ages, and was used in the Civil War, the Exclusion Crisis, and 25 pamphlets during the time of the Glorious Revolution.

7. Demophilus, "The Genuine Principles of the Ancient Saxon, or English Constitution," in *American Political Writing During the Founding Era*, ed. Charles S. Hyneman and Donald S. Lutz (Indianapolis: Liberty Press, 1983), 345-50.

8. Schwoerer, *No Standing Armies*, 142.

9. Schwoerer, *No Standing Armies*, 71; Miller, *Glorious Revolution*, 37.

10. Ashley, *Glorious Revolution*, 162. This was particularly galling to the country gentry, who had always been most powerful in the counties, and who had always prided themselves on their independence.

11. Miller, *Glorious Revolution*, 9.

12. J. Trenchard and W. Moyle, *An Argument Showing that a Standing Army is Inconsistent with a Free Government*, quoted in Miller, *Glorious Revolution*, 113-14. Miller notes that this extract "shows how little the traditional view of the constitution...had changed." He also notes its striking similarity to Charles I's answer to the Nineteen Propositions over fifty years earlier.

13. Quoted in Schwoerer, *Declaration*, 64. See also Miller, *Glorious Revolution*, 102.

14. This is not to say that Catholicism during this era necessarily led to absolutism. Louis' rise to absolute power took place under the ideology of Gallicanism, which declared the primacy of the king over the church in his country. England had experienced absolute government under Henry VIII, who broke with Rome to eliminate restraints on his own power.

15. J. G. A. Pocock and Gordon J. Schochet, "Interregnum and Restoration," *Varieties*, ed. Pocock, 152.

16. James would attempt to regain his throne by bringing French troops to Ireland and recruiting an army there. His flight helps show the peripheral nature of Locke's writings on the Glorious Revolution, before which his *Second Treatise* was largely written, and after which it was published. The convention argued, not over whether to cashier James, but over how to respond to his voluntarily vacating the throne.

17. Schwoerer, *Declaration*, 79-81, notes that inclusion of the quo warranto issue would have been troublesome because the legal procedure itself was legitimate, though misused by James.

18. Ibid., 15-17. Schwoerer's thesis is that many of the provisions of the Declaration of Rights assert new rights, but her own evidence establishes that the convention sought to, first, declare well-established rights and, second, settle for good a number of issues between King and Parliament that had been in dispute, such as the proper extent of the dispensing power, which the convention deemed too dangerous to continue.

19. Miller, *Glorious Revolution*, 42. See also Greene, "Glorious Revolution," 263-4.

20. Donald S. Lutz, "Religious Dimensions in the Development of American Constitutionalism," *Emory Law Journal* 39 (1990): 23-24. Citations omitted.

21. David S. Lovejoy, *The Glorious Revolution in America* (New York: Harper & Row, 1972), 178.

22. Ibid., 39, 90. And note Lovejoy's argument at 186, where he notes that James suspended New England town meetings to the extent possible because they stirred up the people by giving them a forum for talk of natural rights. See also

Pocock, "Political Thought in the English-speaking Atlantic, 1760-1790: The Imperial Crisis," Varieties, 261.

23. Lovejoy, Glorious Revolution in America, 39. See also 348, where he notes that Massachusetts' charters (both 1629 and 1691) guaranteed all colonists the liberties and immunities of free and natural subjects within the realm.

24. Greene, "Glorious Revolution," 265. See also Lovejoy, Glorious Revolution in America, 25, 246-7, 348, 359, 369.

25. Greene, "Glorious Revolution," 264-5.

26. Bernard Bailyn, The Ideological Origins of the American Revolution (Cambridge: Harvard University Press, 1971), ix, xi, and 95. Bailyn sees the roots of Whig ideology not in 1688, but in the radical writings associated with the Civil War and Interregnum—aberrational times lacking the concern for mixed government so common in English history, yet so surprising to Bailyn in the War for Independence.

27. See especially Pocock, "Political Thought," Varieties, 263, 274.

28. Quoted in Greene, "Glorious Revolution," 270-1. Note also that England had "progressed" beyond its mixed constitution toward a theory of Parliamentary sovereignty as dangerous to limited government as royal prerogative. See Bailyn, Ideological Origins, 46. See also Bailyn, 123, where he points out that Jonathan Mayhew and other prominent Americans thought Parliament was attempting to reverse the settlement of 1688-1689.

29. Bailyn, Ideological Origins, 221-3. Bailyn argues that the colonists' Old Whig vision was somehow new and radical.

30. Pocock, "Political Thought," Varieties, 262.

31. On Samuel Adams see "Letter from the House of Representatives of Massachusetts to the Governor, January 26, 1773," in The Writings of Samuel Adams, ed. Harry Alonzo Cushing (New York: Octagon, 1968), 2:425. Other citations can be found in Pocock, "Political Thought," Varieties, 278-9.

32. See, for example, Demophilus in American Political Writing During the Founding Era, 340; Braxton in Ibid., 330-31; and Anonymous, "Four Letters on Interesting Subjects," in Ibid., 381.

33. Quoted in Pocock, "Political Thought," Varieties, 267.

34. Quoted in Bailyn, Ideological Origins, 174-5. Bailyn sides with Seabury in seeing as radical what was in fact a defense of prescriptive rights, and as conservative Parliament's attempts to centralize and make arbitrary its own powers.

35. James Wilson, Works, ed. Robert Greene McCloskey (Cambridge: Harvard University Press, 1967), 149. Jefferson is quoted in Herbert W. Schneider, A

History of American Philosophy (New York: Columbia University Press, 1946), 95. Adams's argument can be found in Hyneman and Lutz, *American Political Writing*, 402.

36. Herbert J. Storing, *What the Antifederalists Were For*, vol. 1 of *The Complete Antifederalist* (Chicago: University of Chicago Press, 1981), 10 and 9.

37. See Brutus, "Essay I," in *The Antifederalist Papers*, ed. Ralph Ketcham (New York: Mentor, 1986), 271. See also Patrick Henry in *The Antifederalist Papers*, 199, where he rejects any government that is not a compact between states as inherently consolidationist.

38. Schwoerer notes that the "eighth article of the Bill of Rights of the United States—'Excessive bail shall not be required, nor excessive fines imposed, nor cruel and unusual punishments inflicted'—was drawn directly from the tenth article in the 1689 Bill of Rights." See Schwoerer, *Declaration*, 290

39. Alexander Hamilton, James Madison, and John Jay, *The Federalist Papers*, ed. Clinton Rossiter (New York: Mentor, 1961), no. 47, 301.

THE THERAPEUTIC THREAT
TO HUMAN LIBERTY:
PRAGMATISM VS. CONSERVATISM
ON AMERICA AND THE WEST TODAY

Peter Augustine Lawler

We conservatives, in recent years, have defended Western thought against various forms of anti-Western multiculturalism, against those who view the imperialism of the West as the leading force for evil in the world. We have defended American founding principles, rooted in the Western tradition, from those on the Left who would disparage them for their ethnocentrism and injustice. Finally, we have defended Western liberty, represented by America, from the monstrous deformation of Western principle embodied in Marxist tyranny. We have, probably too much, viewed ourselves as on the defensive in such battles. We have been too complacent in viewing the West as our own.

But the newest form of American leftist thought, put forward by the nation's most celebrated professor of philosophy, is presented as pro-Western, pro-American, antimulticulturalist,

and anticommunist. Richard Rorty's *Achieving Our Country*[1] is
a particularly clever attempt to revive for the Left the American
perception, first noticed by Alexis de Tocqueville, that pragmatism is the true democratic philosophy and outlook.[2] Rorty's
version of America is now the most interesting and insidious
threat to our conservative efforts to restore a true and invigorat-
ing view of America and the West. Rorty reminds us that the
true conflict of our time is among differing versions of the West,
and that we conservatives support one view of the West over
others.

Rorty's threat takes center stage, in my view, in the wake of
the revolution of 1989, the authoritative discrediting of communism as a human ideal. As Tocqueville observed, not socialist revolution but therapeutic evolution is the deepest threat to
human liberty in democratic times.[3] For Rorty, the revolution
of 1989 stands as proof that pragmatic linguistic therapy is the
only effective road to a fully classless society,[4] or one without
those human distinctions Tocqueville and we conservatives recognize as human liberty.

Unlike Marxism, American pragmatism hardly seems at first
to be a misanthropic defense of tyranny. Pragmatists such as
Rorty favor evolution, not revolution, and they are sincere opponents of all forms of cruelty. What distinguishes them, as
Rorty makes so clear, is a certain Hegelian conception of history. Human beings are completely self-made, and so they re-

create themselves through historical action any way they please. Anything that can be imagined is possible, and so we should imagine a classless, cruelty-free society.

We conservatives are often criticized for being uncritically devoted to the past, and to dogmatic illusions about nature and God. But in fact our first objection to pragmatism is that it is unempirical and uncritical. We have real standards with which to judge the desirability of human projects for reform. We deny that anything and everything is possible, and that human beings are really without limits and purpose. We say that pragmatism, in its way, is as misanthropic and as undisciplined as Marxism. Its hopeful vagueness about the future lies in its rejection of the goodness of the past and present, of the real world of human beings. The vision of the pragmatist, Tocqueville explained, is really a manifestation of the tendency of the democratic poet to be so uninspired by merely human reality that he turns his imagination exclusively to constructing a monstrous picture of an unprecedented and impossible human future.[5] I turn to Rorty as the most impressive American proponent today of a characteristically Western rebellion against the truth about human or ordered, limited liberty.

RORTY'S PRAGMATISM

Pragmatism, for Rorty, is the thought that flows from a certain view of human identity, of what human beings are. Human identity is radically contingent. It has no support in God and nature. Human beings are social, historical, or linguistic beings all the way down. All human experience is a linguistic creation, and so there are no limits to how human beings might create and re-create themselves by using words to alter the imagination. So our identities and the American identity have been created by thinkers and artists who have been successful in using language to form the imagination of our particular place and time. America's future and the future identity of particular human beings will be determined by a struggle among thinkers and poets to form the American imagination.[6]

The problem with most American intellectuals today, Rorty says, is that they make the mistake of believing that they are too good or too insightful to participate in this struggle over American identity. They tend to be Socratics, believing they are pursuing the detached truth about human self-consciousness.[7] They separate themselves from the "many" because they believe they alone value self-consciousness. Culturally-oriented intellectuals, whether they present themselves as being on the Left or on the Right, are all antibourgeois. The bourgeois life is the ordinary life, the one that vulgarly prefers mere enjoyment to cultural excellence or pursuit of the truth. America, our cultural intellectuals on the Left especially believe, has become irredeemably bourgeois. To understand America by freeing oneself from all patriotic chauvinism is, for them, to see how ghastly our country really is. It is, our thinkers have learned from Europeans such as Nietzsche and Heidegger, a wasteland full of last men, human beings who wretchedly prefer contentment to self-consciousness or the truth.

Rorty sees the same cultural tendency on the Right, in Allan Bloom's Socratic aversion to his nice students, whom he portrays as clever animals approximating last men. Rorty's conclusion concerning all our cultural critics is that they view America as the contemporary equivalent of the democracy that killed Socrates. Bloom, in fact, is more honest than allegedly Marxist cultural leftists. He admits he prefers self-consciousness to ordinary happiness, and knowledge to human hope. The truth, for Rorty, is that anyone who preaches political hopelessness, that the achievement of justice is impossible, belongs on the Right.

In the name of justice, Rorty uses pragmatism to mock the illusion of Socratic detachment. There is no true world or true self with which the historical world of today's human beings can be compared. Human beings do not really have religious or cultural longings that cannot be satisfied through political reform. Philosophical talk about God and nature has no foundation. The only standard of truth is utility, its effectiveness in solving human problems. All intellectual controversies can only be resolved through the evaluation of political effects. If thinkers and artists do not use their minds and imaginations to achieve human or political reform in the service of human happiness, they are worthless parasites at best, or cruel tyrants at worst.

So thinkers and artists have no standard by which to shirk their duty to be useful or just, to solve problems human beings share. Rorty says that the liberal or truly humane view of justice is the alleviation of human misery, the reduction of the amount of poverty and cruelty or sadism in the world. Deep down, Rorty admits, his view of justice is as arbitrary as any other. He still gives the argument that, whatever our differences, all or almost all human beings share the goal of not being poor or humiliated.

According to Rorty, intellectuals tend to value self-consciousness over cruelty reduction, but the truth is that there is no true self to discover. If the pursuit of self-consciousness makes human beings miserable, if it causes them to act cruelly by obsessing over God, Being, or death, then it must go. Being cruel is the worst thing we can do, and nothing matters but human happiness. Rorty, in effect, presents his choice of happiness over self-consciousness—the bourgeois choice—as the true choice. He also presents this choice as democratic: he skeptically refuses to privilege views of truth or culture that say that something matters more than the absence of misery and cruelty. Thus pragmatism points human effort in the direction of the classless society, one in which the obsessions of the few are not given preference over the happiness of the many.

Rorty argues that American thinkers and artists, in the name of both truth and justice, must attempt to reform America in a democratic direction. A truthful or pragmatic thinker must be on the Left. He must act as a prideful American citizen, because that is the only way to achieve political progress today. The thinker or artist must use America and Americans as tools to achieve a classless and nationless society.

Americans will not act politically unless they have some pride in their nation. So, Rorty says, the pragmatic intellectual must enter the political struggle by constructing a prideful national identity that will motivate citizens to act for equality and against cruelty. All accounts of a nation's history are really partisan or political, and we should call true whatever we find useful in achieving our political goal. The pragmatist must construct a history of America with Hegel's idea of progressive evolution in mind. Americans should take pride in those heroes and successes that have moved the nation toward a fully classless society, and they should feel ashamed of the persons and events which have resisted this goal. Americans should feel ashamed of conservatives in general.

This prideful history of America, writes Rorty, should be compelling enough imaginatively to be the core of American "civic religion."[8] This religion has nothing to do with God; it concerns what Americans can achieve for themselves. All the devotion to something larger than oneself that used to go to God should now go to the political creation of the nation's future. People do not always need religion to live well. But the pragmatic reformer can use the religious impulse, which he hopes will eventually wither away, to achieve his secular or historical goal.

For Rorty, the prophet who founded America's civic religion was the poet Walt Whitman, who was inspired by the philosopher Hegel. Hegel said history is all there is, putting hope before knowledge by helping human beings to forget about eternity. Thinking about eternity—or the fact that we are not eternal—undermines pragmatism by showing the limits of pragmatic reform. The pragmatic reformer seeks to talk Americans out of their concerns with eternity and mortality and re-focus them on an historical goal they might really achieve.

RORTY'S AMERICA

Rorty begins his inspirational Hegelian history of America with Whitman, but that is surely an error. He notes that Whitman himself was inspired by the Declaration of Independence and Abraham Lincoln, whom he read with Hegelian eyes. Rorty's dismissal of the Founding is needlessly anti-American. Using pragmatic poetic license, I will redescribe America in a comprehensively Hegelian way, correcting Rorty here and there.[9] I will do so to show the contemporary alternative we conservatives must confront and largely reject. The various conservative descriptions of America presented in this collection of essays differ on many of the particulars, but they can all be read as rejecting the pragmatist's Hegelian view of America, one that is not nearly as new as Rorty believes.

The leftist history of America begins with the Declaration of Independence, which devoted Americans to the liberty and equality of all human beings. Nevertheless, that dedication was contradicted by the racially-based slavery and subordination of women in America at that time. That many of the Declaration's signers knew that slavery was wrong and hoped that it would, in the spirit of progressive evolution, gradually disappear is admirable. They might have taken more risks on behalf of their hope. But Whitman was right that the Declaration was a new "dawn," and Americans should take pride in their exceptional, revolutionary dedication.

The Constitution, inspired by the Declaration's revolutionary principles, was the first wholly secular founding document in human history. Its purpose comes from the people, not the people under God. The Constitution of 1787 is silent on religion, except to prohibit religious tests for office. The Constitution intended to create a classless society of free and equal persons. It failed, of course, to do so, but the history of America is the gradual fulfillment of this inspiring intention.

One original failure of the Constitution was that its reach over human experience was limited, that it placed dogmatic restraints on government. The pragmatist holds that all of human experience might be transformed in the service of justice. Not only did the Constitution limit government as such, it divided the authority of government between the nation and the states. Thus the national Constitution did not determine the content of all American law, and so racism, sexism, and so forth could flourish unchecked in the states.

Rorty writes that *the* nineteenth-century example of Hegelian progressive evolution was the Civil War. The synthesis effected by the war's outcome was better than either of the two antagonists in the struggle. The Fourteenth Amendment, properly understood, applied the Constitution's classless principles to state law and thereby devoted the nation to the indefinite expansion of government with equal citizenship in mind. But much of the potential of that amendment was realized only in recent decades. On this point, Rorty cites the U.S. Supreme Court decisions *Brown v. Board of Education* and *Romer v. Evans*, which extended the reach of the national government in eradicating the cruel humiliation connected with racism and heterosexism.

Note that pragmatists usually praise the growth in power of the national government, with its leftist and cosmopolitan intellectual vision, its courts, and its expertise. Pragmatists think that local government tends to be overly influenced by unenlightened and rural populations and so is racist, sexist, homophobic, nativist, and sadistic. A pragmatist does not favor an active citizenry for its own sake, but only when it is imaginatively directed by intellectuals toward the classless society.

According to Whitman, the progress of civilization includes the end of the cruel repression of sexual eros and thus the growth of "the kind of casual, friendly copulation which is insouciant about the homosexual-heterosexual distinction."[10] His vision began to be realized socially and politically in America with the youth culture of the 1960s. Prosperous young people became erotically and morally casual enough not to privilege one form of sexual activity over another. But the sixties' struggle for social justice was not only through casualness. In addition to the more famous Civil Rights movement, Stonewall—the revolutionary uprising of the gays against the police in New York City—deserves to be presented as a key event in American history.

Some pragmatists—such as John Dewey and his schoolmarmish followers—might be a bit hesitant about certain innovative forms of liberation from cruelty. But they cannot deny that sex, drugs, and even rock-and-roll contribute to the production of a fully classless society. Rorty agrees with the Socratic cultural critic Allan Bloom that easygoing sexual promiscuity, recreational drugs, and music to the beat of the mechanical rutting of animals are all signs that today's students have become nicer and so more devoted to the American idea of justice. Rorty laughs at Bloom's serious Socratic objection to the students' unselfconscious contentment, which he considers perverse.

From Rorty's Hegelian perspective, the American Right

wrongly tends to believe that civilization was devastated by the sixties because it wrongly connects civilization to the perpetuation of arbitrary standards of personal virtue. The Left regards that connection as a failure of the imagination, coming from the illusion that human experience is constrained by sin, some ineradicable cruel flaw. For Rorty, all moral restraint is repressive cruelty unless it contributes to progress toward social justice. In a fully classless society, morality will have withered away, but until then a pragmatist may use moral argument to create a world without morality, nations, or citizens. Justice, in fact, will no longer be a virtue, because there will no longer be any need for political reform and no human impulse toward injustice which requires moral resistance.

The fact than an American moral majority opposes sixties' liberation is evidence of their sadism or desire to humiliate. Rorty complains that ordinary people are not yet fully bourgeois, free from the moralistic illusions of cruel societies of the past. He observes that sophisticated students are more bourgeois—or apathetically nice and content—than ordinary people, and he intends to make the workers more like the students.

As important as these sixties' contributions are to the Left, the greatest success of the American Left so far has been the vision constructed for the nation by the Progressive intellectuals. These thinkers realized that the Industrial Revolution had made the individual-rights rhetoric of eighteenth-century

America no longer useful. The selfishness promoted by that rhetoric had produced vast disparities in wealth, and so was replaced with a socialist rhetoric of national fraternity and solidarity. This rhetoric formed "something like a national 'church,'" run out of the universities, which aimed at the redistribution of wealth through government policy, and it united the intellectuals and union members into a national majority.[11]

The Progressive civic religion was remarkably untainted by the reactionary moralism found among the workers. This American brand of socialism owed nothing to Marxism. It did not produce ineffective revolution or cruel tyranny, but aimed at moderating gradually the excesses of capitalism by winning elections and changing laws under the Constitution. According to Rorty, Americans should take pride in the resulting gradual growth of the welfare state, and be ashamed that we have lagged behind European nations in this regard.

Rorty also praises American anticommunism, even calling the Soviet Union an evil empire. He does not dwell on the thought that the American defeat of communism depended on some responsible resistance to sex, drugs, and rock-and-roll. Rorty does not even make this victory a key point of national pride, fearing that it would encourage irresponsible militarism. He makes a point of distinguishing this just crusade against communism from George Bush's merely chauvinistic show of force in the Gulf War. Rorty is also embarrassed by the fact that anticommunism in America was predominately rightist.

Rorty's historical account emphasizes the extent to which the Left was also anticommunist, and he adds that those leftists who were not anticommunist can be forgiven in light of the unjust excesses of American policy. The biggest of these was the Vietnam War, which threatened to turn America into a "garrison state."[12] Leftist opposition to that war is presented as a more noble and selfless defense of liberty than American anticommunism, which was compromised by mixed motives. The worst effect of the Vietnam War was to turn the American Left away from political reform and toward cultural criticism. This turn, Rorty admits too candidly, came as revenge for the unions' refusal to support the intellectual George McGovern in 1972 for patriotic reasons. The Left abandoned the economic platform—redistribution—of the majority coalition. The result was that American political life became less an economic and more a cultural struggle. The Right benefitted in two ways: people were diverted from the results of economic selfishness, and ordinary people revolted against professorial anti-Americanism and antibourgeois contempt.

Rorty does credit the cultural Left with one great political success: political correctness. The university professors—and governmental and corporate bureaucrats influenced by them—insisted that ordinary language be purged of humiliating references to African-Americans, women, gays, and so forth. This cultural reform was easily accepted by sophisticated students at leading universities, and correctly-formed college graduates then imposed it on unsophisticated Americans. With the change in language, human experience changed too. This extension of the reach of political reform really did reduce the amount of racism, sexism, heterosexism, and so forth in America.

In Rorty's eyes, political correctness should also be viewed as a way of removing barriers to the common pursuit of justice by all citizens. All serious "cultural" experiences—religion, race, or whatever—that separate Americans can be talked out of existence. Political correctness, properly understood, opposes multiculturalism with citizenship.

Generally, the influence of the cultural Left has produced a progressively more agreeable cosmopolitanism among prosperous Americans. All that remains to be done, Rorty contends, is universalize this niceness. The problem to be solved today is that the welfare state can no longer guarantee prosperity for most Americans. Its efforts at redistribution are defeated by the globalized economy. Jobs and salaries protected by American law can too easily be moved to other, less prosperous countries. The result is the gradual "immiseration" of the American work force as economic inequality grows.[13]

To address this problem, Rorty encourages the Left to promote economic nationalism in the name of prosperity for all American citizens. Economic cosmopolitanism should be moderated, for now, by the duty of one citizen to another. Progress toward universal prosperity now requires nationalism. The Left should steal the nationalist Republican Pat Buchanan's thunder to reunite the workers with the intellectuals. If Buchanan prevails because the Left does not act effectively, Rorty predicts that the result will be a return of cultural cruelty, and "'nigger' and 'kike' will once again be heard in the workplace" in America.[14]

Rorty, in effect, encourages the cultural Left today to have a prideful, American political vision to keep America nice. Otherwise, working Americans might rebel against college graduates telling them what to say. The Left has to see the interdependence of its economic and cultural agendas: progress toward agreeable cosmopolitanism tomorrow depends upon a certain kind of American citizenship today. The pragmatic goals remain universal prosperity and an eradication, through politically-correct linguistic therapy, of the human experiences that produce cruelty.

OUR AMERICA

I will resist the temptation to challenge many of the details of Rorty's Hegelian American history; but I have presented enough of them for the reader to compare Rorty's account with those proffered in this book. I will say that Rorty is not completely wrong: the reduction in the cruel humiliation connected with racism is progress, and in certain ways women are treated more justly today than ever before. But there is something obviously wrong with the Hegelian idea of progressive evolution.

A conservative knows that things are almost always getting better *and* worse, and that even beneficial reform is usually the cause of decline. Rorty's progressive view is of more or less constant improvement for women, gays, and so forth. Pragmatic reformers believe that there is nothing positive to learn from America's less egalitarian and more cruel past. In contrast, conservatives know that women, for example, may now be treated more justly, but they—not to mention men and children—are on balance less happy.

Women, conservatives observe, used to be encouraged to and often willingly did refuse to be sticklers about justice. They subordinated it to love, to their own and their family's happiness. Now women and men demand that women, in the name of justice, become wage slaves like men. Contrary to the nerve of Rorty's thought, women and families have tended to become less, not more, casual. One statistical trend that is perfectly clear is that, with every passing year, parents are spending less time with and giving less attention to their children. That neglect, we must acknowledge, is often cruel, even when irresponsible parents seem perfectly nice.

To move on to the most comprehensive, conservative observation: Rorty's history is based upon a monstrous exaggeration of two ideals characteristic of the Western world—reason and freedom. That exaggeration—which leads to the denial of the goodness of human life as it actually exists—comes from the refusal to acknowledge the intractable limits to human achievement.

The acknowledgment and acceptance of limits is what has made Western thought, from the beginning, properly human. The denial of limits, a perennial temptation connected with striving to be free and rational, most radically is the effort to eradicate the distinction between human beings and God. But that denial always culminates in the eradication of the distinction between human beings and the other animals. He who would be a God, as Pascal says, ends up acting like a beast.

Rorty's classless society will be filled with nice people incapable of being moved strongly by love or death, and not really self-conscious at all. They won't need God, government, or each other. They will be free from cruelty but not for anything in particular. They will live rationally in the sense that they won't do anything perverse or cruel, but they also will not be particularly curious, engage in theological or metaphysical speculation, or even search for the truth about themselves. They will have been persuaded by pragmatic linguistic therapy that there is no self and no truth to be understood. In the Socratic sense, they won't be rational at all (which is why Rorty calls himself an antirationalist).

"The basic experience of everyone," observed Flannery

O'Connor, "is the experience of human limitation."[15] That is the truth about being a self-conscious mortal, a mixture of mind and body. Human beings will never be able to overcome their fundamental limitations through their own effort. They are stuck with the responsibility of living well with them. Morality is not cruel repression, but living well in light of the truth. Sexual morality is accepting the hard purposes connected with knowing that we are born to die, and so truthful human experience is shaped by the necessities of birth and death. The goodness of human life depends upon those experiences. Human life would be cruelly empty without them.

Rorty is so interested in talking away death—our most fundamental limitation—that he would also talk away love. Rorty's America includes no place for the heart-enlarging experiences that come from the family, local government or communal self-regulation, and love of God in religious community. The family, the local political community, and the church—what Alexis de Tocqueville called America's most precious inheritances from the Western tradition—have, according to Rorty, nearly evolved out of existence. The human or social needs and excellences that brought them into being are in the process of being talked out of existence, and so those heart-enlarging institutions need not and should not stand in the way of the pursuit of justice.

If it ever really came into existence, Rorty's America would have no room for the intense love of one human being for another, for his country, or for God. Love is inegalitarian; it causes us chauvinistically to prefer one or a few to all others. Love puts us out of our mind with "cruel" obsessions. And love—or a strong connection with other mortals—cannot help but bring death to mind. A nice, just, classless society would have to be one with very little love. Its agreeable cosmopolitanism would have to exclude what most Americans now say makes life worth living. The result would be a world with apathetically content people, but no human happiness.

Conservatives prefer the version of America presented by the American Founders because it aimed to perpetuate, not resolve, the tension between love and justice. One expression of that tension was the limited reach of government itself. Personal relationships, the family, and the church were to be largely untouched by the passionless impersonality of political correctness. And the protection of property from government was based on the thought that what is most one's own must be protected from political reform. "Conscience," James Madison contended, "is the most sacred of all property."[16] Another expression of this tension was federalism, or the division of political authority and responsibility. The national government might be more competent and just, but state and local governments are more attuned to the moral and political needs of particular human souls and so better able to care for virtue.[17]

Finally, the Founders all recognized and accepted the distinction between man and God. Religion is not primarily civil religion, or a means to political reform. (And conservatives ought to be particularly careful not to confuse our devotion to America with true religion.) All human beings are free from political domination by virtue of their duties to God, and because they have longings that no political reform could either extinguish or satisfy. All political choices are merely human, or deficient from the perspective of God's wisdom, justice, and love.

SELF-GOVERNMENT RIGHTLY UNDERSTOOD

One way of saying that the American Founders accepted the distinction between man and God is that they were accepting of human beings as they actually are. As Wilfred McClay writes elsewhere in this book, the Founders viewed human beings as sinful and perverse. But they also regarded human or limited liberty as both natural and good. Consequently, they worked to defend human liberty from the excesses of human perversity, and they regarded the Constitution as a noble experiment on behalf of liberty and self-government. The Constitution's political experiment in ordered liberty is modeled on the mixture of order and liberty, goodness and perversity, and virtue and vice that constitutes a true account of the way human beings are. The purpose of that experiment is not to transform human nature through political means—showing pragmatically that what was called natural is not natural at all—but to protect the natural capacity of persons for self-government.

The philosopher-novelist Walker Percy, for one, has reminded us that self-government or personal sovereignty is, most deeply, living well in light of the truth about one's own experiences, capacities, and limitations.[18] Rorty denies both the possibility and the goodness of personal sovereignty, and he would have ordinary people wholly controlled by the sentimental propaganda of experts.[19] For him, America is an unlimited experiment in the transformation of human selves primarily through politically-imposed linguistic therapy.

Percy also helps us to see that the understanding of America as a pragmatic experiment is disintegrating. Human behavior is not, for the most part, becoming more predictable and tranquil. People are more anxious and loony than ever, restless and deranged, as Tocqueville said, in the midst of prosperity.[20] Ours has been both the most sentimental and most cruel century ever. I have already mentioned the cruelty of lonely and empty lives, and even Allan Bloom (but never Rorty) writes of the experience of angry chaos that deranges the children of the divorced.[21] It turns out that our niceness is little more than the desperate mouthing of therapeutic platitudes that do not correspond to our experiences at all.

A fundamental experience of our time, as Percy and the Canadian Christian philosopher George Grant have noticed, is of deprival.[22] We experience ourselves as having been deprived, by failed therapy, of the language that expresses our experiences.

The educational project of our time is to recover that language, which is why Americans, now more than ever, need to recover the classical and biblical sources of their country's founding thought. They need to rediscover why their tradition regards human liberty as a human good.

Rorty's therapeutic pragmatism is finally the result of his moral failure. He uses his vision of a cruelty-free, classless society to divert himself from the wisdom of the West at its best, the truth about human beings and their limitations. He is also deaf to the most philosophical and moral voices of our time. He refuses to learn what the Czech dissident Vàclav Havel said Americans must learn from communism's defeat that being and human being invariably resist human manipulation. There is no American or human alterative to living conscientiously in light of the truth. Rorty is equally deaf to the lesson Aleksandr Solzhenistyn brought to Americans from the Gulag: if human beings were born only to be happy, they would not have been born to die.[23] The secret to happiness lies in renouncing the right to be happy, and in accepting the truth that moral responsibility matters more than happiness.

Today ordinary Americans understand better than Rorty and his fellow leftist intellectuals much of what is implied in the Western distinction between man and God. Thus we are left with the conclusion that they are more realistic and truthful than many professors of philosophy. They are not only more capable of self-government than the experts think; they are more capable of self-government than the experts themselves.[24] The elitism of Rorty's antimoral linguistic therapy leads conservatives to the connection between populism rightly understood and moral realism. That connection is at the heart of the synthesis of Socratic reason and biblical revelation that is the secret to the West's vitality.

NOTES

1. Richard Rorty, *Achieving Our Country: Leftist Thought in Twentieth-Century America* (Cambridge: Harvard University Press, 1998). Much of my essay is a general discussion of themes present in this book.

2. See Alexis de Tocqueville, "Concerning the Philosophical Approach of the Americans," vol. 2, pt. 1, ch. 1 in *Democracy in America*.

3. Ibid., vol. 2, pt. 1, ch. 7 on the seductiveness of the philosophy of pantheism for democratic times, and vol. 2, pt. 4, ch. 6, "What Sort of Despotism Democratic Nations Have to Fear."

4. Richard Rorty, *Truth and Progress* (Cambridge: Cambridge University Press, 1998), 228-43.

5. Tocqueville, *Democracy*, vol. 2, pt. 1, ch. 17.

6. These fundamental premises of Rorty are found in *Achieving Our Country*, but they are often supported more amply in his more philosophical work. See my "Bloom's Ineffectual Response to Rorty: Pragmatism, Existentialism and American Political Thought Today," in *Community and Political Thought Today*, ed. P. Lawler and D. McConkey (Westport, CT: Praeger, 1998) and my *Postmodernism Rightly Understood: The Return to Realism in American Thought* (Lanham, MD: Rowman and Littlefield, 1999), ch. 2.

7. In addition to *Achieving Our Country*, see Rorty, *Truth and Progress*, 230-32.

8. Rorty, *Achieving Our Country*, 15.

9. The basis of my correction will be the view of certain students of Leo Strauss that the American Constitution of 1787, silent on God, positive recognition of religion, race, class, and gender, established the first universal and homogeneous state, one name for the Hegelian end of history. So the Constitution

and the intentions of its Framers do not violate contemporary standards of justice. See my *Postmodernism Rightly Understood*, ch. 1; Michael P. Zuckert, *The Natural Rights Republic: Studies in the Foundation of the American Political Tradition* (Notre Dame, IN: University of Notre Dame Press, 1996); and Thomas G. West, *Vindicating the Founders: Race, Class, Gender, and Justice in the Founding of America* (Lanham,MD: Rowman and Littlefield, 1997). I urge Zuckert and West to read Rorty to see the danger their implicit atheism poses for any conservative defense of human liberty in our time.

10. Rorty, *Achieving Our Country*, 26.

11. Ibid., 50.

12. Ibid., 67.

13. Ibid., 85.

14. Ibid., 90.

15. Flannery O'Connor, *Mystery and Manners* (New York: Farrar, Straus, and Giroux, 1969), 131.

16. James Madison, *The Mind of the Founder: Sources of the Political Thought of James Madison*, ed. M. Meyer (Hanover, NH: University Press of New England, 1981), 187.

17. See Wilfred M. McClay, "Communitarianism and the Federal Idea," in *Community and Political Thought Today*, 101-08.

18. This is the theme of Percy's last novel, *The Thanatos Syndrome* (New York: Farrar, Straus, and Giroux, 1987). See my *Postmodernism Rightly Understood*, ch. 4.

19. See especially Rorty, *Truth and Progress*, 167-85.

20. See Walker Percy, *Lost in the Cosmos: The Last Self-Help Book* (New York: Farrar, Straus, and Giroux, 1983) with Tocqueville, *Democracy*, vol. 2, pt. 2, ch. 15. Also, my *Postmodernism Rightly Understood*, ch. 3.

21. Allan Bloom, *The Closing of the American Mind* (New York: Simon and Schuster, 1987), 118-21.

22. See Percy, *The Thanatos Syndrome*, and George Grant, *Technology and Empire* (Toronto: Anansi, 1969).

23. On Havel and Solzhenitsyn, see my "The Dissident Criticism of America," *The American Experiment*, ed. P. Lawler and D. Schaefer (Lanham, MD: Rowman and Littlefield, 1994). Also, Daniel J. Mahoney, "The Experience of Totalitarianism and the Recovery of Nature: Reflections on Philosophy and Community in the Thought of Solzhenitsyn, Havel, and Strauss," in *Community and Political Thought Today*, 209-26.

24. See Christopher Lasch, *The Revolt of the Elites and the Betrayal of Democracy* (New York: Norton, 1995) and my *Postmodernism Rightly Understood*, ch. 5.

ABOUT THE CONTRIBUTORS

Bruce Frohnen is a speechwriter for U.S. Senator Spencer Abraham and has taught politics at Reed College, Cornell College, Emory University, and Oglethorpe University. He is the author of *The New Communitarians and the Crisis of Modern Liberalism* and *Virtue and the Promise of Conservatism: The Legacy of Burke and Tocqueville*.

Robert P. George is Cyrus Hall McCormick Professor of Jurisprudence at Princeton University and recently completed a six-year term as a presidential appointee to the U.S. Commission on Civil Rights. He is the author of *Making Men Moral* and *In Defense of Natural Law*, and is the editor of *Natural Law, Liberalism, and Morality*. He is a former judicial fellow at the Supreme Court of the United States where he received the 1990 Justice Tom C. Clark Award.

Gary L. Gregg II holds the Mitch McConnell Chair in Leadership at the University of Louisville and is director of the McConnell Center for the Study of Leadership. He has served as National Director of the Intercollegiate Studies Institute and is the author of *The Presidential Republic: Executive Representation and Deliberative Democracy.*

E. Christian Kopff is Associate Professor of Classics and Associate Director of the Honors Program at the University of Colorado. He has been a National Endowment for the Humanities fellow at the American Academy in Rome and is the author of *The Devil Knows Latin: Why America Needs the Classical Tradition.*

Peter Augustine Lawler is Professor of Political Science at Berry College and is the associate editor of *Perspectives on Political Science.* Among the ten books he has authored or edited are *The Restless Mind: Alexis de Tocqueville on the Origin and Perpetuation of Human Liberty* and *Postmodernism Rightly Understood: The Return to Realism in American Thought.*

Donald W. Livingston is Professor of Philosophy at Emory University and is the author or editor of six books, including *Hume's Philosophy of Common Life* and *Philosophical Melancholy and Delirium: Humean Reflections on the Pathology of Philosophy.* He has been a fellow with the National Endowment for the Humanities and the Institute for Advanced Studies in the Humanities at the University of Edinburgh.

Wilfred M. McClay holds the SunTrust Bank Chair of Excellence in the Humanities at the University of Tennessee at Chattanooga. He is the author of *The Masterless: Self and Society in Modern America*, which received the 1995 Merle Curti Award of the Organization of American Historians for the best book in American intellectual history. He has been awarded fellowships from the National Endowment for the Humanities and the Woodrow Wilson International Center for Scholars, and was designated one of the nation's outstanding educators in the Templeton Honor Rolls for 1997-1998.

Barry Alan Shain is Associate Professor of Political Science at Colgate University and is the author of *The Myth of American Individualism: The Protestant Origins of American Political Thought.*

James Stoner is Associate Professor and Director of Graduate Studies in Political Science at Louisiana State University and is the author of *Common Law and Liberal Theory: Coke, Hobbes, and the Origins of American Constitutionalism.*

Bruce Thornton is Chair of the Department of Classics at Fresno State University and is the author of *Eros: The Myth of Ancient Greek Sexuality* and *Plagues of the Mind: The New Epidemic of False Knowledge.*

Graham Walker is Assistant Professor of Government at The Catholic University of America. He is the author of *The Ethics of F. A. Hayek* and *The Moral Foundations of Constitutional Thought: Current Problems, Augustinian Prospects.* The latter book won the Edward S. Corwin Award for the best dissertation in public law from the American Political Science Association.

INDEX